BlackBerry® Application Development FOR DUMMIES®

by Karl G. Kowalski

Software developer for RSA Security

WILEY

Wiley Publishing, Inc.

BlackBerry® Application Development For Dummies®

Published by
Wiley Publishing, Inc.
111 River Street
Hoboken, NJ 07030-5774

www.wiley.com

Copyright © 2010 by Wiley Publishing, Inc., Indianapolis, Indiana

Published by Wiley Publishing, Inc., Indianapolis, Indiana

Published simultaneously in Canada

For general information on our other products and services, please contact our Customer Care Department within the U.S. at 877-762-2974, outside the U.S. at 317-572-3993, or fax 317-572-4002.

For technical support, please visit www.wiley.com/techsupport.

Wiley also publishes its books in a variety of electronic formats. Some content that appears in print may not be available in electronic books.

Library of Congress Control Number: 2010935568

ISBN: 978-0-470-46711-4

Manufactured in the United States of America

10 9 8 7 6 5 4 3 2 1

WILEY

About the Author

Karl Kowalski has traveled the world of software development for far longer than he really wants to remember. He has written code for everything from airplanes, to voice recognition, to robot submarines, to games, and even particle accelerators, and he has developed software on everything from mainframes to cellphones. He lives near Boston and works for RSA, the Security Division of EMC, where his tasks include developing security solutions for mobile platforms, most especially the BlackBerry smartphone. In his spare time, he develops software for smartphones such as BlackBerry, iPhone, and Android as part of his startup, BlazingApps LLC (`www.blazing apps.com`).

Dedication

To my parents, Stanley and Constance Kowalski, who are always there for me, and who at every step helped me to become who I am today. Thanks, Dad, for introducing me to programming computers, back before I could do algebra. To my siblings — Lee Anne, Rosemarie, and Joseph — who always kept me honest about taking time off from writing. Special thanks to Lee Anne who helped me get started when I first mentioned the idea. To my friend Pauline, who saw me through some of the hard parts of becoming a writer. Finally, to the members of the RSA Credentials Everywhere team: I couldn't have done this without your encouragement and support.

Author's Acknowledgments

Many thanks go to Carole Jelen, agent extraordinaire, who never gave up on me nor let me give up on myself. Acquisitions Editor Katie Mohr helped me greatly through my learning to write *For Dummies* experience and also with ideas and motivation for moving ahead. Project Editor Jean Nelson deserves enormous thanks for putting up with a wet-behind-the-ears writer as I worked to stay on target and stick to the schedule. Senior Copy Editor Teresa Artman was very helpful in her efforts to take my typing and turn it into something readable. Special thanks also to Leah Cameron for her feedback as I learned to write *For Dummies*. Thanks to Christopher Parsons for his technical review. Thanks to Robert Philpott at EMC for his work to ensure that I maintained a distinct separation between my EMC efforts and my writing efforts.

Publisher's Acknowledgments

We're proud of this book; please send us your comments at http://dummies.custhelp.com. For other comments, please contact our Customer Care Department within the U.S. at 877-762-2974, outside the U.S. at 317-572-3993, or fax 317-572-4002.

Some of the people who helped bring this book to market include the following:

Acquisitions, Editorial, and Media Development

Project Editor: Jean Nelson

Senior Acquisitions Editor: Katie Mohr

Senior Copy Editor: Teresa Artman

Technical Editor: Christopher Parsons (Bla1ze)

Editorial Manager: Kevin Kirschner

Media Development Project Manager: Laura Moss-Hollister

Media Development Assistant Project Manager: Jenny Swisher

Media Development Associate Producers: Josh Frank, Marilyn Hummel, Douglas Kuhn, Shawn Patrick

Editorial Assistant: Amanda Graham

Sr. Editorial Assistant: Cherie Case

Cartoons: Rich Tennant (www.the5thwave.com)

Composition Services

Project Coordinators: Katherine Crocker, Kristie Rees

Layout and Graphics: Samantha K. Cherolis, Joyce Haughey, Christin Swinford

Proofreaders: Melissa D. Buddendeck, Dwight Ramsey

Indexer: BIM Indexing & Proofreading Services

Publishing and Editorial for Technology Dummies

Richard Swadley, Vice President and Executive Group Publisher

Andy Cummings, Vice President and Publisher

Mary Bednarek, Executive Acquisitions Director

Mary C. Corder, Editorial Director

Publishing for Consumer Dummies

Diane Graves Steele, Vice President and Publisher

Composition Services

Debbie Stailey, Director of Composition Services

Contents at a Glance

Table of Contents

Introduction

The advent and growing popularity of BlackBerry smartphones has changed how corporate users communicate whenever away from their offices. No longer tied to their landline phones, no longer glued to their desktop PCs, corporate users could stay in touch via voice and e-mail as long as cellphone reception was available. Then, Research In Motion (RIM) upped the ante: Independent software developers were allowed to create software to run on BlackBerry smartphones. Developers familiar with Java (the BlackBerry uses the Java programming language) could leverage that knowledge to create BlackBerry apps. This opened the BlackBerry smartphone to the creative power of developers all across the world.

In April 2009, RIM went one step further: The BlackBerry App World was introduced, offering developers a place to market, advertise, and sell their applications to all BlackBerry users.

BlackBerry Application Development For Dummies shows you how to develop an application from concept to completion, from coding to uploading it to the BlackBerry App World to sell it to BlackBerry users.

About This Book

BlackBerry Application Development For Dummies is a guide to developing BlackBerry smartphone applications. No BlackBerry development experience is required, but familiarity with the Java programming language is assumed. After all, Java is the language you use to develop applications for BlackBerry smartphones, and all the API documentation follows the Java documentation guidelines as well as providing coding examples in Java.

The BlackBerry platform enables and encourages you to create minimalist applications that can do some pretty powerful and useful things. You can start small, making simple apps that do a few really important things for your users, and then over time, improve and increase the features and functionality that your apps deliver.

Examples don't tell you how or why

My preferred style of learning is to see lots of examples. Give me good examples, and I can figure out just about everything I need to know regarding programming a BlackBerry. The Java Development Environment (JDE) comes with plenty of examples, and the RIM developer Web site and Knowledge Base provide even more examples.

The challenge I faced when I started coding for the BlackBerry was that I had nothing to show me the all-important *how* and *why*. The application programming interface (API) documentation would tell me what each object did, but gave no instruction for how to coordinate the actions and interactions of the scores of

objects that make up a BlackBerry application. The sample applications were ready to go but provided no reasons for *why* a particular coding choice was made. Those apps are useful to see how a particular feature can be implemented, but there is no "guiding philosophy" shining over the entire set.

All through my early BlackBerry development, I searched for a book that would show me the whys and hows to get my applications working right. I didn't find anything. Eventually, I decided it was time to write the book I had been searching for — *BlackBerry Application Development For Dummies*.

This book helps you sift through the resources of BlackBerry development to reveal only what's absolutely necessary to get you started developing real applications to make the smartphone do real, useful work. You're taken on a path through many areas of the BlackBerry application framework to gain a well-grounded basis for how BlackBerry applications work. And you discover how to go beyond what the book shows when RIM releases new smartphones with updated functionality.

Conventions Used in This Book

Code examples in this book appear in a monospace font so they stand out from the surrounding text. Code blocks look like this:

```
import net.rim.device.api.ui.container.MainScreen;
public  class FirstBlackBerryScreen extends MainScreen
{
    public FirstBlackBerryScreen()
    {
        this.setTitle( "First BlackBerry Screen" );
    }
}
```

Java code is case sensitive, so when you use code that appears in this book, type it *exactly* as it appears. (You can find code samples for this book at www. dummies.com/go/blackberryappdev — download the code samples, and you won't have to type long code blocks!)

All the URLs referenced in this book also appear in a monospace font as well; for example, www.blackberry.com.

And when I define something, it appears in *italic*. And for code/text you enter, it appears in **bold** (unless it's a snippet or block of code).

Foolish Assumptions

In writing this book, I have to make some assumptions about you, the reader. I assume you have the following hardware:

- ✔ A PC
- ✔ A BlackBerry smartphone

I assume that you're familiar with BlackBerry smartphones in general. A lot of smartphones are available; I've had my hands on 20 or so distinct BlackBerry smartphone models. Although it's impractical to try to work with all BlackBerry models, you should at least be familiar with how BlackBerry smartphones operate and how users use them. In addition, you should play around with the standard applications that come with a BlackBerry so you can get a good feel for how users expect applications to behave. You might want to download a few of the free (or inexpensive) apps from the BlackBerry App World to get a sense of what's available.

Further, I assume you have or will obtain the following software:

- ✔ **32-bit Windows XP, Vista, or 7:** As of this writing, only 32-bit versions of Windows support the BlackBerry development tools.

- ✔ **The Sun Java Software Development Kit (JDK), version 1.5 or higher:** The BlackBerry development tools are themselves Java applications and need JDK 1.5 or later to run.

- ✔ **The BlackBerry Java Development Environment (JDE):** You can get the JDE for free, but you must become a registered BlackBerry developer first. Registration is also free. Registering with RIM and downloading the JDE are covered in detail in Chapter 2.

And finally, I assume you have some programming knowledge and that you have at least a basic understanding of object-oriented programming (OOP), specifically in Java. If you're not up to speed with Java, consider *Java For Dummies,* 4th Edition, by Barry Burd, or *Java All-In-One Desk Reference For Dummies,* 2nd Edition, by Doug Lowe and Barry Burd (all from Wiley Publishing). Sun's online tutorials are helpful as well.

How This Book Is Organized

The chapters in *BlackBerry Application Development For Dummies* are divided into seven parts.

Part 1: Getting Started on BlackBerry Apps

Part I takes you into the world of BlackBerry application development. You find out about BlackBerry applications in general, and you discover some of the challenges that your app might encounter on a BlackBerry smartphone. You also discover how to become a registered BlackBerry developer and all the steps you need to take so you're ready to deliver to the BlackBerry App World.

Part II: BlackBerry Application Development

In Part II, you dive right into code. Not the deep end, but not exactly shallow, either. You start with structure and then touch all the pieces of code to make an application do everything it needs to do to communicate with the user and behave like a proper BlackBerry app.

Part III: Developing Enterprise-Class BlackBerry Apps

In Part III, I expose you to the use of BlackBerry devices in the world of a corporate enterprise, which is where many BlackBerry users live. You discover the advantages of a BlackBerry that is tied directly to a corporate network — and I show you the constraints this can place on your application. You also discover the benefits and the challenges for your app to communicate over a network to reach from the corner office to the limits of the Internet.

Part IV: Finishing and Debugging Your App

Part IV provides you with the information you need to put the finishing touches on your application. Here's where you find out how to debug your application on both a simulator and on a real device. I also show you how to submit and upload your app to the BlackBerry App World.

Part V: Securing and Supporting Your App

In Part V, I introduce you to some of the better disciplines I've found to develop solid code. The chapters in this part give you information regarding some of the different tools you can use to keep track of the different pieces of information for the applications you develop. The information found here helps you look to the future of when you'll be writing and releasing multiple applications, and trying to keep track of every piece of all of them.

Part VI: The Part of Tens

Part VI contains some of the "Wish I'd thought of that before I started" kinds of tips that help you get your code prepared to do its job better and make it easier for your app to evolve smoothly. I also point you to some of the many sample applications that can give you ideas or help you overcome challenges with examples.

Part VII: Appendixes

The first of the appendixes informs you about the simulators — including simulated devices and simulated services — that you use to assist in developing your application. The second appendix gives you information about real devices and how to use them to test your application. Some of the real services are a bit beyond the beginner level for setting up, but Appendix B provides you with the information you need to be aware of when your application encounters them in the real world.

Icons Used in This Book

Like all *For Dummies* books, this book makes frequent use of icons to help identify important, helpful, or technical information. Take heed when you see one of the following icons.

This icon indicates a useful pointer that you shouldn't skip. Tips make your coding life easier by showing a shortcut or letting you know the information next to it shows you the easiest approach to a coding problem.

This icon represents a friendly reminder. It describes a vital point that you should keep in mind while proceeding through a particular section of the chapter.

This icon signifies that the accompanying explanation might be informative, maybe even interesting, but is technical and isn't required for your goal of understanding BlackBerry application development. Feel free to jump over these little pieces.

This icon alerts you to potential challenges you may encounter on the way. Read and obey these commentaries to avoid problems down the road.

Where to Go from Here

You're ready to begin the BlackBerry adventure. You can, of course, turn the page and continue reading at Chapter 1. If you haven't registered with RIM to become a BlackBerry application developer and downloaded the JDE, I recommend you hop right to Chapter 2. If you have a particular question or problem, check the Index or Table of Contents to find the information you need.

If you have questions or comments about the book or BlackBerry development in general, contact me at kgkfordummies@gmail.com. You can also find additional information about my BlackBerry application, The Word Locker, at www.thewordlocker.com. You can find sample code for this book at www.dummies.com/go/blackberryappdev.

Good luck, and happy coding!

Part I

Getting Started on BlackBerry Apps

The 5th Wave   By Rich Tennant

"This model comes with a particularly useful app – a simulated static button for breaking out of long-winded conversations."

In this part . . .

Your goal is to develop an application that runs on one of the most widely known and well respected smartphones in the world today — the BlackBerry. You have a great idea, and you know all the pieces needed to satisfy your customers. So now what?

You start here. This part shows you how to start developing BlackBerry applications, including what tools you need, where to get them, and how to use them. This part shows you how to become a registered BlackBerry developer, which will get you access to all the free programs that Research In Motion (RIM) provides to help you develop, debug, and produce your app. From there, you become a card-carrying BlackBerry App World Vendor, which allows you to deliver your application to RIM for review as a submission to the BlackBerry App World.

Also in this part, you get a chance to see what's already in the App World, which presents an opportunity to improve and refine your app idea. Finally, you get your feet wet by producing a simple application that will run on a simulator or a real device.

Chapter 1

Gathering What You Need to Develop BlackBerry Apps

In This Chapter

▶ Discovering BlackBerry apps and why to develop them

▶ Collecting the right tools

▶ Sharpening the right skills

▶ Meeting the challenges of BlackBerry development

A BlackBerry application is meant to be small, fast, and responsive to its users. BlackBerry smartphones are small, fast, and function as mini-communications centers: a phone, text-messaging system, e-mail client, and Web browser. Your app should give the user the same kind of experience as the standard apps that come with the BlackBerry, providing information quickly and easily with a minimal amount of input.

In this chapter, I show you what tools, skills, and ideas you need to gather and discover to start developing BlackBerry apps.

Why Develop BlackBerry Apps?

The BlackBerry App World from Research In Motion (RIM) provides a marketplace devoted to BlackBerry users, and a great many apps of all different kinds have yet to be built. BlackBerry devices have been around a while, mostly as mobile corporate e-mail connections, but the individual consumer is now getting into BlackBerry devices as well, increasing the number of places your app can be running. Figure 1-1 shows the Home Screen of my BlackBerry Curve, with the BlackBerry Browser Application highlighted. Figure 1-2 shows the Browser while running.

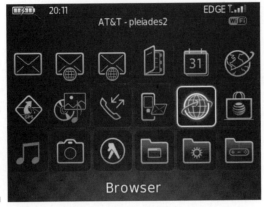

Figure 1-1:
The
BlackBerry
Curve Home
Screen with
the Browser
application
selected.

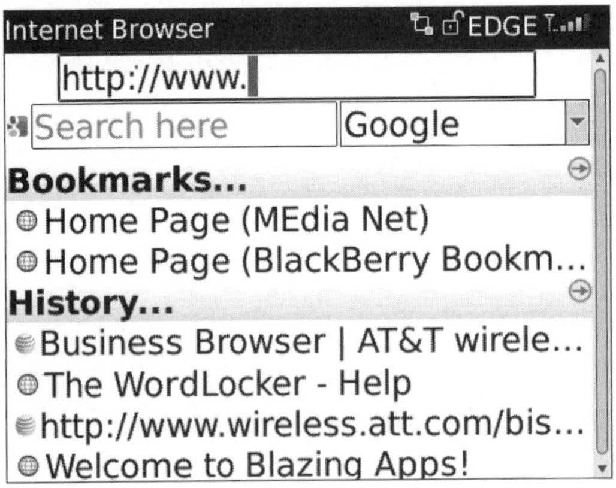

Figure 1-2:
The
Browser
application
in action.

Here are a few other reasons why I see the BlackBerry as a great development opportunity:

- ✔ **BlackBerry applications tend to be small.** This makes them easy to develop and maintain, and they don't require a large development team: You need fewer people to debate the pros and cons of different ways to do the same thing.

- ✔ **BlackBerry apps narrowly focus on delivering what the user wants, and no more.** The apps are simple and direct, providing the user with only the information they want — and the tools to get it.

- ✔ **BlackBerry apps use Java.** You can leverage any desktop PC Java programming experience you have.

- ✔ **The tools and simulators are all free.** You can do all your development on a Windows PC. The simulators all execute the same code as the actual devices, so you can be sure that if your app works on a simulator, it will work on a real device.

✔ **The BlackBerry is widely used in corporate enterprises.** From CEOs to administrative assistants and everyone in between, you have a market for business-specific apps that could link everyone in the enterprise.

✔ **RIM provides the BlackBerry App World for you to showcase and sell your app.** This venue removes the responsibility of credit card handling, hosting, downloading, and notifying users of updates. The App World comes with a variety of pricing tiers, including free and Try & Buy. RIM keeps 20 percent of your application price to cover some of its costs. Submitting your app to the App World incurs a $20 fee per submission, which you can buy in blocks of ten for $200.

Discovering Apps, BlackBerry Style

BlackBerry users are on-the-go, fast-paced, living in the moment, and your app will need to behave accordingly. BlackBerry users are interested in getting their information *now;* they can't wait more than a few seconds after launching your app to get to the stuff they expect your app to deliver. Your application must accommodate your users and provide them with a means of getting to the value your app adds to their mobile existence. Whether it provides a world traveler with a list of restaurants open around the clock for the city they just arrived in, or merely provides a few moments of entertainment while they're waiting to board their next flight, your app must be easy to use, simple to learn — and, as much as possible, fun.

Getting familiar with standard apps

The best way to find out more about BlackBerry applications is, well, to use them. Look at the apps that run on a BlackBerry out of the box. You can use a real device or use the BlackBerry simulator that comes with the JDE. Every BlackBerry comes with the following standard apps:

✔ Browser

✔ Messages (Email and SMS)

✔ Contact Manager

✔ Calendar/Address Book

✔ Memo Pad

✔ Tasks

✔ Calculator

✔ Alarm Clock

Each one of these applications, written by RIM, contains the basic interactions that BlackBerry users expect to see in your application. BlackBerry users will be using the standard applications often, and so you should become familiar with how users get things done with them. Figure 1-3 shows the BlackBerry Email application as I check my mail account.

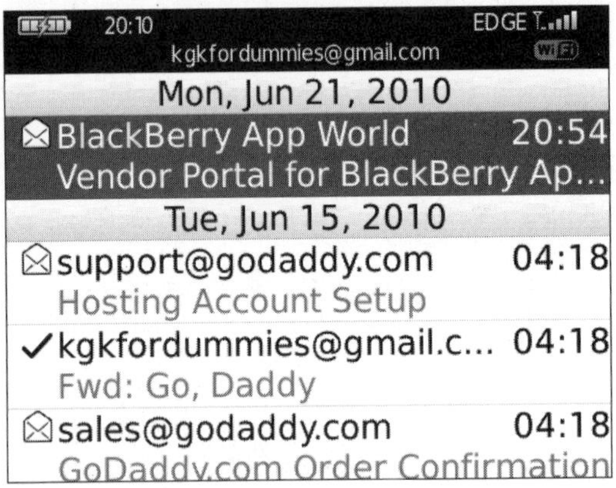

Figure 1-3: The BlackBerry Email app. BlackBerry Email lets you connect to any e-mail service provider, such as Gmail.

Understanding how users navigate and use their BlackBerry smartphones

Most users get most of what they need from a BlackBerry application by using just one hand, and often, just by using their thumbs on the trackpad (or trackwheel/trackball for older devices).

The primary input mechanism for a BlackBerry is the pointing device, which can take one of several forms, depending on which model BlackBerry your user has.

✔ **Trackwheel:** Users move the wheel on the side of the BlackBerry to make the selection highlight move back and forth; users select a highlighted item by pressing in the trackwheel. Figure 1-4 shows a BlackBerry 8700 and its trackwheel.

Trackwheel

Figure 1-4:
The
BlackBerry
8700
smartphone
provides a
trackwheel.

✔ **Trackball:** Users can move across the pointer around the two-dimensional BlackBerry screen; to select a highlighted item, the user clicks the trackball itself. Figure 1-5 shows a BlackBerry 8830 with its trackball.

Figure 1-5:
The BlackBerry 8830 smartphone sports a trackball for input.

Trackball

✔ **Trackpad:** Users touch the pad lightly to move the selection highlight, and press down to click. You can see the trackpad of the BlackBerry Bold (9700) in Figure 1-6.

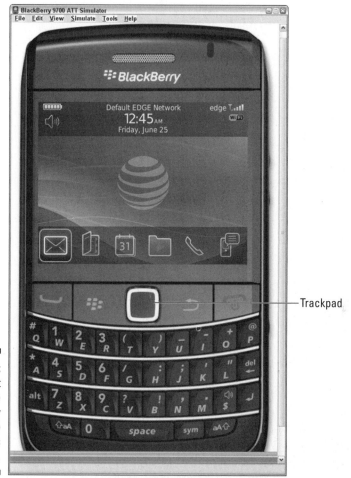

Figure 1-6: RIM's latest offering: the BlackBerry Bold (9700) and its trackpad.

✔ **Touchscreen:** Users touch the screen lightly to move the selection highlight, and press down slightly to click the item selected. Figure 1-7 shows you what a BlackBerry Storm looks like, with its touchscreen.

Each input mechanism comes with its own advantages and disadvantages, and this is important when developing your app. You might discover that your app is easy to use on a touchscreen device, yet difficult to use on a device with a trackwheel. If so, you might decide to create two versions of your app: one optimized for use on a BlackBerry Storm, and one for all the other devices. Keep in mind that you might have to adjust your app based on what type of pointing device the user's BlackBerry supports.

Touchscreen

Figure 1-7:
The
BlackBerry
Storm with
its touch-
screen.

Although all BlackBerry devices have a keyboard for users to enter text data, ideally your app should require very little text input. Typing text into a small BlackBerry keyboard is slower than typing on a full-size laptop or desktop keyboard. Investigate whether there is another way for users to provide information.

As long as I'm talking about keyboards, there's one more thing you need to know. BlackBerry smartphones offer two different types of keyboards for users:

✓ **SureType:** You find this keyboard on the BlackBerry Pearl and Pearl Flip smartphones, as well as a BlackBerry Storm when in portrait mode. Figure 1-8 shows an image of a Pearl with its keyboard. Because the keyboard has fewer keys than a normal keyboard, SureType provides two letters for each key, and the keyboard is laid out like a regular QWERTY keyboard. SureType attempts to predict what a user is typing to speed up the entry of data. Some BlackBerry models with SureType offer a mode called Multitap, where the first tap of a key enters the first letter for that key, and a quick double-tap enters the second letter for that key.

Figure 1-8:
The BlackBerry Pearl and its SureType keyboard, with its guesses for the word I type.

✔ **Full:** You find a regular QWERTY keyboard on every other BlackBerry model, as well as on the BlackBerry Storm when in landscape mode. This is the keyboard I prefer to use because all the keys represent one character and I don't have to press a key twice. Figure 1-9 shows the BlackBerry Storm in landscape mode with its full QWERTY keyboard on display.

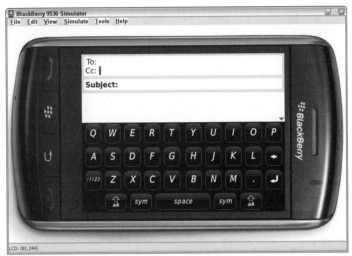

Figure 1-9: BlackBerry Storm rotated clockwise to show the full keyboard on a touch-screen.

Filling Your Toolbox

You are the most important tool in your software development toolkit. Even when you're working as part of a team, your expertise is more important than the other tools you use to create the code. Your skills in using those tools are what make the tools useful. However, you can't develop BlackBerry apps without the right set of software and hardware tools. The following sections describe the software and hardware you need to gather to start creating BlackBerry apps.

Downloading the software you need

The following are the major software tools you use to create BlackBerry applications:

✔ **The BlackBerry Java Development Environment (JDE):** This integrated development environment is available from RIM. The JDE includes the editor, debugger, device simulator, and memory viewer. (See Chapter 2 for the details of choosing a JDE version and downloading it to your PC.)

✔ **The RAPC compiler:** This is the compiler and linker used by the JDE to produce BlackBerry application files. It makes use of the Sun Java compiler (see the following bullet) to compile your BlackBerry Java code, and then packages it into a form that can be installed onto a BlackBerry device. (The acronym RAPC stands for RIM APplication Compiler, and you don't need to download it — the RAPC compiler comes with the BlackBerry JDE.)

✔ **The Sun Java compiler:** This is the Sun Microsystems Java Standard Edition (JSE), which must be version 1.5 or later. You can download the Sun Java compiler from

```
http://java.sun.com/javase/downloads/index.jsp
```

I have run into some difficulty using the JDE on 64-bit Windows machines, including Windows Vista and Windows 7. As of this writing, the RIM JDE requires a 32-bit operating system (OS), with a 32-bit version of Sun's Java, in order to run at all. In addition, there is no Macintosh OSX tool for BlackBerry development, unless you use a *virtualization application* (an application that allows you to run other operating systems within it).

RIM offers a plug-in for the Eclipse development environment. *Eclipse* is an open source (free) Java development environment you can download from `www.eclipse.org`. This book concentrates on development using the RIM JDE, but if you're comfortable using Eclipse, you should definitely investigate RIM's plug-in. As of this writing, the current version of BlackBerry Java Plug-in for Eclipse is 1.1, and makes use of the BlackBerry OS 5.0 APIs. Information about the RIM Eclipse plugin can be found at

```
http://na.blackberry.com/eng/developers/devbetasoftware/javaplugin.jsp
```

Gathering BlackBerry simulators

The BlackBerry JDE comes with several supporting applications to assist you in developing a quality BlackBerry application. You use smartphone simulators to execute your app just as if it were running on a real BlackBerry device. You use the service simulators to represent the real-world services for the BlackBerry to access the Internet (through your PC) or to simulate sending and receiving e-mail. You use simulators in your development process to test your apps before you run them on an actual BlackBerry smartphone. You can download the smartphone simulators from RIM at the following URL:

```
http://na.blackberry.com/eng/developers/resources/simulators.jsp
```

Appendix A contains more information regarding smartphone and service simulators.

Basically, here are the four types of simulator applications you want to use:

- ✔ **JDE device simulators:** These come with the JDE, and you launch them with your application already installed. Each JDE comes with its own set of simulated devices, and the newer JDEs have the newest device types simulated. Read more about the device types per JDE version in Appendix A.

  The smartphone simulators that each JDE includes in its set simulates a version of the smartphone OS for that particular version of the JDE. For instance, the BlackBerry JDE 4.5.0 comes with a simulator for a BlackBerry smartphone 8320, and this smartphone shows that it is running smartphone OS 4.5.0.44.

- ✔ **Downloaded device simulators:** RIM provides new simulators on its Web site on a regular basis. You can download and install these simulators for free. RIM updates its JDEs less frequently than it releases new devices, so check for new simulator downloads, even while you're in the middle of developing your app. Figure 1-10 shows my application, The Word Locker, running on a simulated BlackBerry Curve (8900).

- ✔ **The Mobile Data Service (MDS) simulator:** This comes with the JDE. A BlackBerry device can talk to the Internet only with the help of an MDS. A real BlackBerry will be associated with either the RIM-hosted BlackBerry Internet Service (BIS) or a corporate BlackBerry Enterprise Server (BES). Each of these associations provides MDS services, allowing the device to connect to the Internet. A *simulated* device can't connect to a *real* MDS service, and so the MDS simulator provides Internet access for device simulators. If your application needs to communicate using the Internet, you will have to use the MDS simulator while using a device simulator.

- ✔ **The Email Service Simulator (ESS):** This comes with the JDE. BlackBerry users love their e-mail, and RIM has created an e-mail simulator that can act as a gateway to a real e-mail server for a BlackBerry device simulator.

The best thing about all these simulators: They're free!

Building or buying a development computer

When you're creating apps for the BlackBerry, your choice of computers is limited to a PC running Windows — Windows XP, Windows Vista, and Windows 7 all work with the BlackBerry development tools, but only as long as they are 32-bit versions (not 64-bit versions). Your choice of programming languages is limited to Java, version 1.5 or later, again using the 32-bit version. This pretty much spells out what you need computer-wise to do BlackBerry development. I've worked on several different computers to do BlackBerry development. In general, it's better to have a fast machine with lots of RAM, though you certainly don't need to buy the most expensive new computer on the market.

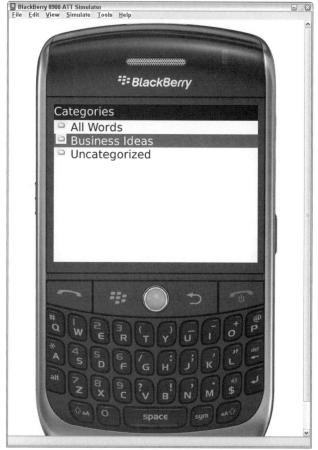

Figure 1-10:
A
BlackBerry
smartphone
simulator
running the
application
WordLocker.

Your development machine will need to handle the following tasks when you're developing BlackBerry software:

✔ **Editing code:** Any computer running Windows XP can support the requirements of the JDE or any other text editor you prefer. Any machine that can run Windows Vista or Windows 7 is also an appropriate choice.

Because Microsoft is no longer supporting Windows XP, you might want to use a newer version of Windows. While Windows XP still works well for developing BlackBerry apps, you should consider the advantages of using a newer Windows OS such as Windows 7 because keeping XP running will get more and more difficult as time goes on.

✔ **Compiling the code into an application:** This is one of the most power-hungry operations you will be performing again and again. Compiling Java code is very CPU- and memory-intensive, so you want a machine that has good processor speed, and as much memory as you can give it.

As mentioned previously, only 32-bit versions of Java and the Windows operating system can be used for BlackBerry development with RIM's tools.

✔ **Executing and debugging the application using a simulator:** The device simulators are Windows applications that completely mimic the operations of a real BlackBerry device. The service simulators provide functionality that you use to enable your simulated BlackBerry to access the Internet and send or receive e-mail messages. This requires a machine that has good processor speed and a lot of memory.

A good midrange computer with a large amount of memory, as much as it can use, will support your needs for BlackBerry application development. Table 1-1 shows the requirements for a bare-bones development PC and for a development PC with power to spare.

Table 1-1	Requirements for a Development PC	
Equipment	*Minimum Requirements*	*Optimum Requirements*
Processor	2.0 GHz processor	3.0 GHz multi-code CPU
RAM	2GB	4GB
Operating system	Windows XP (Service Pack 3)	Windows 7/32-bit
Java version	Java 1.5.0	Java 1.6.0
Network connection	DSL	Cable

Choosing a BlackBerry device

The BlackBerry models available as of this writing are

✔ Bold (9000, 9650, and 9700)

✔ Curve (83xx, 85xx, and 89xx)

✔ Pearl and Pearl Flip (81xx and 82xx)

✔ Storm and Storm2 (95xx)

✔ Tour (9630)

✔ 8800 series

These models are available through the major wireless carriers. A particular model may be exclusive to a particular carrier — for instance, the Storm and Storm2 devices are currently Verizon-only, whereas the Bold and Curve devices were originally AT&T-only. AT&T and Verizon strike deals with RIM to be the sole providers of a particular model, but usually the exclusivity is time limited. For instance, Verizon and Sprint have been selling models of the Curve for a couple of years now, after AT&T's contract with RIM to be the only provider selling the Curve ended.

There are pretty much just two ways to acquire a BlackBerry:

✔ **Purchase one, new or refurbished, from a wireless service provider.** This requires a service contract with the wireless service provider, which might not fit into your budget.

✔ **Buy one used.** This way is usually less expensive than buying from a wireless service provider but comes with its own set of advantages and disadvantages.

See Appendix B for more information on buying new or used smartphones.

Using Your Programming Skills

You will need some general skills to develop BlackBerry applications:

✔ **Java programming:** The Java programming language is the development language for BlackBerry applications. Your source modules must represent Java classes, which get compiled into Java class files and then packaged for the BlackBerry device OS to execute.

✔ **Debugging:** After you code your app, there's a statistical likelihood that it won't be perfect. If you're lucky, the imperfections will show up rather quickly and obviously. As you develop more applications, you'll find that the obvious and quickly fixed problems happen less often, which leaves the subtle and more-challenging bugs. Your skills at debugging — looking at code as it runs, keeping track of what is going right and what is going wrong, and so on — will play an important part in completing your apps.

✔ **Software design patterns:** Like with most modern computing platforms, your app will benefit from using software patterns where appropriate. You can certainly create a functional and usable BlackBerry application without relying on any of the canonical design patterns, but applications that are to have a long-duration existence will require a solid structure for operation that the use of software patterns will support. The most obvious is the Model-View-Controller (MVC) pattern, which enforces the separation of your app into pieces that are easy to manage. (See Chapter 4 for more information about MVC.)

Java programming for BlackBerry

For BlackBerry development, you should be familiar with Java programming in general, and you should know the basics of Java syntax. BlackBerry Java development is somewhat different from desktop PC Java development. The major difference is BlackBerry Java has a somewhat smaller set of classes that you can use to develop applications. Several of the basic Java packages are available:

✔ `java.io.*`: This package contains the input/output classes you can use to manage retrieving data from and delivering data to various locations, such as Web services and data files.

✔ `java.lang.*`: You will find the familiar Java base classes such as `String` in this package.

✔ `java.util.*`: Some of the classes available in the desktop version of Java are available here, such as `Vector`.

Not all the classes available in the JSE version of these packages are available in the BlackBerry version. For instance, the BlackBerry `java.util.*` package consists of only a dozen or so classes and interfaces, whereas the JSE `java.util.*` package comes with almost ten times as many.

RIM removed many classes because of size and performance constraints. For instance, one of the major changes to the Java language was the addition of *generics* in version 1.5, for use with collection classes such as `Vector` (`java.util.Vector`). RIM has not implemented generics for use with BlackBerry development in part because this feature requires a great deal of overhead (such as OS functionality) that doesn't provide a dramatic improvement in the end result in terms of performance.

In addition to these standard Java packages, several of the `javax` and `org` packages are also available:

✔ `javax.microedition.*`: The Java Micro Edition (JME) packages are all available for you to use. If you've developed a JME application, you can run it without modification on a BlackBerry.

✔ `javax.bluetooth.*`: Your application can access the Bluetooth hardware on a BlackBerry, if it's available.

✔ `javax.xml.*`, `org.w3c.dom.*`, `org.xml.*`: These packages provide classes your app can use to read and write blocks of XML data.

RIM provides a fairly rich framework of classes and interfaces that you can use to make your application do just about anything you need. The RIM classes fall into the following three categories:

✔ **Device interactions:** Your applications use the classes in this category's packages (`net.rim.device.*`) to perform operations that make use of the various parts of the BlackBerry device, such as using the smartphone's GPS or communicating with Bluetooth devices. In addition, the classes you use to create every visual user interface object can be found in this category.

✔ **BlackBerry application interactions:** You can use the classes in this category (`net.rim.blackberry.*`) to interact with the standard BlackBerry applications. For instance, your app can create an e-mail message and send it, all without the user having to launch the BlackBerry Mail application.

✔ **Plazmic Media Engine:** This category (`net.rim.plazmic.*`) contains classes your app can use to deliver audio and video content to your users.

Debugging

The BlackBerry development tools come with a source-level debugger. However, your own skills in debugging Java software are what matter most.

I assume that in your software application development experience, your apps didn't always work perfectly. I'm guessing that you've presumably spent time analyzing code to find where the problems were hiding, and ruthlessly eliminated them. In general, debugging is still something of an art. Sure, tools can assist with finding the place where code goes wrong, but you still need creativity and imagination to know where to start looking. Small applications are usually easy to debug, but when your app has several dozen classes and interfaces, bugs find more places to hide.

You can find resources online and in print regarding debugging, as well as techniques and habits that you can use to make your code easier to debug. I've worked on only a few applications where debugging of some sort was not necessary, and that includes the sample applications I show you in the chapters that follow. All of them had quirks and gotchas that required analysis and imagination to overcome.

Using software patterns

The world of software has been around long enough that a lot of the ways to solve problems have become standardized. You'll find that using software patterns can greatly simplify your code. This leads to code that's easier to maintain. Patterns tend to be simple and effective, focusing on delivering a limited set of functionality within your app. A class in your application that represents a particular software pattern for achieving a particular objective is straightforward and easy to test.

The simplest example of a software pattern that you might use is one I employ in a great many of my applications: the Singleton pattern. Only one instance of a `singleton` class will exist in an application. Most `singleton` classes have the general appearance shown in Listing 1-1.

Listing 1-1:   The Smallest Form of a Singleton Pattern, Implemented in Java

```
public class SingletonClass
{
    private static SingletonClass m_instance;

    public static SingletonClass getInstance()
    {
        if (null == m_instance)
        {
            m_instance = new SingletonClass();
        }
        return (m_instance);
    }

    private SingletonClass()
    {
        // initialization code
    }

    //
    // the remainder of the methods
    //
}
```

Any code that makes use of this `SingletonClass` will execute `Singleton Class.getInstance()`. This method will instantiate *(create)* and initialize the solitary instance of this class available for the application the first time the method is called, and return that instance that time and every subsequent time the method is called.

Your application can make use of the Singleton pattern when you want to restrict access to one specific location for information. This pattern comes in useful for a large number of different parts of an application, such as

- ✔ **User settings:** You will normally have only one user of your application, and so storing that user's preferences for your application in a `singleton` class makes perfect sense.

- ✔ **Resource connections:** Access to resources such as a database should be funneled through one object because opening a connection to a resource usually requires substantial code execution. Opening the connection once and maintaining it through your application's lifetime incurs less overhead than multiple openings and closings. You can use a `singleton` class to ensure that a connection is opened only once.

Understanding BlackBerry Application Development Challenges

If BlackBerry programming were easy, you wouldn't need this book. So you need to be prepared for the inevitable difficulties that will appear. Sometimes these challenges are caused by the BlackBerry device or its OS, and you will have to "code around" these types of problems. Sometimes you will discover you have coded yourself into a corner: for example, a particular decision of how to code something at an earlier moment has forced responsibilities upon your code further down the development path.

The following sections describe the challenges that you'll face in writing BlackBerry applications.

Choosing an OS version

You have to decide what version of the BlackBerry OS your application will execute on. This is the most significant decision you must make because it will influence and constrain your application's capabilities.

RIM produces new BlackBerry devices — and, therefore, new BlackBerry OS versions — several times per year. In 2009 alone, the following new devices were released:

- ✔ Storm2
- ✔ Bold 9700
- ✔ Curve 8900
- ✔ Tour

Each of these devices came with its own new version of the BlackBerry OS. OS versions are usually represented by four numbers separated with dots, such as 4.7.0.113. The first two numbers are usually the most important; they are the major and minor version numbers. The difference in behavior between OS 4.6.0.49 and OS 4.6.0.75 is likely to be minor although I have come across times when such a version upgrade has fixed a bug that my code encountered.

It's true! Sometimes you will discover that your perfectly debugged and packaged code comes across a bug in the OS!

The differences between minor OS versions — say, OS 4.6 versus OS 4.7 — will likely be significant. Of the two just mentioned, OS 4.7 is interesting because it's the only OS that runs on the BlackBerry Storm and Storm2 devices. What's interesting about these devices? Two things:

- ✔ Storm and Storm2 use the touchscreen as their primary input mechanism. This permits your app to make use of users sliding their fingers around the screen, enabling your app to perform some actions more fluidly.

- ✔ Storm and Storm2 have accelerometers to indicate the orientation of the display. Your app can take advantage of knowing whether the user has switched the device's orientation from portrait (taller than wide) to landscape (wider than tall). You can see the Storm showing its landscape mode in Figure 1-9.

Each JDE has a version number as well, and this version number corresponds to the version number of the OS that you can code for. I can't stress this fact enough:

The version of the JDE you choose will limit which devices your app can run on.

For more information about choosing a JDE version, see Chapter 2.

The JDE version is the minimum device OS version that your app will execute on. Your application's code will usually be *forward compatible:* That is, newer device OS versions will usually execute code created using an earlier JDE version. This isn't always true, but it's a safe bet for the next several subsequent versions of the OS. This also depends on what BlackBerry classes your app uses to do its job. A bare-bones minimalist application that does something simple such as take user text input and store it in memory isn't likely to run afoul of changes in the device OS for several versions to come.

RIM releases a device OS about once every year that runs on all of a set of the currently available devices. As of this writing, a version of OS 5.0 can run on all the devices that were released in 2009, plus several others that came out in 2008. Currently, the OS version that runs on the greatest number of smartphones is OS 4.5.0.

Using version 5.0 of the JDE, you can develop applications that will run on every device using OS 5.0. This will mean your app can use classes that take advantage of the features listed above for the Storm series of devices but still run (without any ill effects) on non-Storm devices. However, because a non-Storm phone (such as a BlackBerry Pearl Flip) has neither a touchscreen nor an accelerometer, code written to take advantage of these features won't install on the device because the OS won't know what to do when it comes across those specific features in your app. However, a Pearl Flip running OS 5.0 will allow code implemented to use those specific features to execute, although that part of the code will simply do nothing.

The BlackBerry App World, RIM's online marketplace for BlackBerry applications, allows you to deploy separate apps that differ only based on which device each one is intended to run on. RIM recognizes that you want your application to run on as many different devices as can access the App World, but that you also want your application to take advantage of the features each device provides, instead of just coding to one common-denominator, lower-level device OS.

Thus, your application can exist in the App World in multiple forms. For example, if you intend for your app to be used only by those users who have accelerometers in their BlackBerry devices, you can restrict your app to an OS 4.7-only zone, and no other device will be able to install it. ***Note:*** If you want your app to run on all devices but also take advantage of accelerometers when running on a Storm, you have to develop two versions of your app: one for Storm devices and then one for all the rest.

The key point is that these two different applications only constitute one app submission to the App World, so you're only paying for one submission instead of two. Chapter 12 goes over the details you need to know about the App World, and your app's life there.

Programming defensively

Your application hopefully will be used by tens of thousands of people worldwide. When that happens, each user becomes a stress test for your app. These users will inadvertently discover ways of breaking your application — causing unforeseen consequences to occur — that you never thought of. Your users will be your next major challenge.

Users follow a bell curve in terms of their use of your app. Most will behave exactly as you expect, following a "happy path" of operation where they never encounter shortcomings in your app and never try to make the app do something incorrect. But a small faction of users either intentionally or unintentionally drives your app into a situation it's not prepared to handle. If you're working for a large organization with a Quality Assurance department, a great many of these situations can be discovered and resolved before your code hits the outside world. If you're a solo entrepreneur, the burden falls on your shoulders.

Most abnormal situations are a result of invalid user input. This specific cause can be eliminated through the use of fixed-input entry fields: UI elements that restrict user input to particular data types or specific values. In addition, your app should "sanitize" the data that users can provide as input, to make sure that nothing bad gets inside your app to wreak havoc.

For instance, your app may want users to enter a date value, perhaps for a birthday reminder. You could use a simple text-editing component, such as an `EditField`, for users to select and start typing in a date. But you would then have to make sure that what they enter is actually a real date — this could be any of the following:

- 09/01/10
- September 1, 2010
- 2010-09-01

As you can see, letting users enter arbitrary text data forces you to implement the appropriate conversion method for turning their entries into a form more suitable for your app to make comparisons and calculations with. However, a basic text-entry field also allows your users to enter text such as *Karl's Birthday* just as easily.

This text will pretty much crash your application if it tries to add or subtract days, months, or years to or from it. A better way to ensure that only valid date values, easily converted to a usable form, are entered is to use UI components that *limit* what a user is permitted to enter. In this case, using a component such as a `DateField` would be much more appropriate. Unless you want to give your users more flexibility — which forces you to convert every possible input to an appropriate, usable form within your app.

 Another potential cause of problems is users who download a version of your app that is not valid for their smartphone OS. Luckily, the BlackBerry App World gives you the ability to provide multiple versions of your application customized to the different smartphones that RIM supports. You discover all this in Chapter 12.

Entering a Brave, New BlackBerry App World

With the success of the Apple App Store for delivering software to iPhone devices, major smartphone manufacturers and even some wireless service providers are designing and deploying their own storefronts to sell applications designed for their platforms. As mentioned earlier, RIM hosts the BlackBerry App World, which is an online marketplace for all kinds of BlackBerry applications. The App World provides many categories of applications for BlackBerry users to download, such as Business, Education, Games, News, Shopping, and Utilities. (For the complete list, see Chapter 12).

Each category is further subdivided, allowing prospective buyers to drill down through the store and find the app that's right for them. You, as a developer, should become familiar with the user's experience of searching and finding apps in the BlackBerry App World, to place your app in the right category and to make sure your app shows off its best face. You find out about all the App World categories and their subcategories in Chapter 12.

Deciding what kind of app to create

If you already have an idea for an app, great! You've passed one of the most difficult steps on your way to BlackBerry App World riches! Figuring out what you want to develop can be challenging, so I recommend that you review the apps available in the App World in a variety of different categories. Think of this exercise as window shopping. Your imagination will be working in the background while you look at what's for sale already, and all it takes is one example to trigger something wonderful.

Brainstorming, alone or in groups

I am a co-founder of a small startup, BlazingApps. The other co-founders and I sit down irregularly for a brainstorming session. We go around the table and contribute an idea or many about different apps we've thought about since the previous meeting. I enjoy this kind of imaginative collaboration and highly recommend it. Granted, you might find it difficult to brainstorm all by yourself, so for the solo entrepreneur, I highly recommend writing down any thoughts or ideas somewhere so that you can easily find them again. You should write down everything, no matter how small or unimportant you might think it is. This way, you'll have a collection of thoughts and imaginings that you can use to spark more of the same. Or else, some combination of your thoughts and imaginings across a spectrum of your recorded notes will group together and prove to be an app worth creating.

How one idea leads to another

For instance, in a project on another smartphone device, I once had a need to display text in a variety of the available fonts to demonstrate to the user experience specialist what the device's different fonts would look like. Several apps were available at this platform's marketplace to do this, and even writing my own was fairly straightforward.

But it got me thinking: The fundamental problem I was trying to solve was an inability on the part of the development team to quickly and clearly see what the results of our choices for user interface elements would actually end up looking like. There was no way for the user experience specialist to "play around" with different settings and get an instant reaction to the settings on a real device.

Unless.... What if I created an app that allowed a user of the smartphone to mix and match fonts and buttons and labels and menus and all the other user interface objects on the phone itself? In essence, this would be an "interface creator" application, running on the actual device, so that anyone with a device could "try out" different combinations of user interface items. Developing such an application would be helpful to anyone in an organization who wants to prototype user interface development, without actually having to write code.

This is the kind of imagination-behind-the-scenes that can lead to applications that your users will want to use. I haven't gone out to build this particular app, yet, but you have my permission to make the attempt.

Even if you're a solo entrepreneur, talking with other developers or even just acquaintances can generate ideas. You can scan the BlackBerry online forums to pick up what issues users are running into and develop ideas based on problems they are encountering and — obviously — want a solution for.

Becoming a BlackBerry developer and App World vendor

Your first step toward BlackBerry app development is to register with RIM as a BlackBerry developer. You then gain access to a treasure trove of all things BlackBerry, including

- ✔ All BlackBerry JDE downloads
- ✔ All BlackBerry simulator downloads
- ✔ Articles pertaining to BlackBerry development (the Knowledge Base)
- ✔ The official BlackBerry online development forums
- ✔ All developer documentation

The developer registration process is pretty straightforward. I go over the steps involved in Chapter 2.

Becoming a BlackBerry App World vendor is a little more complicated, with more steps to follow because (you guessed it) money is involved. You need a PayPal account. I go over these details as well in Chapter 2.

Chapter 2

Registering and Downloading

· ·

· ·

*B*efore you can create and sell your killer BlackBerry app, start off by arming yourself with the right hardware.

When you're ready to start creating apps, you need to join the ranks of BlackBerry developers by first registering with Research In Motion. After you confirm your registration, you'll have access to all the resources you need to download the Java Development Environment (JDE) as well as device and service simulators from RIM.

At your disposal, too, is a plethora of BlackBerry technical documentation — and you can even communicate with other developers on the forums. You can find an overwhelming amount of information and tools available at the BlackBerry Web site, and in this chapter, I give you assistance to navigate that Web site and the resources you find there.

Registering with RIM

With your development hardware and software ready at your end, it's time to get connected to Research In Motion. The process is pretty straightforward and easy to get through:

1. **Point your browser to www.blackberry.com.**

   This is the entry point for all things BlackBerry.

2. **Select your country from the drop-down list and then click Go.**

   If you're in the United States, Canada, the UK, or Germany, click the appropriate link beside the Go button.

3. **Click the Developers link at the top of the page.**

   Now you're getting to Developer Central. You see the page shown in Figure 2-1.

4. **Click the Register For Free button.**

5. **On the registration page shown in Figure 2-2, fill in the text boxes so RIM has information about who you are. Then click Next.**

   You need to enter information into all the fields marked Required. Otherwise, the Web site will throw a tantrum and hold its breath until it turns blue.

Figure 2-1:
The BlackBerry Developer Zone for preregistrants.

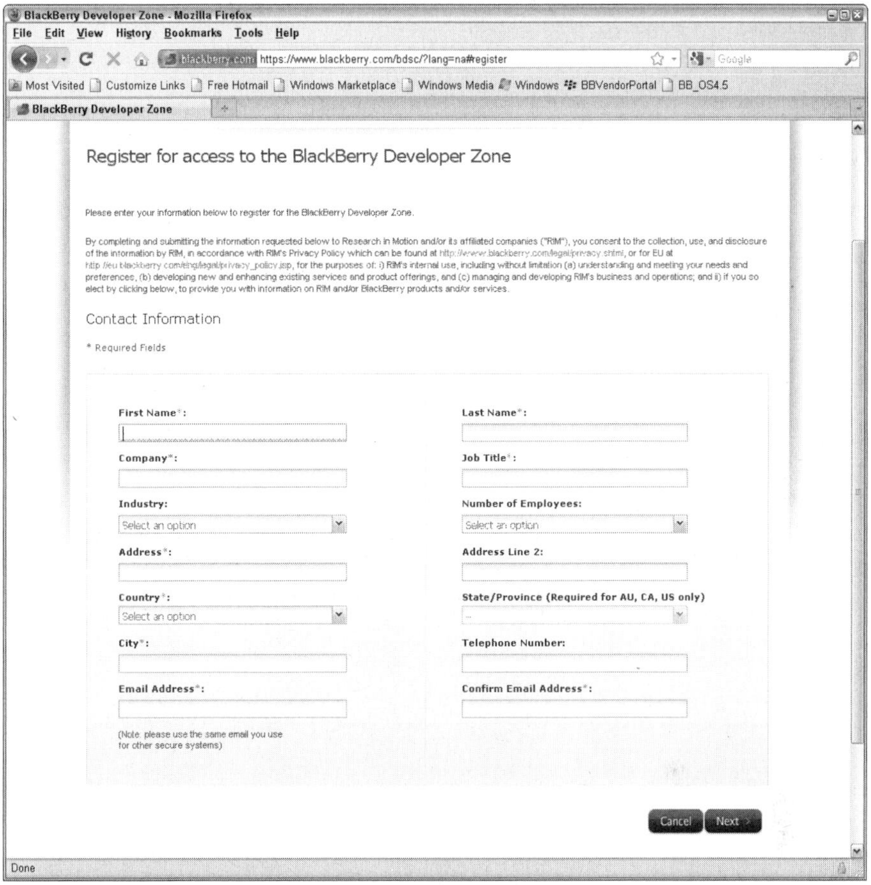

Figure 2-2:
The first
registration
page, to be
filled with
your basic
"Who
am I?"
information.

6. **On the second registration page shown in Figure 2-3, fill in more information about yourself, and then click Next.**

   • Again, you have to provide information in the fields marked Required.

   • RIM wants to know what your role as a developer is, so you select that from the Developer Role drop-down list. I chose the Commercial Consumer Developer item because that's the type of app I intend to release.

   • Under Technology, select the check box(es) for the items you intend to program. For example, I selected the Java, BlackBerry Enterprise Server, and BlackBerry Internet Service check boxes.

- RIM also wants to know your technical level, so you need to select that from the Technical Level – Mobile drop-down list. Select a level you feel comfortable with. Don't worry, there's no wrong answer here.

- Your choice from the list of check boxes in the Specialization section gives RIM an idea of the type of applications you're planning to develop. You can select some, none, or all of these check boxes.

- RIM also wants to know which developer forum you want to subscribe to. As of this writing, you can select only one (which doesn't make a lot of sense to me), but you can access all the forum topics. Lastly, RIM has thoughtfully provided you with two check boxes already selected, enabling RIM and RIM's authorized partners to send you messages about BlackBerry products and services, as well as the Blackberry Developer Newsletter. If you don't want extra messages in your inbox, clear these two check boxes.

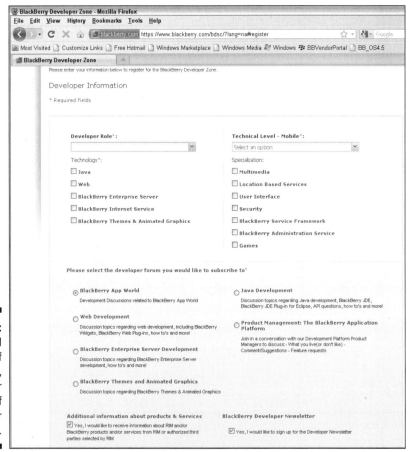

Figure 2-3:
The second part of registration, looking for what kind of developer you are.

7. **Finally, you arrive at the BlackBerry Developer Zone Agreement page. Select the I Agree radio button, and then click the Next button.**

   You must agree to the license agreement to become a registered BlackBerry developer. You see one more page to confirm all the contact information you've just given, and after you submit that, RIM sends you an e-mail containing a link. Click that link to enable your developer account. Then you can log in and access the resources available to developers at the BlackBerry site.

That's it! You are now a fully registered BlackBerry developer. You have access to all the tools and resources available for BlackBerry developers from RIM. The next step: becoming a part of the BlackBerry App World. Onward and upward!

Signing Up to Be a Citizen of the App World

You will find the tools and resources you need for developing your BlackBerry application ready for download from RIM when you complete the developer registration process (described in the previous section). In Chapter 10, I go over the steps necessary for you to purchase signing keys from RIM to allow you to deploy your application onto a real BlackBerry device so you can see it running there — that will mark the completion of your development needs. To sell your app through the BlackBerry App World, one more registration will be required, though: PayPal.

You need a PayPal account before you can be part of the BlackBerry App World. If you don't have a PayPal account, go to www.paypal.com to register. If you need help setting up your account, check out

www.dummies.com/how-to/content/setting-up-your-paypal-account-and-profile.html

BlackBerry App World hired Digital River to manage the behind-the-scenes transaction processing, and payments are made through PayPal for both ends of the transaction. Users who buy your app can use PayPal or a credit card to purchase it, but you receive your share of the proceeds as a payment made to your PayPal account.

Your PayPal account is also how you will pay RIM to become a vendor in the BlackBerry App World, coming up in Step 10 in the following list.

The following steps assume you already have a PayPal account. Follow these steps to link your PayPal account to BlackBerry App World so you can start banking your profits:

1. **Point your browser to**

   ```
   http://na.blackberry.com/eng/developers/appworld
   ```

   If you're already logged in as a registered BlackBerry developer, click the BlackBerry App World Vendor Support link in the upper left of the BlackBerry Developer Zone page (refer to Figure 2-1). You see the page shown in Figure 2-4.

2. **Click the Submit an Application or Theme to BlackBerry App World or Learn How to Register link.**

   I'm not altogether positive why this link is not more prominent; as a BlackBerry developer looking to sell apps through the App World but not knowing where to start, I expected something more obvious. Figure 2-5 shows the results of clicking this link.

3. **Click the Get Started button.**

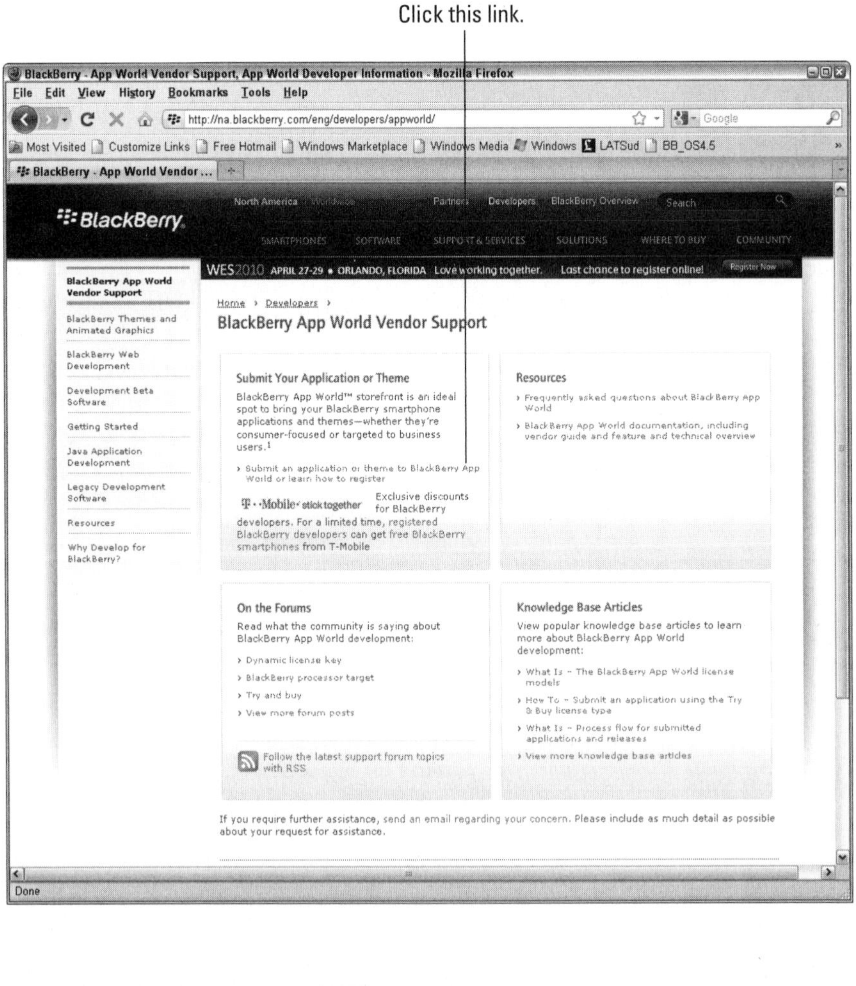

Click this link.

Figure 2-4:
The gateway to the BlackBerry App World for developers.

Figure 2-5:
The Web page where you will begin to enroll as an App World citizen.

4. On the Vendor Registration page that appears, scroll to the bottom of the list box and select the I Have Reviewed the Agreement and Am Prepared and Authorized to Accept the Terms and Conditions Set Out in the Agreement check box.

Undoubtedly for legal reasons, RIM requires that you read (or, more accurately, scroll) to the bottom of the agreement before allowing the check box to be accessible.

Do review the agreement, especially if you're doing corporate development and your company's legal team is required to review it before you accept the agreement. If you're like me, as an individual entrepreneur, agreeing to this agreement is pretty much a no-brainer: Agree and continue, or refuse to agree and be denied access to the App World.

5. Select the Yes radio button if you want to sell your applications using the payment facilities of BlackBerry App World.

If you don't plan to sell your app — that is, you want to provide it for free — select the No radio button.

If you select Yes, the Digital River terms and conditions appear, with yet another agreement you have to commit to.

6. **Scroll to the bottom of the list box, and then select the Do You Agree to the Digital River Terms and Conditions? check box to agree to Digital River's terms and conditions.**

   Digital River handles the payment transactions between the App World and PayPal.

7. **You need to agree to the Bango terms and conditions, so scroll to the bottom of the next list box, and then select the Do You Agree to the Bango Terms and Conditions? check box.**

   Bango is the service that supports selling applications through the wireless carrier's network. This is the last of the agreements for you to agree to.

8. **Click Next.**

9. **Enter your e-mail address, first and last names, phone number, and password in the appropriate text boxes. (See Figure 2-6.) Click Next.**

10. **Enter your vendor information: company name, address, phone number, homepage URL, e-mail, support e-mail, and fax number in the appropriate text boxes. (See Figure 2-7.) Click Next.**

    The Homepage URL and Fax Number text boxes are optional; you must fill out all the other text boxes.

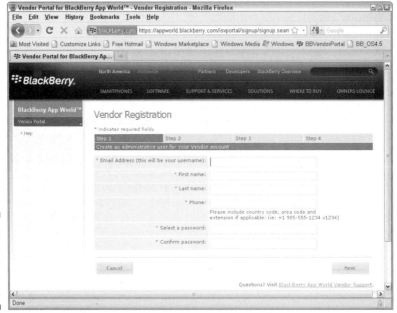

Figure 2-6:
Fill in the form to register as a vendor.

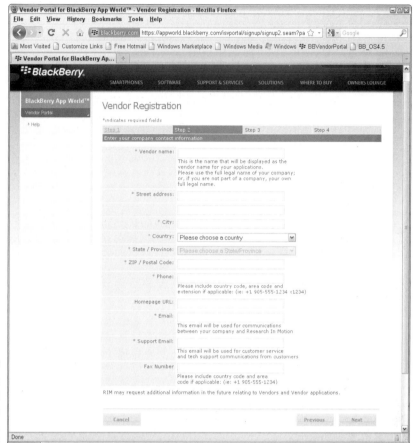

Figure 2-7:
More text
boxes to
fill in.

11. **On the next page, click the Checkout with PayPal button.**

    RIM requires you to pay a $200 service fee to complete your registration and to submit your apps. You go through the standard PayPal payment process to pay the fee. After you complete the payment, you return to the BlackBerry App World Vendor Registration page.

12. **Click Next, and on the final page, click the Done button.**

    Whew! You're finally done.

    Make sure your PayPal account is set up with a valid credit card *before* you start the App World registration process. I set up the PayPal account with a credit card while in the middle of registering, and the App World registration Web page timed out before I was through. This meant I was forced to go through the process from the beginning.

Getting the JDE

RIM has designed and built a great many BlackBerry smartphones to support the myriad needs, likes, and dislikes of business users and consumers. This wealth of devices presents you with a large marketplace in which to sell your app. The flip side is that because there are so many models, each smartphone comes with a different version of the BlackBerry OS to support the unique features of that particular device. Here are just a few of those features:

- ✔ **GPS:** Some BlackBerry devices can determine a physical location via Global Positioning System (GPS). Your app can take advantage of the user's physical location on BlackBerry smartphones that include this feature.

- ✔ **Storage card:** Most BlackBerry devices come with an option for a removable storage card, but some models do not. Your application can use a storage card to preserve large amounts of information; 2GB and larger storage cards are pretty affordable.

- ✔ **Touchscreen:** The BlackBerry Storm and Storm2 smartphones incorporate a touchscreen for user input. Your app can accommodate the user of a touchscreen in a manner different from the other BlackBerry input mechanisms (such as the trackball or the trackpad).

- ✔ **Accelerometer:** The BlackBerry Storm and Storm2 smartphones also incorporate *accelerometers,* which are small electronic components that provide information regarding how the device is being moved and held. You might incorporate acceleration data in an application to track a user's movements through time, such as to move a ball through a maze game.

The challenge comes when deciding what JDE you want to use. The normal approach in the world of desktop PC development is to select the Java development system that contains the best selection of classes that your application wants to use to implement features and functionality for your users. You would then ship your desktop application with a notice that indicates what Java Runtime Environment (JRE) is required to execute your app.

You use a similar approach when developing BlackBerry applications, but here are a couple of points to keep in mind while deciding what version of the JDE you should use to develop your app:

- ✔ **1, 2, 3:** BlackBerry JDE version numbers are related to the first three numbers of the BlackBerry device OS version. Thus, the BlackBerry JDE version 4.5.0 contains code libraries that support devices running OS version 4.5.0 and higher.

- ✔ **Old to new, good:** A BlackBerry application developed with an older OS version *most likely runs* on a BlackBerry device using a newer OS version. For example, if you create an application using version 4.5.0 of the JDE, it almost always executes equivalently on a BlackBerry smartphone that has OS version 4.6 installed. I am being intentionally non–fully committal here, though, because sometimes things don't always work out this way.

✔ **New to old, bad:** A BlackBerry application developed with a newer OS version will *most likely not run* on an older OS version. You encounter this restriction with every platform for which you develop apps for: Namely, the executable you develop for a current OS generally won't run on a prior version of the OS. This is true for BlackBerry OSes just like for any PC OS. And even if you find that the app you developed using BlackBerry JDE 4.5.0 does run on a device using OS 4.2.1, you can never be sure whether some big crash is waiting just around the next corner of code.

As of this writing, the following JDE versions are available for download from RIM, starting with the latest and greatest first:

5.0	4.7.0	4.6.1	4.6.0
4.5.0	4.3.0	4.2.1	4.2.0
4.1.0	4.0.2	4.0.1	4.0.0

I avoid any development environment — BlackBerry or otherwise — in beta. This doesn't mean that JDE 5.0 (as of this writing) is untrustworthy, but that's not something I'd like to find out after shipping an application built using it, especially an application that I expect users to buy. Your mileage may vary.

To find the version number of a BlackBerry device or a simulator, follow these steps:

1. **Turn on the BlackBerry smartphone or open the simulator.**

   Simulators are covered in Appendix A.

2. **Press the Menu button and click the Options icon.**

   You might have to click Settings first to get to the Options icon. Figure 2-8 shows the Options menu.

3. **Select About.**

   Figure 2-9 shows the top of the About screen on my BlackBerry 8900.

   The version number of the OS that your device is running appears near the top of the screen. My BlackBerry 8900 has version 4.6.1.315 of the OS installed — the fourth number (315) is the platform number, and for comparing with the JDE version, this number can be safely ignored. This version numbering means that

   • Applications built using JDE versions 4.6.1 and lower operate on this BlackBerry.

   • Applications built using JDE version 4.7.0 or 5.0.0 (as of this writing, the two highest versions) do not operate on this BlackBerry.

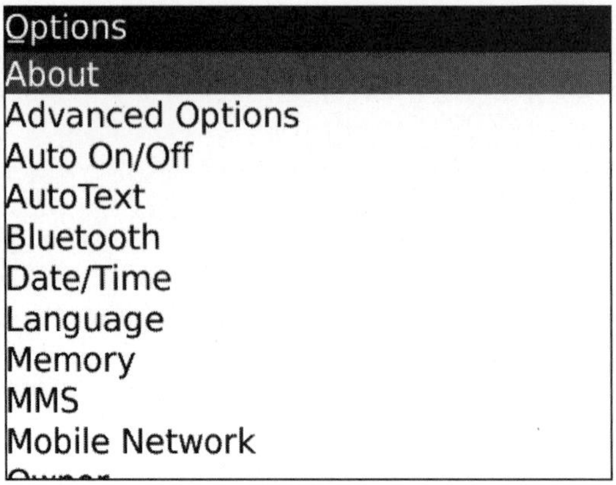

Options
About
Advanced Options
Auto On/Off
AutoText
Bluetooth
Date/Time
Language
Memory
MMS
Mobile Network
Owner

Figure 2-8:
Start from
the Options
menu to find
your version
number.

BlackBerry.

BlackBerry® 8900
smartphone (EDGE, Wi-Fi)
v4.6.1.315 (Platform 4.2.0.108)
Cryptographic Kernel v3.8.5.50a
Branding Version: 1.0.102.117
Micro Edition Configuration: CLDC-
1.1
Micro Edition Profile: MIDP-2.0
Micro Edition JTWI Version: 1.0

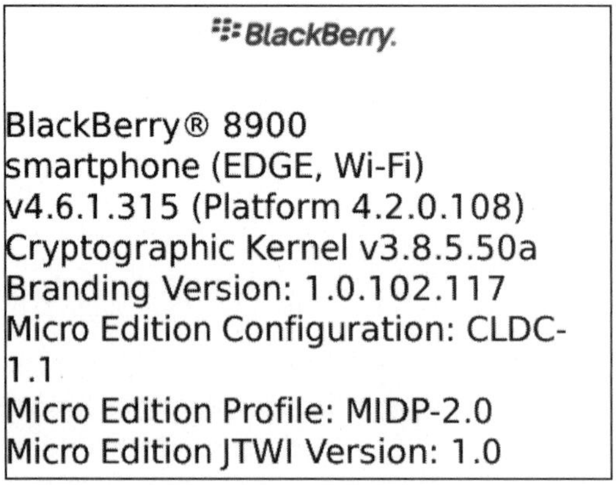

Figure 2-9:
Find your
version
number
here.

Which JDE version is right for you?

You want to pick the JDE that best suits your application. Keep one thing in mind, though, to make that decision easier. Periodically, RIM releases a "One OS for All" — a version of the BlackBerry device OS that's available for an entire set of devices. This means that no matter which previous OS version a device has, it can be upgraded to this "universal" OS. You would then write applications using the equivalent JDE version, and your applications would then be able to run on any device that upgrades to this OS.

Each OS version differs from the versions around it in ways that are either small or large, depending on the features RIM has added or changed. While accelerometer information and touch events required major changes to OS 4.7 (with respect to OS 4.6.1, the previous version), other minor improvements in terms of new classes and methods were also included. And this leads to one of the most beautiful things about the universal versions: Any BlackBerry device running a universal OS executes code developed for previous OS versions. This might not sound very "beautiful" as I promised, but think of it this way: If you wrote an application using JDE 4.7 to take advantage of the accelerometer on a Storm device, that same application executes on any device running OS 5.0, *even if the device does not have an accelerometer*. Now, your accelerometer-using application might not work correctly on a BlackBerry Curve that's upgraded to 5.0, but most of the functionality implemented for your app still works correctly. Normally, your app wouldn't install onto a device that doesn't have the accelerometers your app has been implemented to make use of.

At the time of this writing, device OS version 4.5 is the universal OS. If you use JDE version 4.5.0 to create your apps, you can run your apps on any of the devices that have that OS version or higher. Version 5.0 of the OS is the next universal OS, and devices are now becoming available using that version. Watch out for the following, though, when developing code for such a universal version:

- ✔ **Some devices can be excluded from the universal version.** For instance, the 4.5.0 OS excludes the 71*xx* series of devices.

- ✔ **Users aren't required to upgrade to the new version.** Sad, but true; some users (myself included) find the prospect of upgrading to a new version of an OS to be a scary prospect. Yeah, I know I can always get back to the prior version of the OS, but I'm always fearful of losing all my contacts, e-mails, calendar appointments, and so on. And sure, I can back up all that information. Still, upgrading a BlackBerry to a new OS is the equivalent of erasing your desktop PC's hard drive and then reinstalling everything. There's always a chance that something won't work right.

- ✔ **New OS versions come out frequently, usually with every new device.** RIM releases a new BlackBerry several times per year and always adds capabilities to new devices, which means a new library of code with each new device. Your app can be coded to use the previous set of features but would be unable to take advantage of any new stuff on the new device.

- ✔ **Your application can use features available only in the universal version.** Your app can't use newer features available on devices released after the universal version arrives.

As of this writing, the most important decision for you to make, regarding which version of the BlackBerry JDE to use, is this: Do you want to take advantage of the touchscreen and accelerometer features of the BlackBerry Storm and Storm2 devices? This is a most important consideration because your choice confines your choice of JDE to 4.7.0 or later. Your application is blissfully unaware of the accelerometer and touchscreen code available on the Storm and Storm2 devices if you choose to use any JDE with a lower version number than this. Any application you write using JDE 4.5 can execute on a smartphone running OS 4.7, but the application won't be able to read any accelerometers or detect "touch" events while doing so.

By the time you read this book, the latest-and-greatest BlackBerry OS version 5.0 will be available and in general use by BlackBerry aficionados across the world. OS 5.0 includes the following improvements, aside from it being a universal OS:

- ✔ **SQLite database support:** You can store your application's data in a real SQL-standard database, and make use of SQL queries to access and manipulate data. *SQLite* is a self-contained SQL database that gives you the capability to manage your BlackBerry app's data as if using an SQL database.

- ✔ **New UI fields:** A variety of new fields has been added to enhance your application's capability to interact with your users.

- ✔ **New UI layout manager:** Your application can lay out its UI elements in a grid style. I've worked with a variety of different layout managers on different platforms, and I prefer grid layouts because they seem easier to use and the code to implement the layout of the UI elements seems to track the resulting display of those elements more closely.

- ✔ **New screen transition management:** Your application can provide a variety of transitions when the user moves from one screen to another.

- ✔ **Improved network connection management:** Network connections are created by using a `Connection-Factory` class that provides you the connection that your application requests. In addition, you can fine-tune the connection attempt by setting values for the instance of the factory class.

Playing it safe

The safest, most consistent OS version number is 4.5, so that's the JDE version I use through the rest of this book. True, using this version prevents my app from making use of the 4.7 features for the touchscreen and accelerometer BlackBerry devices (read about this earlier in the chapter), but using JDE 4.5.0 allows me to ship my app to the widest possible set of BlackBerry devices available. Because I want to make some money with a shipping application, the more devices that can run my app, the more money I can make.

I do pay close attention to how my application behaves on touchscreen devices, though. For example, Storm and Storm2 users can rotate the device's visual orientation, switching from portrait (taller than wide) to landscape (wider than tall). With that knowledge, I can be wary enough to know how my application behaves when the user does something that I can't anticipate or react to in my code.

So that's my advice: JDE 4.5.0 is the current best choice for development of BlackBerry applications for wide use.

Downloading and Installing a JDE

The BlackBerry JDEs are available at one place: `www.blackberry.com`. To download a JDE, follow these steps:

1. **Point your favorite browser to `http://na.blackberry.com/eng/ developers`.**

   This displays the main developer Web page for the site, and you need to navigate deeper.

2. **Click the Java Application Development link from the list on the left-hand side of the page.**

   The left-hand list is redisplayed, this time with more items under Java Application Development.

3. **Click the Java Application Development Tools & Downloads link from the expanded list.**

4. **Click the Learn More About and Download the BlackBerry JDE link.**

5. **Scroll down the page until you can see the BlackBerry JDE Downloads section.**

   This contains links to all available JDE versions, as you can see in Figure 2-10. The Get Help link on the right side leads to a small article that advises, "When building applications, you should use a BlackBerry JDE version that matches the lowest version of the BlackBerry Device Software you want to support."

Figure 2-10: The links leading to the available BlackBerry JDE versions.

6. **Select the JDE version that fits your application's needs best.**

   As I mention previously, I'm going with JDE version 4.5.0.

7. **Fill out the form on the page that's displayed and then click Next.**

   Most of this form is already filled out for you, assuming that your browser keeps track of the same form you filled out to register with the RIM developer network, as described earlier in this chapter. Some of the information might be missing. And honestly, I haven't spent enough time figuring out the pattern of when this happens. I only know that if I don't review it carefully, the Web page admonishes me to Please Fill Out All The Required Fields.

8. **Fill in the text boxes on the Eligibility Requirements page that appears, and then click Next.**

   You see yet another Do You Agree? page with a lot of licensing agreement statements in rather small type. If you're a solitary entrepreneur, it's a go/no-go kind of decision. But because you purchased this book, my assumption is that you select whatever choices get you to the end result you're looking for, which in this instance is downloading the JDE. If you're doing any other kind of development, be sure to get permission as necessary to complete these steps.

9. **Agree to the licensing statements by selecting the Agree radio button and then clicking the Next button.**

   Finally, this delivers you to the BlackBerry JDE 4.5.0 download page displayed in Figure 2-11.

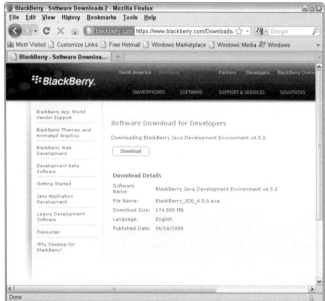

Figure 2-11: At last! The BlackBerry JDE 4.5.0 download page.

10. Click the Download button.

Follow the standard procedures for downloading executable files from the Internet, making sure to check for viruses and so on. The file I downloaded is `BlackBerry_JDE_4.5.0.exe`.

Congratulations! You've taken the first step to developing BlackBerry applications. The preceding steps take you through downloading the 4.5.0 version of the BlackBerry JDE, but this same process works for all JDE versions available.

Installing the JDE is easy:

1. Navigate the Windows file system to the location of the executable you downloaded.

My browser requires me to tell it where to download stuff, so I know where to find it. Your downloads may arrive in the Downloads folder of Windows Vista or Windows 7, or the My Downloads folder of Windows XP.

2. Double-click the JDE installer.

This will be the `BlackBerry_JDE_4.5.0.exe` application.

3. Follow the instructions on the installer screens.

I haven't yet found a need to modify the default values found in the installation screens, so I just click on the appropriate "continue until installation succeeds" buttons.

Now I congratulate you on the successful completion of the second step to developing BlackBerry applications. Choose Start➪All Programs➪Research In Motion (as shown in Figure 2-12) to see your installed version of the JDE and the following menu items:

Figure 2-12:
The BlackBerry JDE 4.5.0 successful installation.

➤ **BlackBerry JDE API Reference:** When you select this menu item, your browser launches and loads a page providing the Javadoc API (application programming interface) documentation for the version of the JDE you just installed. This is an invaluable resource. I typically bookmark it within my browser. It's available from the Start menu, too.

✔ **Device Simulator:** This menu item launches the default BlackBerry smartphone simulator for this JDE. *Note:* This might not be the same simulator that's set to be launched from within the JDE as the JDE has a drop-down list you can use to launch any of the simulators that installed with it.

✔ **ESS:** Your JDE installation comes with an Email Services Simulator (ESS). This simulator can be used to demonstrate an e-mail service that interacts with a BlackBerry device simulator so that you can create and test applications that work with e-mail messages. Appendix A reveals details regarding the ESS.

✔ **JDE:** This is the workhorse: the application you use the most to create your application.

✔ **JDWP:** You can debug a BlackBerry application using a simulator, or you can debug it running on an actual device. The Java Debug Wire Protocol (JDWP) tool allows the JDE debugger to connect to a BlackBerry device across its USB cable. I prefer not to use this approach because it adds an extra layer of processes between the debugger and the executing code, but sometimes it's the only way to see what's happening on a real device.

✔ **MDS-CS:** The JDE installation also provides a Mobile Data System- (MDS) Connection Service (CS) simulator, which allows a BlackBerry device simulator to connect to the network through the desktop PC's network connection. The MDS simulator *must* be executing when your application is running on a simulator if you intend your app to communicate to network-based resources. I go over details of the MDS simulator in Appendix A as well.

✔ **Uninstall BlackBerry JDE:** Last but not least, the installation of your JDE includes an "undo everything you installed" menu item. You may choose to use this when you're ready to use a newer version of the JDE, although you can install all the currently available ones together with no problems.

That's it! You've downloaded and installed the BlackBerry JDE to develop your BlackBerry applications.

Downloading and Using Alternate Device Simulators

I expect to see something new from RIM every three months or so. Sometimes it's a revamped model of an older device; sometimes it's something completely new. RIM also updates the operating systems on its devices. All these changes mean that you have to keep up to date on what RIM has delivered to the marketplace to make sure that your app doesn't run afoul of either a new device or a new OS. If you have a large amount of money to devote to purchasing a new device every time RIM makes one, you can just order a new one from the carrier's Web site, and you're all set. Or, if you're more like me, you periodically check the BlackBerry Web site for new versions of simulators.

Each new JDE comes with a set of simulators matched with the JDE's version of the BlackBerry OS. However, because RIM introduces more new devices and more new OSes faster than it introduces new JDEs, you'll discover that you need to download the new device simulators as RIM provides them. These simulators exist separately from the JDE and are installed apart from it.

You download new device simulators to your PC from the RIM Web site by following these steps:

1. **Point your browser to**

   `http://na.blackberry.com/eng/developers/resources/simulators.jsp`

   This brings you to a page similar to the one shown in Figure 2-13.

2. **Select a device simulator from the Select a Smartphone drop-down list.**

   The simulators in this list represent almost all the BlackBerry devices that your app is likely to be running on. However, you can find even more simulators by clicking the View All BlackBerry Smartphone Simulator Downloads link. For this example, I'm going with the BlackBerry 9700.

Figure 2-13: The device simulator downloads the Web page.

3. **Choose a wireless provider from the Select a Carrier drop-down list.**

   I'm a card-carrying AT&T customer, so I'll choose that carrier. You can also choose the OS for the device instead, if you prefer. Selecting AT&T reveals one or more links for the device simulator and its OS version. As of this writing, there are two links for the two different OS versions: 5.0.0.296 and 5.0.0.405.

4. **Click the link for the device simulator and OS version you want to download.**

   I selected the BlackBerry Smartphone Simulator v5.0.0.405. This will take you to a registration page, similar to the one you saw when you registered as a BlackBerry developer (described earlier in this chapter).

5. **Fill out the required text boxes, and click Next.**

   This takes you to an Eligibility page, where you are required to affirm that you're eligible to download the simulator and that your promise to do only good things with it.

6. **Select Agree and then click Next.**

   This takes you to the Software Download for Device Simulators page, which shows you the details of the simulator you're about to download.

7. **Click the Download button.**

   You see a standard Windows dialog box from which you choose where to put your simulator installer file.

8. **After the simulator installer file downloads successfully, navigate through Windows Explorer to the file and double-click the file to launch the installer.**

   The file I downloaded is named

   ```
   BlackBerry_Simulators_5.0.0.405_9700-ATT.exe
   ```

9. **Follow the installation instructions to install the simulator.**

To use the new simulator you just installed, here's all you do:

1. **Choose Start⇨All Programs⇨Research In Motion⇨BlackBerry Smartphone Simulators X.Y.Z⇨*your device simulator*.**

   For example, I choose Start⇨All Programs⇨Research In Motion⇨BlackBerry Smartphone Simulators 5.0.0⇨5.0.0.405⇨9700-ATT, which is a simulator of the AT&T BlackBerry 9700.

   My selection of the BlackBerry 9700 shows a simulator as in Figure 2-14.

2. **Choose File⇨Load Java Program and load your app.**

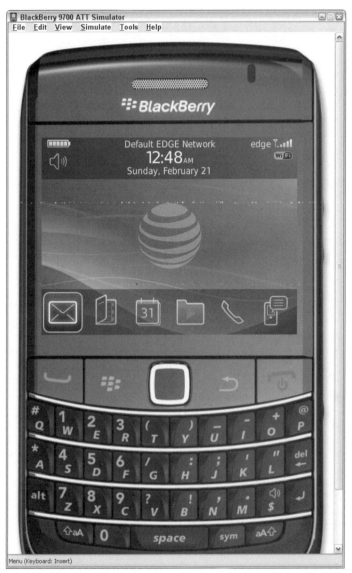

Figure 2-14:
The
BlackBerry
9700
simulator.

You can now see what your app looks like and how well it behaves on simulators of devices (so you don't have to purchase those devices!). Oh, by the way: You are welcome to send me half the money you just saved.

Tapping Helpful Resources

Sooner or later, you are going to need help. The problem will seem insurmountable: The network communication that your app needs works on some devices, but not the specific one you want it to. Your e-mail attachment handling worked perfectly yesterday, but today, nothing is going right. The larger your project, the greater the chance that at some point, you're going to run into a dead end. You could remove that one feature that's causing the trouble, thereby avoiding the problem, but eventually, you're going to have to turn to some form of outside assistance. And that's where online help becomes necessary.

Three principal resources can help you find solutions to the challenges that arise in the course of developing your apps. These resources overlap somewhat, and each has its own benefits and caveats, as I describe in the following sections.

Perusing the API documentation

The BlackBerry JDE installs with a set of HTML files that contain the API documentation in Javadoc format. This is the place to start when you want to know what a particular class in the BlackBerry OS can or should do. I place a bookmark in my favorite browser to the main page installed by the JDE. For the default installation, that location is

```
C:\Program Files\Research In Motion\BlackBerry JDE x.y.z/docs/api/index.html
```

$x.y.z$ is the version number of the JDE that you installed (see Chapter 3).

This resource is great if you already have a class you know you want to investigate, such as `net.rim.device.api.ui.UiApplication`, which is the standard application class used to build applications that provide a user interface. The API documentation provides descriptive information about many different aspects of a class, such as

- ✔ **The class inheritance tree:** For example, the `UiApplication` class descends from `net.rim.api.system.Application`. This is useful for figuring out whether a particular class can pose as another.

- ✔ **Highlights of the class:** Most of the classes you work directly with are pretty specialized. They embody certain patterns of behavior, and the API documentation provides you with the unique traits of the classes you use. In addition, you find suggestions for making use of various aspects of each class.

✔ **Descriptions of the class methods:** You find the answers to many of your questions within the method descriptions, so you can determine which methods you should override in your own further specialized version of the class.

✔ **Example code:** Some of the class descriptions in the API documentation contain sample code that shows you the proper ways to use the class to achieve certain goals. For instance, the `Connector` class (`javax.microedition.io.Connector`) comes with sample code showing how to open various types of network communications channels.

The API documentation is great: that is, when you know what class you're going to use to achieve something. (Kind of like looking in a dictionary for how to spell something.) But you'll find that the API documentation doesn't easily allow you to search for something based on keywords. It's just simple Javadoc, which can't tell you what class to use to determine the screen dimensions. (Hint: It's not `net.rim.device.api.ui.Graphics`.) In addition, the API documentation can't provide you with a BlackBerry application "world-view." The Javadoc can deliver mountains of details about any one particular class, but it doesn't come with information about how to put one class together with another. To solve this information problem, you need to go to the developer documentation at the BlackBerry Web site itself.

Digging into online developer documentation

Your next stop is the support sections on the BlackBerry Web site. The online developer support is available at

```
http://na.blackberry.com/eng/developers/resources
```

Figure 2-15 shows the developer resources page.

The links on the right side of the page are extremely useful if you run into problems in your quest to create a BlackBerry application. Here's what they are, and what they contain:

✔ **Documentation:** This link gives you access to all the developer documentation, which includes the API documentation you get with the JDE. You can see the API documentation for all the different versions of the BlackBerry OS, which can help you resolve why some things work on one version of the OS and not on another. The documentation here is available in HTML and PDF form. In addition, detailed programming documentation is also available via this link, including development guides on specific device features and functionality.

Figure 2-15:
The entry
point for
BlackBerry
development
documenta-
tion.

✔ **Online Forums:** Your developer registration allows you to become involved in the community of online BlackBerry developers available through the BlackBerry development forums. I explain more about the forums in the next section.

✔ **Knowledge Base:** The BlackBerry Developer Knowledge Base contains information not available in either the API documentation or the development guides. Occasionally, you find that your application development halted because of something the API documentation claimed to be true, but isn't. The Knowledge Base is set up to provide information about known issues, and is fully searchable. Articles in the Knowledge Base point out problems in the OS, and sometimes provide code samples to enable you to work around the problem. For instance, one of my recent challenges involved changing the application icon at runtime, based on the type of device on which my application was executing. A class in the BlackBerry OS allows this; however, using this class and its methods to change the application icon caused the program to crash. The Knowledge Base explained what was going wrong and also provided example code to get my application around the problem.

- ✔ **Developer Tutorials:** Tutorials are always welcome additions to your learning process when you're trying to get familiar with something new. The BlackBerry development tutorials are available in PDF format.

- ✔ **Video Library:** RIM recently added some video tutorials in addition to its PDF tutorials.

- ✔ **Developer Labs:** This resource provides you with some hands-on walkthroughs of BlackBerry development. Each lab comes with source code and a set of instructions for building a BlackBerry application to demonstrate different parts of development.

I have made the most use out of the developer documentation, and I continue to do so today. I still check the PDF files available for download, and when I'm looking for example code to do something new, that's the first place I start. So I rank the online programming guides and developer documentation slightly higher in value than the API documentation in its usefulness for helping solve problems. But I consider the online developer forums the best of all.

Exercising your Google-fu

If you're having trouble tracking down the solution to a problem in the API documentation and the online developer documentation, it's time to open up a search engine. If the information you seek is on the Web, Google can find it. The big difficulty is searching the results. The more you use Google, the more you discover that you must uniquely identify the problem with the most appropriate words to narrow the cascade of results.

If your Google-fu fails you, it's time to ask for help on the developer forums.

Asking for help on the developer forums

Online forums have existed for BlackBerry users pretty much since the first BlackBerry was produced. A forum is a great way to interact with other BlackBerry users and developers, and you can discover new things and new hints and rumors about upcoming changes and devices and operating systems.

I recommend frequenting two forums; when I'm doing BlackBerry development, I make use of them both.

✔ **RIM BlackBerry Developer Forum**

```
http://supportforums.blackberry.com/rim/?category.id=BlackBerryDevelopment
```

The RIM Developer Forum is new to the scene. There is one nice thing about using this forum hosted by RIM: Developers at RIM are paying attention. Your question may go unanswered because you stumped the expert developers in the field. At that point, maybe someone at RIM will add to your thread, and provide you either with the answer, or make suggestions for work-arounds. For some reason, I find this aspect of using the Developer Forum quite seductive, knowing that some developer at RIM might be looking at my problem and might know how I can fix it.

✔ **CrackBerry.com developer forum**

```
http://forums.crackberry.com
http://forums.crackberry.com/f9
```

CrackBerry.com hosts forums on wide variety of BlackBerry topics beyond application development. Because these forums aren't supported by RIM, you find a lot more commentary (some of it less than pleasant!) about the BlackBerry and other platforms as well. In addition, you see rumors and wild guesses from the community about unreleased devices, operating systems, and changes in general.

Both forums are great places to visit when you run into issues doing BlackBerry development. Sometimes you find your question answered almost immediately. Sometimes all you find is a group of other developers also interested in finding a solution to the same problem.

I think the forums are the best place for finding answers because of the large number of BlackBerry developers who are there trying to find answers themselves. Your question just has to reach the right eyes, and it only takes one pair to find you a solution. But there is a catch: *You must ask the question correctly.* Check out this Web page to see some of the rules for posing questions on the Internet: www.catb.org/~esr/faqs/smart-questions. html. You should review this Web page before posting a question to any of the forums. The suggestions in this Web page apply well to posting forum questions. Bottom line: You want to appear as though you made a serious attempt to solve the problem on your own before asking someone to help you solve it.

Chapter 3

Coding with the BlackBerry Java Development Environment

Your main tool, friend, actor, assistant, and crash-test dummy for creating BlackBerry applications is the BlackBerry Java Development Environment, also known as the JDE. You use the JDE for almost every task you must complete to turn your idea into a fully functional application that will win the hearts of millions of BlackBerry users.

In this chapter, I show you how to find and install the best version of the JDE for your development needs. I also demonstrate the construction of a simple application, from start to finish, so that you can see the basic approach to follow when you create your own apps.

Getting Familiar with the JDE

The BlackBerry JDE is a graphical user interface (GUI) application, both written in Java and used to write Java code for BlackBerry applications. You use the following components of the JDE for most of the work developing and testing your application:

✔ **Source code editor:** You use the JDE editor to create and edit Java source modules for your BlackBerry application. You can use your own editor if you prefer (such as Windows Notepad or WordPad), but the BlackBerry JDE editor incorporates some context-sensitive help that can assist your development tasks, and a third-party editor might not provide such assistance.

✔ **BlackBerry build tools:** The JDE comes with its own command-line compiler, `rapc.exe`, for interpreting your Java code and creating a BlackBerry application. During this multistep process, several intermediate products are also produced when you tell the JDE to build your project. I go over these details later in this chapter.

✔ **Source-level debugger:** You'll find it convenient to run your application in a simulator after you make changes or additions to your application's source code. (I cover BlackBerry smartphone simulators in Appendix A.) When something goes awry, you use the source-level debugger to perform standard debugging tasks.

✔ **BlackBerry simulator:** The JDE installs with one or more simulators that are equivalent to actual BlackBerry devices. The source-level debugger I mention earlier in this list launches one of the simulators when you debug your application. Each simulator contains the actual code of the BlackBerry device it represents, so you can be assured that your app is running as it would really run on an actual device.

The BlackBerry JDE is available for free from RIM, and it runs only on 32-bit versions of Microsoft Windows XP, Windows Vista, and Windows 7. Chapter 1 contains more information about the baseline hardware and software requirements for BlackBerry app development.

You might run into some difficulty getting the JDE to execute on 64-bit versions of Windows (Windows 7 and Windows Vista). I believe the problem is related to the JDE being unable to correctly find the installed version of Java. Unfortunately, at the time of this writing, this issue has not yet been resolved.

Creating a BlackBerry Application with the JDE

You are now on the path to creating a BlackBerry application, using the JDE you selected to manage, edit, and build your code. The download and installation were both pretty straightforward, but now things get interesting. The rest of this chapter describes the following tasks:

✔ Finding out what files are needed by the JDE to produce your application

✔ Discovering what files are produced by the JDE for your application

✔ Building the sample applications that were installed with the JDE

✔ Creating and building a very basic application using the JDE

What does the JDE actually do?

You use the JDE to achieve your goal of creating a BlackBerry application. That goal sounds pretty simple, but the JDE creates many subtle, smaller products when you issue the Build My Application command. In addition, there are a lot of pieces to keep together before you can tell the JDE to perform a build. Here are the files you need to create for the JDE to make your application:

✔ **JDE workspace file:** All BlackBerry development takes place within the context of a workspace, which has .jdw as its file extension. A *BlackBerry workspace* is a text-based file that contains information regarding the set of projects displayed when the JDE opens the workspace. A workspace can contain multiple projects.

✔ **JDE project files:** An individual BlackBerry application is based in a project file, which has .jdp as its file extension. One application equals one project. The JDP file is a text-based file containing information regarding how the JDE is to build the application.

✔ **Source code files:** These files represent your code; you create your application using them. This is where your Java source code resides, so these files have .java as their extension.

✔ **Image files:** You can add image files to your application to use in a variety of ways. One of the most important is to provide an application icon, also known as a *home screen icon,* to be displayed as the icon your users see to select your app from all the others on a BlackBerry screen. The following image file types can be added to your application: GIF, JPG, and PNG.

✔ **Language resource files:** You can add files to use for localizing your BlackBerry application, following standard "resource bundle" rules. The JDE assists you in creating and maintaining the file types used for letting your application speak languages other than American English.

Here are files that the JDE produces when you build your application:

✔ **Application COD file:** This is the primary output file: your application to be installed on a BlackBerry device. All the files and data you contributed to the project housing your application are mixed and folded and put together into this one file. Your application is represented by this file, named *your_app*.cod.

✔ **Application JAD file:** The Java Application Descriptor (JAD) file is used to allow Web-based over-the-air downloads of your application. If you were to host your application on a Web server to allow users to download and install your application from their BlackBerry connected to the Internet, this file is required. Your users enter the URL path to the JAD file, which provides enough information to the browser for it to attempt to download the application (assuming that the user okays the attempt). The JAD file references your application COD file.

In certain instances, I have determined that the JAD file doesn't necessarily get updated when I make a change in the application's code. There is some information within the JAD file related to the time of the build, as well as the size of the COD file. I make it a point to delete the JAD file by hand before a new build occurs, especially if I'm running an automated build — then I'm always rewarded with a new JAD file that I'm certain represents the current build.

✔ **Application JAR file:** You might not find a lot of use for this file, but I include it here for completeness. The JAR file is a standard Java ARchive file, and it contains the full hierarchy of classes from your source modules as well as all the other files incorporated into the project. I sometimes check the JAR files produced by the JDE to make sure that the hierarchy of resources and classes is what I expect.

When you tell the JDE to build your application, it does the following things:

1. The JDE compiles each source module using its compiler (`rapc.exe`).

   The compiled code for each module is used to create a Java Class file in memory, which is placed into its appropriate place in the JAR file hierarchy.

2. The JDE creates the COD file from the JAR file.

3. The JDE creates the JAD file containing descriptive information needed by the BlackBerry browser for downloading and installing the application COD file.

Depending on the resulting size of the COD file, the JDE might split the COD file into separate, smaller COD files. These COD files are then packaged together using the ZIP archiving utility, and the resulting file is *also* given the COD file extension. This can make things a little confusing, but don't worry: The BlackBerry device OS knows how to make use of the entire file, regardless of the actual contents. This is a historical feature that has to do with limitations (long since removed) on how much memory could be allocated to store data coming in from a network connection.

The JDE display

The JDE display has a great many elements, but you mostly work with only a small subset. Figure 3-1 shows the display you encounter when you launch the JDE for the first time.

When you first launch the JDE, you see the workspace as well as a group of preloaded projects. This is the "samples" workspace, which I talk about in the next section. For now, the major items in Figure 3-1 are

- **Menus:** The standard menus are here (File, Edit, Window, and Help) along with menus for dealing with different aspects of the JDE and the build process.

- **Toolbar:** Right below the menus is the toolbar, which holds some buttons for performing some of the tasks available through the menus. The most interesting part of the toolbar is the Default Simulator drop-down list, which shows a list of the simulated BlackBerry devices that were installed with the JDE.

Files and projects   Editor

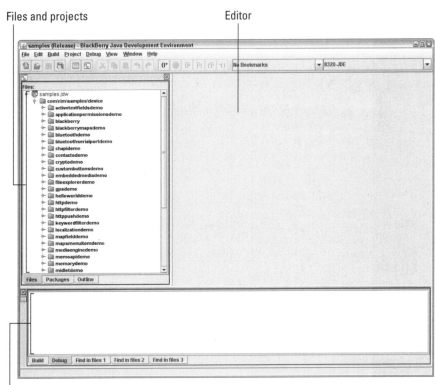

Figure 3-1:
The JDE
main
display at
first launch.

Status zone

✔ **Files and projects:** This is your workspace navigation zone. Your workspace file and its contents are displayed in a hierarchical fashion. The workspace contains projects, and the projects contain files for building the project's application. The hierarchy corresponds to the file system hierarchy into which the Samples workspace was deployed. For instance, the `samples.jdw` workspace file references a project named `ActiveTextFieldsDemo`, which is located in a folder named `activetextfieldsdemo`, which itself is at the path `com\rim\ samples\device`, relative to the location of the workspace file. You spend much of your time moving through this section of the display selecting files to edit.

✔ **Editor:** You spend most of your time in this section of the JDE display. When you double-click a source code module from the files and projects pane, the source code shows up in the JDE's text editor.

✔ **Status zone:** This portion of the JDE main display shows messages that the JDE delivers to you from a variety of sources, which I explain later.

Building and Running Your First BlackBerry App

When you first launch the JDE, it's already set to open with a workspace and about 40 projects. You can build and play with the sample applications, but for now, I'm going to walk you through the creation and implementation of a very simple BlackBerry application so you can get used to the process. You use the same procedure every time you start a new BlackBerry app, so becoming familiar with this process now prepares you for the rest of the code projects in this book. I go over some of the sample applications in Chapter 15.

The first thing to do now is to clear the JDE of the sample apps by choosing File⇨Close Workspace. With a clean workspace, you're ready to create a working BlackBerry application. The general sequence to create an app follows these steps:

1. Create a workspace.

2. Create a project within the workspace.

3. Create the main Java source module within the project.

   This source module is your application's `main` class, which is a subclass of a BlackBerry `application` class.

4. Implement the `main` routine code in the Java source module.

The BlackBerry OS looks for a `public static main()` method in the `main` application class, which is just like the `main()` method of a desktop PC Java application.

5. Implement the application's `main` class.

6. Create a Java source module to implement the display screen for the application.

7. Implement the display screen class.

8. Build the application.

9. Launch the application in the default simulator.

Whew! It sounds like a lot to do, but you'll soon breeze through it. Just follow the steps I provide in the rest of this chapter, and you'll create a simple but complete app!

Creating your first app

To get started creating your first app, follow these steps:

1. **Choose File⇨New Workspace.**

    The Create Workspace dialog box appears, as shown in Figure 3-2.

2. **Enter the name and location for your workspace in the Workspace Name field and the Create in This Directory text boxes, respectively, and then click OK.**

    For this example, I enter the workspace name **FirstBlackBerryApp** (the JDE adds the `.jdw` file extension text for you) and the directory **C:\Business\Authorship\Development\Chapter03**.

    This creates the JDW (Workspace) file, and loads it into the JDE main display. In addition, if the path you selected for the Create in This Directory text box has any missing elements, the JDE asks whether you want it to create them for you. When the JDE is set, you see the No Workspace entry at the top of the files and projects pane replaced with the name of your workspace.

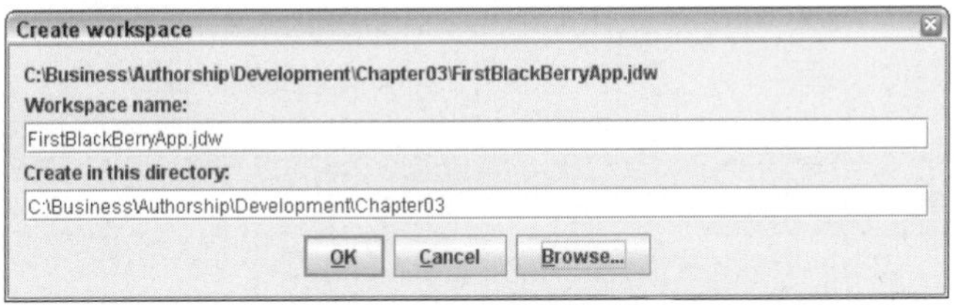

Figure 3-2:
Create a
workspace.

Create workspace

C:\Business\Authorship\Development\Chapter03\FirstBlackBerryApp.jdw

Workspace name:

FirstBlackBerryApp.jdw

Create in this directory:

C:\Business\Authorship\Development\Chapter03

OK   Cancel   Browse...

3. **Right-click the workspace name and choose Create New Project in *YourWorkspaceName*.**

   You see another small dialog box, like the one used to create the workspace, but this time asking you to create a named project, as shown in Figure 3-3.

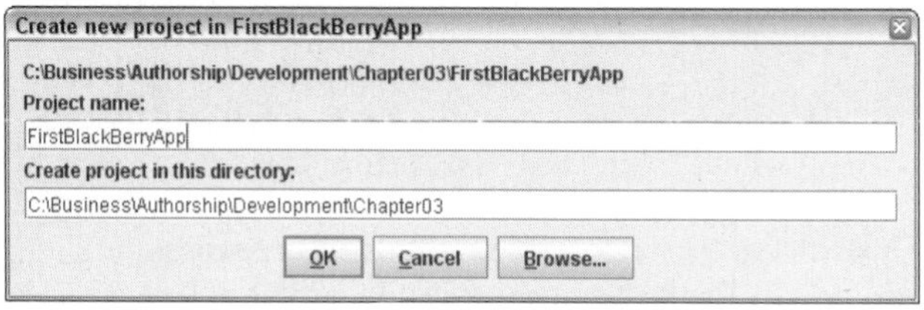

Figure 3-3:
Create a
project.

Create new project in FirstBlackBerryApp

C:\Business\Authorship\Development\Chapter03\FirstBlackBerryApp

Project name:

FirstBlackBerryApp

Create project in this directory:

C:\Business\Authorship\Development\Chapter03

OK   Cancel   Browse...

4. **Enter the project name and location in the Project Name and the Create Project in This Directory fields, respectively, and then click OK.**

   I use FirstBlackBerryApp as the project name, and also leave the setting for it to be created in the same directory as the workspace (again, the JDE adds the .jdp file extension for you).

   This creates a JDP (Project) file in the same folder as the workspace on your file system, and it also adds the project as a child node of the workspace in the JDE.

5. **Choose File⇨Save All, or click the Save All button on the toolbar.**

   Save early; save often.

6. **Right-click the project name and choose Create New File in Project.**

   Once more, you see another small dialog box like the first two.

7. **Enter the source file name and location in the Source File Name and the Create Source File in This Directory fields, respectively, and then click OK.**

   Figure 3-4 shows my modification to the empty dialog box: I'm telling the JDE to create a Java source file (extension .java), and I add **com\karlgkowalski\firstblackberryapp** at the end of the path to create a series of subfolders from the folder containing the workspace and the project. Figure 3-5 shows the message window that appears when the JDE discovers the path you entered does not exist.

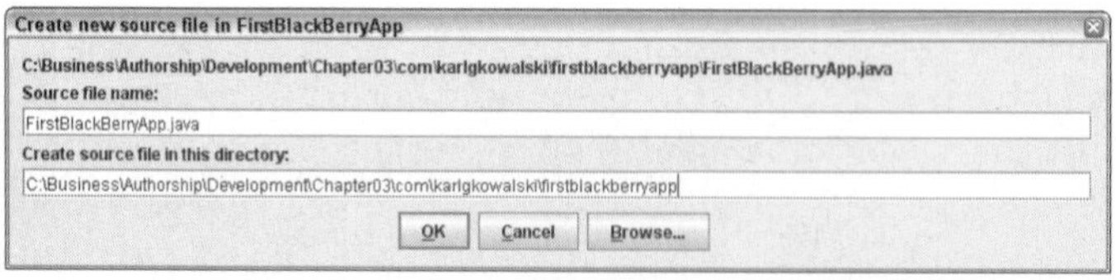

Figure 3-4:
Create the
Java source
module.

Create new source file in FirstBlackBerryApp

C:\Business\Authorship\Development\Chapter03\com\karlgkowalski\firstblackberryapp\FirstBlackBerryApp.java

Source file name:

FirstBlackBerryApp.java

Create source file in this directory:

C:\Business\Authorship\Development\Chapter03\com\karlgkowalski\firstblackberryapp

OK   Cancel   Browse...

Figure 3-5:
Create
folders.

When writing a Java application, the compiled code that represents each class is placed into a hierarchy of folders, called a `package`. Most commercial Java applications, including BlackBerry Java applications, create their package hierarchy using the reverse order of their Internet domain names. So the classes I create in my applications all start in a folder tree, the base of which is named `com`, which contains a folder named `karlgkowalski`, and below that are the folders grouping all my classes in some order. You can make the names of these folders anything you'd like; however, as you make more apps and earn more money selling them, you will want to ensure that your code contains something that identifies it as belonging to you (or your company). While using the reverse-domain name does not guarantee no one will steal your code, it is recognized as a means of some copyright protection.

You can avoid query by clicking the Browse button (in Figure 3-4) and creating the folders yourself, but I find it easier to type the names and have the machine do the work for me.

The JDE does several things at this point. It creates the path of folders leading to where you directed it to place the Java source file. It also creates the source file, adds it as a child to the project, and then opens the file and displays its contents in the editor. Figure 3-6 shows what this looks like.

Pay attention to the basic text already added to the source module. Here's what you see in my example `FirstBlackBerryApp.java` source module:

- ✔ **A copyright statement at the top:** You'll want to change `<your company here>` and the copyright date, just to stay legal.

- ✔ **The `package` directive:** The JDE presumes that your selection of folders for where to place this source file is intended to represent a Java package hierarchy, so it adds the appropriate packaging directive.

- ✔ **The `class` directive:** Every Java source module requires that a class named the same as the module's filename (without the `.java` extension) be implemented within the module. The JDE creates a text file containing a bare minimum of code, consisting of the `class` directive and an empty constructor for the class.

You need to modify the source module to implement the class as needed for it to be a BlackBerry application class. So, for this running example, edit `FirstBlackBerryApp.java` to include the `main()` method so that it matches the code shown in Listing 3-1.

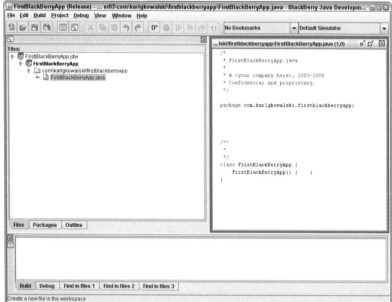

Figure 3-6:
The first
project
containing
the Java
source file,
ready to
edit.

The main() method is the starting point for all Java applications, and you must do the typing to add one to your BlackBerry app. This is the first code that the BlackBerry smartphone OS will execute when a user launches your app.

In Listing 3-1, you can see the line that starts with import. This is a command that informs the Java compiler about where to find a particular BlackBerry OS class, the UiApplication class. This class is used as the basis for the FirstBlackBerryApp class that this file implements, and the compiler needs to know where to find it in the BlackBerry OS libraries. The line that starts with public class is the declaration of the class named FirstBlackBerry App, which extends the UiApplication class — the FirstBlackBerryApp class will inherit all the functionality in UiApplication, and will operate as one.

Listing 3-1: Including the main() Method

```
/*
 * FirstBlackBerryApp.java
 *
 * © Karl G. Kowalski, 2011
 * Confidential and proprietary.
 */

package com.karlgkowalski.firstblackberryapp;

import net.rim.device.api.ui.UiApplication;
```

```
public class FirstBlackBerryApp extends UiApplication
{
   public static void main( String[] inArgs )
   {
      FirstBlackBerryApp bbApp = new FirstBlackBerryApp();
      bbApp.enterEventDispatcher();
   }

   public FirstBlackBerryApp()
   {
   }

   public void activate()
   {
   }
}
```

The code so far looks pretty simple. Nothing really exciting is happening, and the main() method simply creates an object of type FirstBlackBerryApp and then executes enterEventDispatcher().This is the only interesting part: the entry point into the BlackBerry OS event mechanism. Every BlackBerry application depends upon a queue of events delivered by the OS to the application. Each time the OS gives your app an event, your app executes code to handle it — sometimes using default code provided by the OS, sometimes using code you implement yourself. For instance, an event is generated and delivered to your app when the user clicks a button on a screen your app creates.

You can download sample code for this book from www.dummies.com/go/ blackberryappdev.

Creating the display class

The FirstBlackBerryApp constructor is empty because it doesn't need to do anything. But the activate() method is also empty, and that's something you change soon. Right now, it's time to create the application's one and only display class.

1. **Right-click the FirstBlackBerryApp.java item in the files and projects pane and choose Create New File in *YourAppName*.**

2. **Enter a source filename in the Source File Name text box; you can accept the default location in the Create Source File in This Directory text box. Click OK.**

   The default location is wherever you placed FirstBlackBerryApp. java. The JDE assumed that because you clicked that file in the hierarchy, you probably want to place the file you're creating right at the same place. You can adjust this location by right-clicking a different item in the files and projects pane and choosing Create New File in *YourAppName*, but for now, this works fine. Figure 3-7 shows the dialog box I filled in with the name of the new source file, FirstBlackBerryScreen.java.

Figure 3-7:
Create the screen source module.

The JDE again creates a new Java source module in the file system, adds it to the project, and opens it in the editor. You can see the result in Figure 3-8.

Figure 3-8:
The JDE with the new module added and ready to edit.

Once again, you created a BlackBerry Java source module that has almost nothing in it. You have to change that. This is meant to be a display class, which means it will inherit all of the features and functionality of a BlackBerry OS class that is used to show information to your users on their BlackBerry smartphone's screen.

Edit `FirstBlackBerryScreen.java` so that it matches the code in Listing 3-2. This listing contains a small amount of code, really just the least needed to show something to the user when they launch the app. The code contains a constructor, and the one method that the constructor calls, `initialize()`. I have declared this method to be `private` because no other code should execute it, only the code found within `FirstBlackBerryScreen`.

Listing 3-2:   Your First BlackBerry Display Class

```
/*
 * FirstBlackBerryScreen.java
 *
 * © Karl G. Kowalski, 2011
 * Confidential and proprietary.
 */

package com.karlgkowalski.firstblackberryapp;

import  net.rim.device.api.ui.container.MainScreen;


/**
 *
 */
public  class FirstBlackBerryScreen extends MainScreen
{
    public  FirstBlackBerryScreen()
    {
        super();
        this.initialize();
    }

    private void   initialize()
    {
        this.setTitle( "First BlackBerry App!" );
    }
}
```

This is now a little more interesting than `FirstBlackBerryApp.java` although not really much.

- ✔ The class extends `MainScreen` (`net.rim.device.api.ui.container.MainScreen`). As you can probably guess, this is a `display` class. For BlackBerry applications, this class provides basic display features, including supplying a `Close` menu item. This is achieved by the call to `super()` in the constructor.

- ✔ Any object of this class initializes its title with the text found in the call to `setTitle` in the class' `initialize()` method. I generally add an `initialize()` method to all my display classes because it provides a consistent location to perform any setup for the class before the user can interact with the display, so you'll see this often in later chapters.

Now you link this display class to the main application class. Edit FirstBlackBerryApp.java to modify the activate() method as follows.

```
public void activate()
{
    this.pushScreen( new FirstBlackBerryScreen() );
}
```

Building your application

The activate() method now does something useful: It creates a FirstBlackBerryScreen object and passes it as a parameter to pushScreen(). Assuming that you typed the source code properly, you're now ready to build your first BlackBerry application.

1. **Choose Build⇨Build or press F7.**

   This runs the JDE build process, which compiles and links your application. You see text appear in the status zone of the JDE display, indicating the operations that are proceeding. If everything went smoothly, the screen shown in Figure 3-9 should be visible.

   Of course, building the application is never enough. Now you have to run it in the simulator.

2. **Choose Debug⇨Go to launch the simulator.**

   The default BlackBerry simulator launches in a separate window. (Nearly all BlackBerry simulators take a long time to start.) Figure 3-10 shows what takes place in the JDE Debug pane in the status zone when the BlackBerry simulator is ready to go.

The BlackBerry simulator is now launched and operational. However, for some reason, the JDE doesn't automatically launch the application that you just created. You now have to use the simulated BlackBerry to navigate to your application and launch it yourself. Figure 3-11 shows what the display on my default BlackBerry simulator looks like when I navigated to the FirstBlackBerryApp, sitting among all the other simulated applications. To launch the app on the simulator after you've highlighted it with the selection cursor, simply click the simulated trackball.

Assuming that everything went according to plan, you're now looking at the main screen displayed by the FirstBlackBerryApp. You're now a BlackBerry programmer! You can create applications, and you can make your applications put screens on a BlackBerry display.

Figure 3-9:
The results
of building
the
FirstBlack
BerryApp.

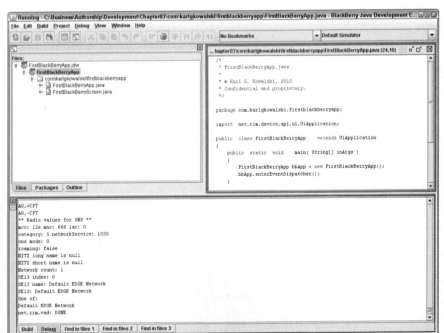

Figure 3-10:
The
BlackBerry
simulator
sends
messages to
the Debug
pane.

Figure 3-11:
The
FirstBlack
BerryApp
running on
a simulated
BlackBerry.

Adding an Alternate Entry Point

Most UI applications you write are a standard form: a Project file and all the Java code files to make the app do what it does, with a few image files added as well. And that's all you need to create a quality BlackBerry app. However, there are a couple of reasons why this standard form might not be enough:

- ✔ **Your app must perform an operation before the user first launches your app.** You might want to do this if your app needs to provide an object to the smartphone OS to pay attention to certain user actions that take place outside your app, such as receiving or sending messages.

- ✔ **You want your app to launch into the background of the OS when the device is first turned on.** Your app might need to initialize lots of data or initiate a connection to a remote server to make sure that everything's ready when the user launches your app later.

Neither of these two features is possible if you use the standard form of BlackBerry application development. To provide these features, you need to create an *Alternate Entry Point* (AEP).

You create an AEP by doing two things:

- ✔ You add and configure a new Project to your Workspace in the JDE.
- ✔ You add some code to your application's `main()` routine.

Creating and configuring an AEP Project

I assume that you've already got the FirstBlackBerryApp already put together from the previous section, "Building and Running Your First BlackBerry App." Follow these instructions to add an AEP Project to your app:

1. **Right-click the Workspace name and choose Create New Project in FirstBlackBerryApp.**

2. **Enter the AEP project name in the Project Name field, and Click OK.**

   Because this is an AEP project, I recommend entering **FirstBlackBerryApp_AEP** to indicate that fact.

3. **Right-click the AEP Project you just added and choose Properties.**

   This displays the project's Properties dialog box.

4. **Click the Application tab in the Properties dialog box, as shown in Figure 3-12.**

Figure 3-12:
The Project Properties dialog box for the Alternate Entry Point Project.

5. **Select Alternate CLDC Application Entry Point from the Project type drop-down list.**

6. **Select FirstBlackBerryApp from the Alternate Entry Point For drop-down list.**

   This will happen automatically if it's the only other project in the workspace.

7. **Enter** aepInit **in the Argument Passed to "static public void main(String args[])" text box.**

8. **Select the Auto-Run on Startup check box.**

9. **Click OK.**

Your FirstBlackBerryApp workspace now contains two projects: the FirstBlackBerryApp project, and the FirstBlackBerryApp_AEP project. The AEP project is set to be an Alternate Entry Point into the FirstBlackBerryApp project, and it will automatically launch when the BlackBerry smartphone is turned on.

That was pretty simple, and didn't take any coding — you've really just provided configuration information that the BlackBerry OS will interpret when your application is installed. In order to use the AEP, you now have to add some code.

Adding AEP code to your app's main ( ) routine

The AEP project you just added puts some information into your application's COD file when the JDE builds it. This information is delivered into your app as text in one of the String objects passed into the main() routine of your application. The text you entered in Step 7 in the previous section is aepInit. This is the text that the code in your main() routine will check for, and will operate one way when it finds this text, and another way if it does not.

The code in Listing 3-3 shows you how this is done. First the number of elements in the inArgs parameter is checked to see if there is one, and if so, its value is checked against the text it expects to see from the AEP configuration. The OS will launch the AEP project at startup because you checked the Auto-Run on Startup check box, and the OS will provide the aepInit text to your app when it launches the AEP project. The FirstBlackBerryApp project will run when the user launches your app from the BlackBerry ribbon, and will not pass any String data into main() when it's launched. So if there are no String objects passed into main(), the FirstBlackBerryApp functions as normal.

Listing 3-3:   Updated FirstBlackBerryApp.java to Watch for AEP Input

```
public static void main( String[] inArgs )
{
    if (inArgs.length > 0 && true == inArgs[0].equals("aepInit"))
    {
        // perform AEP initialization here
    }
    else
    {
        FirstBlackBerryApp bbApp = new FirstBlackBerryApp();
        bbApp.enterEventDispatcher();
    }
}
```

That's all there is to an Alternate Entry Point project.

Part II
BlackBerry Application Development

"As an application developer, I never thought I'd say this, but your app needs more bells and whistles."

In this part . . .

After you have the tools you need to develop BlackBerry apps, it's time to get deeper into the life of a BlackBerry application. This part first shows you the importance of creating your app with a plan so that you provide a structure for your app while you implement the different parts. Then you proceed to the surface layer of the app itself: the screens, buttons, menus, and everything else that your users interact with.

You also see how to maintain information for your users, sometimes just temporarily (and why that can be important) and sometimes permanently (and why you might not always want a permanent record). In the last chapter of this part, you delve into application threads and how to make them work for you, like the brooms of the Sorcerer's Apprentice.

Chapter 4

Designing and Organizing Your BlackBerry App

In This Chapter

▶ Brainstorming and recording ideas for new apps

▶ Planning what your app will do

▶ Embracing BlackBerry application fundamentals

▶ Using screen management and callbacks

*Y*our BlackBerry application could be downloaded by potentially millions of users. Those users have expectations about how your app should run and behave, and they will compare your application against other apps built for the BlackBerry. You know this, of course, but sometimes while writing your app, it's easy to get focused on the little details and forget about the actual end users and their experiences. I've done that more often than I can remember, and it's sometimes a shock to pull myself out of the code and try to see the bigger picture.

In this chapter, I go over how to design your code to make it easier for you to add the features and functionality your users want, and also to make it easier to understand why things go wrong. You will find BlackBerry development easier if you start from a plan, rather than starting by writing code and then trying to plan around what you wrote. Essentially, you will become an architect, making the plan for your app, and then building the app from your plan.

Getting Creative and Keeping a Record

One of the most fun things I've done is brainstorming — sitting with friends and co-workers and dreaming up all kinds of crazy ideas. The sessions of brainstorming have been some of the most creative moments I've experienced. Some thread of those sessions lingers on inside, and I find myself tripping over new ideas on a regular basis, even out of simple conversations that are totally unrelated to BlackBerry apps or even software development.

But these sources of ideas are only useful if the ideas get *recorded*, somewhere, somehow. It's fun to dream, but it's more helpful to keep a record of these dreams for future reference: not necessarily to relive the fun, but to make something profitable from it. You likely have some means of keeping track of your multi-million dollar ideas already. Certainly, the least-expensive is to use Notepad or its equivalent on your computer, but that's really just a computerized version of sticky notes or writing things down on random pieces of paper on your desk (both approaches I've used in the past). I've come to believe in the power of a computer to maintain this information better than I can by myself — and, more importantly, to link pieces of information from one topic to another.

For that, a *wiki* is a fabulous tool you can use to keep track of just about any kind of data you would write down. A wiki uses a simplified version of HTML to display text on Web pages produced by the wiki application. Like bug-tracking software (see Chapter 11), a wiki requires a Web server and a database server to operate. This makes it more complicated than Notepad to set up, but after you configured it, the wiki pretty much just works.

I use a free wiki package called MediaWiki to support my creative recordings. You can find it at `www.mediawiki.org`. If you've already installed bug-tracking software that uses a database server, you can use the same database server to support wiki applications such as MediaWiki. And backing up all the information stored in both the bug tracker and the wiki is as simple as performing a normal database backup.

A wiki is great for keeping your creative impulses organized. That might sound contradictory: sort of like keeping your inspirations on a leash. But I think you'll discover that each of your creative moments is over much too quickly, and without a record to look back at, the flashes of insight and imagination will be lost. If you could capture those moments, as close as possible to the moment they occur, you will be creating a repository of all your creative results. I find that reviewing what I've recorded in my wiki brings me back to the feelings of creative power I experienced during the actual event of dreaming up my ideas. And having all the ideas together generates more possibilities simply due to the power of combining an old idea with a new one.

Regardless of what tool you choose to record the products of your imagination and creativity, having such a record is a productive step toward coming up with the next Killer App.

Planning What Your App Will Do

When you've narrowed down your ideas to The One App, it's time to start thinking about all the different ways your app will make your users' lives easier. Long before you start typing code into the JDE, before creating your very first `UiApplication` class, you will find the development of your app will go along much more smoothly if you have planned what your app will do ahead of time. One of the best ways I've found for starting off is to create a one-sentence description of what your app is going to do. For my app, The Word Locker, that description was this:

> *The Word Locker is a password-protected memo pad.*

I find it helpful to have this statement written down nearby, usually in a text file where I store the workspace and project files. Knowing that the statement is recorded somewhere close reminds me of what the app's purpose is, and keeps me focused on developing code to accomplish it. Even if you never look at your app's statement once you've put it down in writing, you will remember where it is and what it says.

After you've made the app's purpose clear, you'll want to start planning how to achieve that purpose. Because your customers are going to use your app, a storyboard or a flowchart is a good way to move forward. A *storyboard* is a series of images displayed in sequence in order to help in visualizing a set of interactions, such as the interaction of a user using your app on their BlackBerry smartphone. Don't be frightened: You don't need an art degree to create a storyboard. A *flowchart* is a block diagram showing the general movement of a user through the application — a less artistic form of the storyboard. Either graphic provides a visual representation of what the user will see when she tries to use your app. Figure 4-1 shows a simple flowchart I wrote for creating The Word Locker.

Your first flowchart or storyboard is just a beginning. You might find yourself returning to it and adding new places for your user to go to within your app. Or, you might find yourself completely rewriting it. I have found that the most difficult part is creating the very first one, but getting it done was very helpful and made my development much easier as I could see what I meant for the app to do.

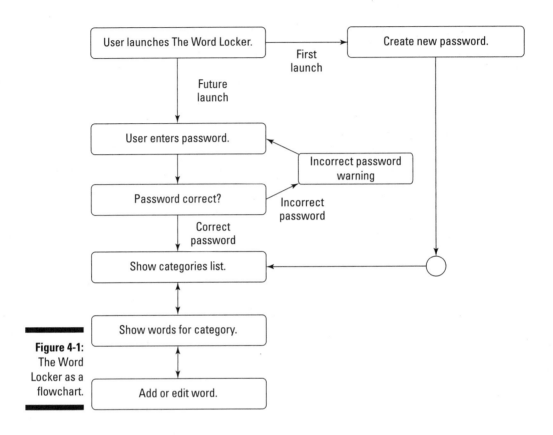

Figure 4-1:
The Word
Locker as a
flowchart.

The Fundamentals of BlackBerry Applications

I confess: I have committed the crime of implementing before architecting. It's very easy to sit down and get code running. *Architecting* — that is, sitting down and *thinking* about coding — is much more difficult. The best place to start convincing you to do this is by going over the fundamental aspects of BlackBerry applications. This is a halfway point between showing you how to implement BlackBerry code, and showing you how to plan the code of your application. I present the information in this chapter using my app, The Word Locker.

Parts of every BlackBerry app

The fundamental pieces of BlackBerry applications include the following:

- **Every application has a "main" function in its application class.** The BlackBerry OS finds the class in your app that extends `UiApplication` and looks for the `main()` function that must be there. It then executes that function as the first part of your application to be run when the user launches your app.

- **Applications with a user interface (UI apps) display screens to the user.** This book discusses only applications that provide some display for your users.

- **Users interact with UI apps through user interface components displayed on their screens.** Chapter 5 discusses the care and feeding of UI components, but I discuss them in broad strokes in this chapter.

- **UI apps usually have multiple screens for displaying information to and retrieving information from users.** At the very least, an About this Application screen will be a second screen for your app, so I show you how to manage simple situations of multiple screens and then advance into more complex scenarios.

- **The BlackBerry OS receives input from the user and delivers that input to your application.** Your users want to make your app do something, so you rely on the OS to intercept what your users want to do, and interpret the commands the OS delivers to your app.

- **The BlackBerry OS receives input from other sources, such as the network, and delivers that input to your application.** The OS sends information to your application — usually because you request it, sometimes even if you don't — and so your app has to prepare to receive the information and make use of or ignore it.

The phases of a BlackBerry application

Table 4-1 is a list of the major events, in order, that your application will move through.

Table 4-1	An App's Life from Start to Exit	
Event	*Object*	*Method*
User launches app.	`UiApplication`	`main( String[] args )`
OS tells app to begin.	`UiApplication`	`activate()`
Screen is pushed onto stack.	`MainScreen`	`onDisplay()`
Screen about to be drawn.	`MainScreen`	`onUiEngineAttached()`
Menu or dialog is removed.	`MainScreen`	`onExposed()`
Screen is closed.	`MainScreen`	`close()`
OS puts app in background.	`UiApplication`	`deactivate()`

These events can be lumped into three main phases in a BlackBerry application's runtime life:

✔ **Startup:** Your app starts this phase as a result of the user selecting your app from the BlackBerry Home screen and launching it.

✔ **Running:** This phase covers everything between the user launching your app and the user exiting your app.

✔ **Exiting:** Finally, your app has an opportunity to tighten things up (for instance, storing information your user has added in the persistent storage) when the user exits your app.

Each phase contains different parts that make up the pathway of operations your application will execute from start to finish. Most of the time, your app is waiting for the user to do something. The average user operates much more slowly than your application does, so your app's operations in the running phase are somewhat intermittent.

Startup

Listing 4-1 demonstrates code that implements the following steps. Here are the general operations that happen during the startup phase (see Figure 4-2):

1. The user selects your app on the BlackBerry Home screen or ribbon and launches it.

2. The BlackBerry OS determines the class of your application that extends the RIM class `UiApplication` and looks for a method called `main()` inside that class.

   For my app this would be `WordLocker`.

3. The BlackBerry OS executes the `main()` method of your `UiApplication` subclass.

4. Your application creates an object from your `UiApplication` subclass `UiApplication` within the body of the `main()` method.

5. Your `UiApplication` object's `enterEventDispatcher()` method is executed.

6. The BlackBerry OS sets up the Event Dispatcher for your application.

7. The BlackBerry Event Dispatcher executes your application's `activate()` method.

8. Your `UiApplication` object's `activate()` method begins.

9. Your `activate()` method creates the first screen-based object and places it on the screen stack.

10. Your application's first screen is displayed for the user.

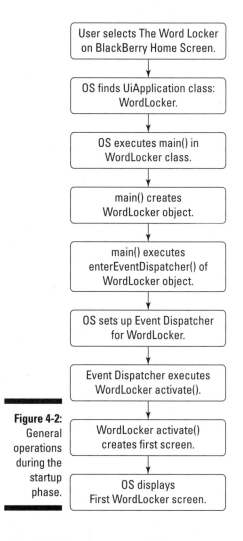

Figure 4-2:
General
operations
during the
startup
phase.

User selects The Word Locker on BlackBerry Home Screen.

↓

OS finds UiApplication class: WordLocker.

↓

OS executes main() in WordLocker class.

↓

main() creates WordLocker object.

↓

main() executes enterEventDispatcher() of WordLocker object.

↓

OS sets up Event Dispatcher for WordLocker.

↓

Event Dispatcher executes WordLocker activate().

↓

WordLocker activate() creates first screen.

↓

OS displays First WordLocker screen.

Listing 4-1:   A Code Implementation of the Startup Phase

```
public class WordLocker extends UiApplication
{
  // steps 2&3 start here
  public static void main( String[] inArgs )
  {
    // step 4
    WordLocker wlApp = new WordLocker();
    // step 5
    wlApp.enterEventDispatcher();
    // step 6 & 7 - the OS takes over now
  }

  public WordLocker()
  {
    // creating the wlApp object above
    // will execute code in here
    // you can take care of any initialization
    // for your app before the OS takes over
  }

  public void activate()
  {
    // step 8 - the OS returns control to your app
    // step 9
    this.pushScreen( new WordLockerMainScreen() );
    // step 10 - the OS takes over now
  }
}
```

Running

When the user can interact with your application, the app is in the running phase. Its general flow is like this (see Figure 4-3, and see Listing 4-2 for the code):

1. Your application's `Screen` subclass object is created and placed on the screen stack.

2. The OS calls the `onUiEngineAttached()` method of the `Screen` object.

3. The `Screen` object draws itself and its components on the BlackBerry screen.

4. The user performs some operation: clicks a button, enters text, selects a menu item, and so on.

5. Your screen object accepts the user's action, and reacts accordingly.

6. If the action affects the contents of the current screen, your application updates the screen and continues at Step 4.

7. If the action requires a new screen to be displayed, your application creates a new `Screen` subclass object and continues at Step 1.

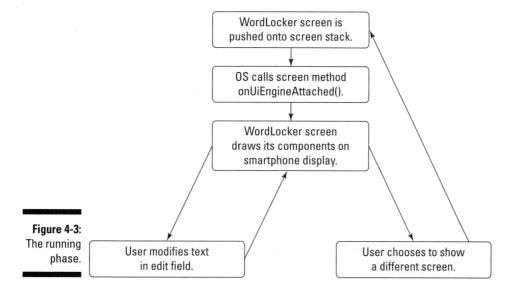

Figure 4-3:
The running
phase.

Listing 4-2: The Running Phase in Code

```
// step 1 as executed from within
// a different class, such as the activate()
// method in WordLocker
public void activate()
{
  // step 1
  this.pushScreen( new WordLockerMainScreen() );
}

// the remaining steps happen within the screen
// class
public class WordLockerMainScreen extends MainScreen
       implements FieldChangeListener
{
  private EditField m_editText;
  private ButtonField m_showHelpScreen;

  public WordLockerMainScreen()
  {
    // the creation part of step 1
    this.initialize();
  }

  private void initialize()
  {
    // create UI elements and
    // add them to the screen
```

(continued)

Listing 4-2 *(continued)*

```
    m_editText = new EditField( "", "" );
    this.add( m_editText );
    m_showHelpScreen = new ButtonField( "Show Help" );
    this.add( m_showHelpScreen );
}

public void onUiEngineAttached()
{
  // step 2
  // this sets up the screen to
  // handle the user clicking
  // the button for steps 4&5
  m_showHelpScreen.setChangeListener( this );
  // after this, the OS executes
  // step 3 behind the scenes

}

public void fieldChanged( Field inField, int inContext )
{
  if (inField == m_showHelpScreen)
  {
    // step 7, which performs like step 1
    UiApplication.getUiApplication().pushScreen(
      new HelpScreen() );
  }
  this.setDirty( false );
}
}
```

Your application's screens constantly accept user input and update themselves or display new screens, all throughout this phase of the application's operation. There are two ways out of the running phase:

✓ **The user exits the application.** This can occur as a result of the user selecting the Close menu item (if the default functionality is present) or pressing the Escape button.

✓ **The user selects the Switch Application menu item or presses the End Call button.** This does not exit the application, but instead places it into the background in a holding pattern. Your users might choose to do this, for instance, if a different application on their BlackBerry can provide them some information for use in your application or vice versa. For instance, your application might require a login ID or a temporary password that has been e-mailed to your user's BlackBerry Mail program: The user will launch your app, switch to Mail, copy the required data from the e-mail message, and then switch back to your app to paste the data as directed.

Switching applications

The Switch Application menu item deserves a little more detail. When a user selects Switch Application from your application's menu, the BlackBerry device OS executes a method in your application class called `deactivate()`. The Application superclass' implementation of this method does nothing. However, your app can override this method and execute any operations that you prefer to support when the user leaves your app running while switching to a different app. When the user selects your now-backgrounded app to switch back to, the OS again executes the `activate()` method. This can lead to a memory leak if your `Application` subclass simply creates a new `Screen` subclass and pushes it onto the screen stack, as if your app were starting up from scratch. So, in your `activate()` method, it's a good idea to check whether any `Screen` objects are currently on the screen stack. Your application should be a subclass of `UiApplication` (`net.rim.device.api.ui.UiApplication`), which provides a method that you can use to determine how many screens are currently on the stack:

```
public int getScreenCount();
```

If there's a screen already there when your `activate()` method is executed, your application has not been newly launched, and you can simply call a different `UiApplication` method to refresh the screen:

```
public void updateDisplay();
```

Exiting

Lastly, the exiting phase of your BlackBerry application operates as follows (see Figure 4-4, and Listing 4-3):

1. Your user selects Close from the menu.

2. The OS executes the `close()` method of your `Screen` subclass.

   This is where your app has its last chance to perform any needed cleanup such as storing user input. The screen object then calls its parent class's `close()` method. Your app can also shut itself down by executing the `System.exit(0)` method.

3. The BlackBerry OS terminates your application.

   The OS does this by executing `System.exit(0)` on your application's behalf.

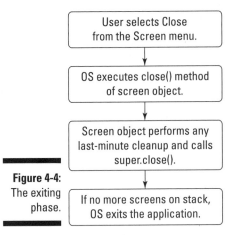

Figure 4-4:
The exiting
phase.

Listing 4-3:   The Exit Phase Implemented in Code

```
public class InfoScreen extends Screen
{
  public InfoScreen()
  {
  }

  public void close()
  {
    // the OS executes this method as a result
    // of step 1
    // step 2
    // perform any last-minute cleanup here
    this.storeUserInput();
    // and call the MainScreen.close() method
    // step 3
    super.close();
  }
}
```

The most interesting thing about the exiting phase is that the OS will terminate
your application if the last `Screen` object on the screen stack is removed.
When there are no more screens to be displayed, the OS kills your application,
and does not give your app any opportunity to do anything before it goes away.
This is just the way the OS behaves, and you must be careful when you code
your app to remove screens from the screen stack because you might find
your app exiting when you didn't intend it to. Listing 4-4 shows a screen
class that causes an application exit without any warning, while Listing 4-5
demonstrates a screen class that provides an opportunity for your app to
handle its responsibilities smoothly.

Listing 4-4: This Screen Terminates Your App When Closed

```
public class TerminatorScreen extends MainScreen
{
  public TerminatorScreen()
  {
  }

  public void close()
  {
    // if no other screens are on the stack
    // the OS will terminate the app
    super.close();
    // this statement will never execute
    UiApplication.getUiApplication().pushScreen( new FollowUpScreen() );
  }
}
```

Listing 4-5: Avoiding Termination while Closing a Screen

```
public class StayingAliveScreen extends MainScreen
{
  public StayingAliveScreen()
  {
  }

  public void close()
  {
    // push the follow-up screen first
    UiApplication.getUiApplication().pushScreen( new FollowUpScreen() );
    // then close this screen
    super.close();
  }
}
```

Sometimes, you might want your app to do some cleanup just before your application is terminated. This will become a challenge because the OS doesn't call back into your application to give it a chance to do something before it closes. This means you will have to override each `Screen` subclass' `close()` method to take care of any application cleanup before your app terminates. Listing 4-6 shows a `close()` method that takes care of storing any changes the user made while the screen was visible.

Listing 4-6:   Cleaning Up Just Prior to Exit

```
public class SettingsScreen extends MainScreen
{
  private EditField m_textField;

  public SettingsScreen()
  {
    super(); // make sure parent class is initialized
    String storedText = this.getTextFromStorage();
    m_textField = new EditField( "Stored Text: ", storedText );
    this.add( m_textField );
  }

  private String getTextFromStorage()
  {
    // return a string from the persistent store
    return (aString);
  }

  private void storeTextInStorage( String inText )
  {
    // store string in persistent store
  }

  public void close()
  {
    // get the original text
    String storedString = this.getTextFromStorage();
    // check the edit field for whether
    // the user has entered new text
    String editText = m_textField.getText();
    if (false == editText.equals( storedString ))
    {
      // text is different, so save it
      this.storeTextInStorage( editText );
    }
    super.close();
  }
}
```

Handling Screens and Callbacks

From the fundamental behaviors of startup, running, and exiting, you might be able to sense two abstract features that your app is going to have to support:

✔ **Managing screens:** Your app is going to create and display multiple screens. Consequently, you need to find some way to manage them.

✔ **Handling callbacks:** Everything that happens in your application occurs as a result of the OS executing a callback method. So you need to know how to set up and manage callbacks in just about every class needed by your application — at least those classes that do interesting things.

The following sections describe the Model-View-Controller method of screen management and how to handle callbacks.

Screen management

Your application creates screens as the primary means of communicating with the user. Your users see the information your app provides to them on a screen. Your app provides components that allow users to deliver information to your app, and these components are shown onscreen as UI elements such as buttons, menus, and so on.

What this amounts to is your app has to manage the screens it generates and displays to your users. *Screen management* is a process by which your application keeps track of which screen is on display, and what happens when the user performs an action that requires a new screen to appear.

You can find a variety of ways to manage the screens in your apps. Some approaches work well when your app has a small number of screens. In The Word Locker, there are only four or five screens in total, and each screen keeps track of what screen (if any) should be displayed when the user selects a particular menu item. This approach works well because the number of screens is small, and there are only a limited number of choices the user has on each screen. However, one disadvantage appears when new screens get added or old ones are removed as the app evolves. The remaining old screens have to be recoded to make use of the new screens and to stop using the removed screens.

Another approach might be to remove the decision of what screen is displayed next from the code within the currently displayed screen and place that decision-making process within a separate screen-controller class. Your screens would no longer be required to know what screen comes next; instead, each of your screens would send a message to the screen-controller class indicating that some event had occurred — for instance, that the user had selected the Close menu item — and letting the screen-controller class decide what to do next.

Although you aren't obliged to follow any particular approach to managing your app's screens, here are a few good reasons for providing some form of screen management:

✔ **Consistent operation:** Your users are going to expect that when looking at a screen they've seen before, the same action on their part will produce the same response your app performed the previous time. This might sound obvious, but as applications start to provide more features and functionality — always adding more screens in the process — a lack of screen management will lead to code that at some point misbehaves.

✔ **Flow control:** When your app's user commands your app to perform a specific task, your application is going to obey by executing a sequence of programmed steps and delivering the result of those actions back to the user. For instance, a doctor using your app to retrieve a patient's medical history might enter the patient's identifying data into your app and then wait for your app to display the patient's temperature readings for the past 24 hours. Your application will have to perform a set of steps in order, and consequently, display multiple screens in their proper order. When you implement a screen manager, you will find it much easier to control the flow of your application, especially when a future version of your app (or even one going through the standard development process!) requires a modification to the flow in order to enhance an old feature or add a new one.

The BlackBerry class libraries don't provide a ready-made set of classes for managing screen objects: You get to make your own. I go over some of the important issues to consider, and give you some reasons why I prefer the Model-View-Controller method.

The way of MVC: Model-View-Controller

The *Model-View-Controller* (MVC) pattern is an approach to designing software that accomplishes a solution to the problem of mixing *business logic* (how data is manipulated by the app) with *interface logic* (how the app presents data to the user) and *interaction logic* (what actions the user can take). When you implement code that combines all three types of logic, you will find it difficult to separate the code that displays a button from the code that reacts when that button is clicked and the code that changes the data as a result of the button click. These three separate types of code should be logically separated from each other: This is what applying the MVC pattern accomplishes. The MVC pattern is made of three components, as shown in Figure 4-5:

✔ **The model:** The *model portion* of MVC represents those parts of the code that handle the data associated with the software application. This code includes what's commonly called *business logic,* which your app uses to make decisions about what data to deliver to the view and controller portions of the code.

✓ **The view:** The *view portion* of MVC takes care of the display of information to the user. This is the simplest part of the MVC paradigm because its job is to display information and UI elements to the user. On a mobile device, the view and the controller can be merged together (see the next bullet).

✓ **The controller:** Finally, the *controller part* of MVC is the code that handles input from the user or other parts of the operating system. On a mobile device, the controller and the view are often merged together because the user interacts with components of the view, and the controller picks up these interactions to pass along to the model.

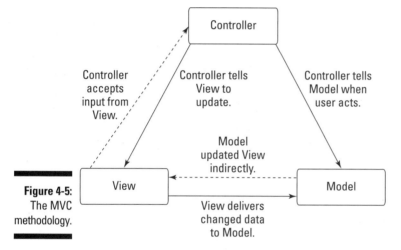

Figure 4-5: The MVC methodology.

As an approach to managing screens, the MVC pattern divides the responsibility for screen management (in the View & Controller objects) from the code needed to supply the screens with information to display. So MVC will assist your app in managing screens, but also provides more capability to perform general application management beyond taking care of your screens.

How MVC controls the flow of an app

Here's a simplified description of the flow of control in an MVC application (see Figure 4-6):

1. The user presses the BlackBerry's trackball on a button displayed on a screen in your application.

2. The controller receives the input event, usually as a result of registering a callback.

   Read about callbacks in the upcoming section, "Callbacks: The Java version of phoning home."

3. The controller informs the model that the user just clicked a particular button.

4. The model changes the data that it's maintaining about the application's current state.

5. The model notifies all view objects that its data changed.

6. The view on display receives the notification from the model about the current state, and updates itself as necessary.

The update might simply be a change in a graph being displayed, or the update could be the replacement of the current screen with that of a new screen.

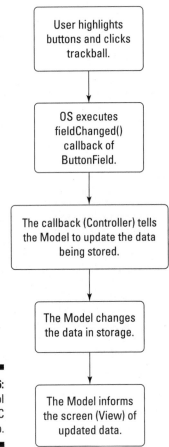

Figure 4-6:
Flow control
in an MVC
app.

The preceding steps cover the general flow of control when using an MVC design for a BlackBerry app. The controller is represented by UI element callbacks, the views are represented by BlackBerry screen objects, and the model coordinates the actions performed by the user (through the controller) with the display of information on the screen (through the views).

You're not obligated to implement an MVC to deliver your app to the BlackBerry App World, but having a defined structure before you begin coding will reduce the challenges you face when developing your app.

What state are you from?

One choice for implementing a model component is a *state machine,* which is a model of behavior that controls the execution of an application by breaking up the operations of the app into separate pieces. State machines are very useful for managing software applications in general as well as for managing screens (the view component) in particular. I won't go into too many details here, but in general, a state machine operates as follows:

- ✔ The application hovers in one state, until an event causes a *transition.* An event may be a user action, or a callback from the OS.

- ✔ A transition is a message delivered to the state machine. The state machine uses the message to determine what state the application should hover in next.

- ✔ Each state can transition to a limited number of other states.

The view component of an MVC application updates itself when it gets a notification from the model component. Because the view component is only responsible for painting pixels, the model component must provide the information about which pixels to paint and with what color. To perform this function, the model has to maintain information about the current "state" that the application is in, which itself is a combination of a prior "state" and input delivered from the controller component.

You use a state machine as follows (see Figure 4-7 and Listing 4-7):

1. The controller delivers input events from the user or OS to the model.

2. The model's current state determines what the subsequent state should be, based on the current state and the input from the controller.

3. The model resets to the subsequent state, which now becomes the current state.

4. The model notifies the view to update itself.

5. The view determines what the current state is, and displays itself as appropriate.

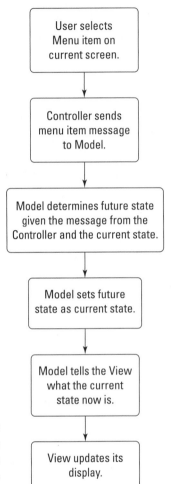

Figure 4-7:
The state
machine.

Listing 4-7: Simplified Model Implementing a State Machine

```
// step 1 happens as a result of
// a callback which executes
// Model.changeState()

public class ModelObject
{
  private State m_currentState;
  private ViewObject m_view;

  public ModelObject()
  {
  }
```

```
    public void changeState( String inMessage )
    {
      // step 2
      State futureState = m_currentState.getFutureState( inMessage );
      // step 3
      m_currentState = futureState;
      // step 4
      m_view.updateUsingState( m_currentState );
    }
}


public class StateObject
{
  private Hashtable m_futureStates;

  public StateObject()
  {
    // initialize the future states Hashtable
    // each message acts as a key to retrieve
    // the State object stored in the Hashtable
  }

  public State getFutureState( String inMessage )
  {
    //
    return ((State)m_futureStates.get( inMessage ));
  }

}

public class ViewObject
{
  private Screen m_currentScreen;
  public ViewObject()
  {
  }

  public updateUsingState( State inState )
  {
    // step 5
    // using information contained in inState
    // update the display
  }
}
```

Point of view

The view component can be something as simple as one screen, or it could be a class that maintains a set of screens. I tend to implement the latter. The applications that I build for users all have multiple screens, so the view component that I construct is a class that manages a fixed set of screens.

When a notification arrives from the model component, my view component performs the following actions; see Listing 4-8:

1. Determines which screen must be on display based on the information provided by the model

2. Updates the contents of the screen to be displayed

3. Displays the screen

Listing 4-8:   View Object Updating Based on State

```
public class ViewObject
{
  private SettingsScreen m_settings;
  private AboutScreen m_about;
  private HelpScreen m_help;
  private Screen m_currentScreen;

  public ViewObject()
  {
    m_settings =  new SettingsScreen();
    m_about = new AboutScreen();
    m_help = new HelpScreen;
    m_currentScreen = m_settings; // first screen to be seen
    UiApplication.getUiApplication().pushScreen( m_currentScreen );
  }

  public void updateUsingState( State inState )
  {
    // step 1 is the Model object
    // calling this code
    // step 2
    Screen noLongerCurrent = m_currentScreen;
    if (inState.getName().equals( "Help" ))
    {
      m_currentScreen = m_help;
    }
    else if (inState.getName().equals( "About" ))
    {
      m_currentScreen = m_about;
    }
    else if (inState.getName().equals( "Settings" ))
    {
      m_currentScreen = m_settings;
    }
    else
    {
      System.exit(0);
      // we exit
    }
    UiApplication.getUiApplication().pushScreen( m_currentScreen );
```

```
    // remove screen since not needed
    UiApplication.getUiApplication().popScreen( noLongerCurrent );
  }
}
```

Pretty simple and straightforward. And you will find it easy to track down problems because the view's job is to get data from the model and show it. The model's job is to tell the view what's supposed to be displayed; the view's job is to make sure it displays what the model has in its current state.

Controller freak

The controller component is sometimes combined with the view component in GUI-based applications. The reason for this is that the controller component passes information to the model from user input, and user input elements are created and managed from within the view component. You will generally add callbacks (discussed in the following sections) to UI elements that will execute as a result of user actions; having this as part of the view consolidates the actions with their UI elements within the same block of code. For mobile devices, you'll find it makes sense to combine these two objects into one. You'll find that developers still call this Model-View-Controller because the three components are all still there, but the View-Controller has become merged code.

Callbacks: The Java version of phoning home

You can write Java programs to support the BlackBerry OS when the OS wants to execute something in your app as a result of external inputs. Regardless of how the input arises, the OS might need more information from your application to proceed. Or, more likely, you want your app to react when something happens so that it gives the OS a piece of code to execute when the correct circumstances arise.

The OS getting information from your app or receiving code from your app to execute is a *callback;* there are two ways to provide them:

✔ **Your application subclasses an OS class and overrides a method in that class which the OS will call.** The OS will eventually call that method as a result of a user's actions, executing your application's code. Note that you don't always have to create a *complete* subclass; your code can instantiate an object of the class you want and override the appropriate methods in that class on the fly. You can see this in Listing 4-9, where a BlackBerry OS `MenuItem` object is created and its `run()` method is implemented as part of creating the object.

Listing 4-9: Creating a MenuItem and its run() Method at Once

```
public void makeMenu( Menu inMenu, int inContext )
{
  MenuItem helpItem = new MenuItem( "Help", 10000, 10 )
  {
    public void run()
    {
      UiApplication.getUiApplication().pushScreen( new HelpScreen() );
    }
  };

  inMenu.add( helpItem );
}
```

✔ **Your application creates a class that implements an interface, and then provides an object of that class to the OS for its use.** The OS treats the object provided by using the interface's methods without knowing that it's your class' implementations of those methods that are being executed. Listing 4-10 shows the implementation of an e-mail attachment handler that will read certain types of files that arrived with the user's e-mail.

Listing 4-10: The KarlEmailAttachmentHandler Imports ".karl" Files

```
public class KarlEmailAttachmentHandler implements AttachmentHandler
{
  public KarlEmailAttachmentHandler()
  {
    // constructor for the class
  }

  public String menuString()
  {
    // return the text for use to see in menu
    // when an attachment we'd like to read
    // is selected
    return ("Open Attachment for KarlEmail" );
  }

  public boolean supports( String inContentType )
  {
    if (inContentType.toLowerCase().indexOf( ".karl" ))
    {
      return (true);
    }
    else
    {
      return (false);
    }
  }

  public void run( Message inMessage, SupportedAttachmentPart inPart )
```

```
{
   // import the contents of the attachment
}
}
```

You might already know about the different ways that Java programs running on a desktop PC make use of callbacks to provide mechanisms for handling all kinds of user and other external inputs. The BlackBerry OS, although it has fewer reasons for making calls into your code, still provides a lot of opportunities for you to implement callbacks, such as

✔ Responding to a menu selection made by the user

✔ Reacting to the user clicking a button

✔ Handling a keystroke

✔ Reacting to a timed operation

✔ Reacting to a screen change

✔ Retrieving data coming in from a network connection

✔ Responding to an incoming e-mail

All these situations require using callback-handling mechanisms. Some are easily implemented by creating a subclass that overrides its parent's methods for handling behaviors that the OS will expect to execute; your application's version of the class can do something different from the OS version of the class. Listing 4-11 shows you a subclass of MainScreen that overrides close() to provide its own functionality. Others might have to be implemented through the use of an interface, depending on what the OS requires you to deliver. You can see this kind in Listing 4-11. And sometimes you can provide classes "on the fly," exploiting the Java language's syntax that lets you implement a class as a parameter to be passed into an OS routine. The MenuItem implemented in Listing 4-11 is an example of this kind.

Listing 4-11: A Subclass of MainScreen that Overrides close() to Provide Its Own Functionality

```
public class MyScreenSubclass extends MainScreen
{
  public MyScreenSubclass()
  {
  }

  public void close()
  {
    // this method will be called instead
    // of the close() method implemented as
    // part of MainScreen.
  }
}
```

The following sections take a look at some of the situations in the preceding bullet list and describe the approaches for handling them.

Selecting from a menu

BlackBerry users make use of the menus that applications provide. (I imagine there's a repetitive-stress injury soon to be called "BlackBerry Left-Thumb" caused by excessive use of the BlackBerry menu button.) Figure 4-8 shows you the BlackBerry menu button on a BlackBerry Bold 9700.

Figure 4-8:
The
BlackBerry
menu
button,
on every
BlackBerry
device.

Pressing this button brings up the BlackBerry *menu,* a list of possible actions that the user can select from to do something.

Your application can add its own menu items to each of its screen objects, and each screen can have its own unique set of menu items. When the user selects one of the items from the menu, your application will have to respond, and the BlackBerry OS will be calling your "menu item callback" code. Listing 4-12 shows you how to create a menu item and override its "run" method on the fly:

Listing 4-12:   Creating a Menu Item and Overriding Its Run Method

```
public class MenuApplicationScreen extends MainScreen
{
    // the Screen's constructor will handle
    // initialization of the items on display
```

```
public void makeMenu( Menu inMenu, int inContext )
{
    inMenu.add( new MenuItem( "Start Timer", 1000, 10 )
    {
        public void run()
        {
            handleStartTimer(); // call back into the class
        }
    });
    super.makeMenu( inMenu, inContext );
}

protected void handleStartTimer()
{
    // start the timer
}
}
```

You can see in the overridden `MainScreen.makeMenu()` method that
a `new MenuItem` object is created as the parameter to the `Menu.add()`
method. In addition, the `MenuItem.run()` method is overridden on the fly,
simply by adding the new `run()` method to the object created from the `new
MenuItem()` statement.

You could also create a completely separate class for this particular menu
item, especially if this particular menu item were to be used in more than
one screen. For instance, an About this Application menu item that appears
on more than one screen and that displays a dialog screen detailing information about your app is a perfect candidate for creating a unique `MenuItem`
subclass. An About screen usually doesn't carry information that changes
as a result of user action, which means an `AboutMenuItem` class is pretty
self-contained. About screens don't have to communicate details about user
actions while the dialog is displayed, and About screens usually aren't interested in retrieving information from the screen users were on when they
selected the About this Application menu item.

Clicking buttons

If you give users a button to click, they will click it eventually. For your application to handle the user's button-push action, you provide a callback via the
implementation of an interface.

Adding a button (`ButtonField` object) to your screen is easy; getting it to
respond to a user clicking it is easy, but not obvious. Listing 4-13 shows a
code snippet that does this.

Listing 4-13:   Adding a Button to Click and Code to Execute as its Callback

```
public class ButtonApplicationScreen extends MainScreen implements
            FieldChangeListener
{
   private ButtonField m_button;

   public ButtonApplicationScreen()
   {
      super();
      m_button = new ButtonField( "Press Me First!" );
      this.add(button);
      aButton.setFieldChangeListener( this );
   }

   public void fieldChanged( Field inField, int inContext )
   {
      if (inField == m_Button)
      {
         // handle button click
      }
   }
}
```

The code implemented in Listing 4-13 demonstrates the use of an interface-implementing class to function as a callback. `FieldChangeListener` is an interface that requires you to code the method `fieldChanged()` in any class that wishes to masquerade as a listener for changing fields. Within the `fieldChanged()` method in Listing 4-13, my code snippet is checking whether the incoming `Field` object that has changed is the button that was created in the constructor. Although it doesn't occur in this code snippet, your code can use the same object (the screen) as the `FieldChangeListener` for multiple UI elements. Your `fieldChanged` method will be executed for each element that has your screen class as its `FieldChangeListener`. As such, you will have to code your `fieldChanged` method to determine which of the multiple elements caused the OS to call into your code.

Responding to keystrokes

As you can see from Figure 4-8, BlackBerry devices come with many different keys. Your application can react to a user pressing a key on the keyboard when one of your application's screens is on display. The code snippet in Listing 4-14 shows you a very simple example of this.

Listing 4-14: Implementing a Screen's Capability to Handle Key Presses

```
protected boolean keyDown( int inKeycode, int inTime )
{
    boolean result = true;
    switch (inKeycode)
    {
        case Keypad.KEY_ENTER:
            this.handleKeyEnter();
            break;
        case Keypad.KEY_ESCAPE:
            this.handleKeyEscape();
            break;
        default:
            // let the parent class handle it
            result = super.keyDown(inKeycode, inTime);
            break;
    }
    return (result);
}
```

Listing 4-14 represents a method in a `MainScreen` subclass that overrides the `MainScreen.keyDown()` method. There are actually several different keyboard-related methods in `MainScreen`:

✔ `keyDown(int keycode, int time)`: Your application's screen object will execute this method when the user presses a key while the screen is on display. However, some UI elements — such as an `edit` field — will intercept the user's key presses because the OS delivers the key-down event to a field that has the focus first. You could use this to move jigsaw puzzle pieces around the screen.

✔ `keyRepeat(int keycode, int time)`: Because a user may hold a key down to repeat it, the OS will tell your application when this happens. I've rarely made use of this method, but it's available if your application wants to take advantage of a particular key being held down. You might make use of a specific repeating key in a *Space Invaders* kind of game to sweep a cannon from left to right as aliens try to bombard your home planet.

✔ `keyUp(int keycode, int time)`: This method will be called by the BlackBerry OS when the user releases a key just pressed, just in case you want to execute code when the user releases a specific key. This method seems to behave the same as `keyDown()` because it's pretty difficult to press a key and not release it while your app is running.

Your app can use the preceding methods to respond to user keyboard actions, and respond in different ways when keys are pressed. For instance, your code might decide to handle the user's pressing the Escape key differently from the default action provided by the `MainScreen` superclass, which normally executes a close this screen operation. I don't recommend modifying the behavior of the Escape or Menu keys, because users depend on their proper behavior as implemented in all the RIM-supplied applications. Your users will be confused if Escape does not perform as expected, and smashing your users' expectations isn't very friendly.

Chapter 5

Setting Up Screens and User Interfaces

. . . .

In This Chapter

▶ Creating screens to display your info

▶ Managing a screen's contents

▶ Creating menus

▶ Working with an interactive environment

▶ Communicating with background threads

▶ Managing the screen stack

. . . .

*Y*our BlackBerry application delivers information to your users — and gets information back — through screens. A *screen* is a container for UI elements, which provide the visual part of your application. The screens that your application uses must deliver content in a way that is helpful (tells the users what to do), efficient (minimizes scrolling, clicking, and reading required), and appropriate (focuses on achieving the application's goal). This chapter guides you through the various aspects of creating the visual pieces of your application, including how to present information to your users and how to enable users to provide information back in kind.

The BlackBerry development libraries contain a rich set of classes that enable your application to deliver its information in a variety of forms. These classes include items such as simple text labels and buttons as well as graphic images and hierarchical trees of data.

In this chapter, I give you the basic information you need to create and manage the screens that your application will employ to exchange information with your users.

The Screen

BlackBerry devices have a small color LCD screen where users find important information in their mobile lives. In combination with a keyboard and a mechanism for navigation — a trackwheel, trackball, trackpad, or touchscreen — the screen enables users to discover new details from and also contribute new data to your application. The screen is the focal point for users, and therefore you need to master this part of your application to control the information you want your application to deliver.

Choosing a screen type

You can use several different classes to display information on a BlackBerry screen:

- ✔ `Screen` (`net.rim.device.api.ui.Screen`): This is the basic screen class that provides a bare minimum of features and functionality.

- ✔ `FullScreen` (`net.rim.device.api.ui.container.FullScreen`): This class inherits the basic screen features and functionality, and adds a layout manager for performing vertical layout of its contents.

- ✔ `PopupScreen` (`net.rim.device.api.ui.container.PopupScreen`): This is the basic class used for dialog screens that pop up when something interesting happens.

- ✔ `MainScreen` (`net.rim.device.api.ui.container.MainScreen`): This class inherits the features and functionality of `FullScreen`, and adds features common to standard BlackBerry applications.

- ✔ `Dialog` (`net.rim.device.api.ui.component.Dialog`): This class is used to display transient dialog boxes to the user, and wait for the user to provide more data.

- ✔ `Status` (`net.rim.device.api.ui.component.Status`): This class is used to display a dialog box to show ongoing status. The user may dismiss this dialog by clicking the trackwheel, or by pressing the spacebar or the Escape key.

I develop the displays for my application using screens based on the `MainScreen` class because it provides a good set of features and functionality right out of the box, and adding anything to or replacing anything in that set is very easy. Most of the information the user provides to my application comes from direct interaction with the screens I create; some interaction results from the use of dialog boxes as well. In Figure 5-1, you can see a `MainScreen` created for a user to enter first-time password information.

First Time Password
Password:
Confirm:
OK

Figure 5-1:
A
MainScreen
object
created
and dis-
played on a
BlackBerry
screen.

Creating a screen

In this section, I describe what it takes to show a screen in a BlackBerry application. The example in Listing 5-1 is very simple: An application initializes itself and creates a blank screen with one menu item, and puts it on the BlackBerry's display. After the code, I give you the steps to use Listing 5-1 to build the app.

Listing 5-1:   SimpleScreenApp.java contents

```
/*
 * SimpleScreenApp.java
 *
 * © Karl G. Kowalski, 2011
 * Confidential and proprietary.
 */

import  net.rim.device.api.ui.*;
import  net.rim.device.api.ui.component.*;
import  net.rim.device.api.ui.container.*;

public  class SimpleScreenApp    extends UiApplication
{
    public  static  void    main( String[] inArgs )
    {
        SimpleScreenApp ssa =   new SimpleScreenApp();
        ssa.enterEventDispatcher();
    }

    public  SimpleScreenApp()
    {
```

(continued)

Listing 5-1 *(continued)*

```
    }

    public void    activate()
    {
       this.pushScreen( new SimpleScreen() );
    }
}

class   SimpleScreen    extends MainScreen
{
    public  SimpleScreen()
    {
       super();
       this.initialize();
    }

    protected   void    initialize()
    {
       this.setTitle( "Simple Screen App" );
    }

    public  void    close()
    {
       Dialog.alert( "Closing the app" );
       super.close();
    }
}
```

Follow these steps to take the code in Listing 5-1 and create a simple app that
displays a screen and menu:

1. **Create a workspace, project, and a main Java file in the project as
   described in Chapter 3. Name the project `SimpleScreenApp` or
   choose your own favorite name.**

2. **Enter the code found in Listing 5-1 into the Java file.**

3. **Build the application and execute it as described in Chapter 3.**

   The JDE compiles the Java code you entered and packages it as an
   application for the BlackBerry simulator, and then launches the
   simulator.

4. **When the simulator launches, navigate to the application you created
   and launch the application.**

   I'm not sure why the JDE needs you to do the actual launching instead of
   just running it on its own, but this is the way the JDE does things.

   The main screen is displayed, as shown in Figure 5-2.

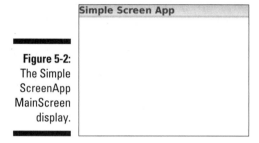

Figure 5-2:
The Simple
ScreenApp
MainScreen
display.

5. Click the Menu button in the simulator.

A menu is displayed, as shown in Figure 5-3. The menu contains only one item, Close. This is part of the functionality provided by MainScreen.

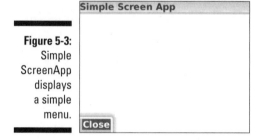

Figure 5-3:
Simple
ScreenApp
displays
a simple
menu.

6. Click the Close button.

The dialog box shown in Figure 5-4 appears.

Figure 5-4:
Simple
ScreenApp
showing the
Close dialog
box.

7. Click the OK button in the dialog box.

The application closes, taking the screen and the dialog box with it, and returning you to the display of the applications in the BlackBerry ribbon.

Extending a screen's basic functionality

The standard `MainScreen` class is a great starting point for creating your own screens. `MainScreen` inherits a wealth of features and functionality from its ancestor classes, and you can override some of these methods to enhance the behavior of your application at certain significant points during your `MainScreen` subclass' lifetime:

✔ `void onUiEngineAttached( boolean )`: This method is called by the BlackBerry OS when your screen is pushed onto the screen stack, after layout has occurred, but before the screen is drawn on the display. This provides an opportunity for you to make last-minute adjustments to the screen's contents such as setting the time display of a digital clock and launching a thread to update it. This method is also called when the BlackBerry OS is about to remove your screen from the screen stack, which gives your app the opportunity to tidy up, such as halting the thread that updates the digital clock. The input parameter is `true` when the OS is about to display the screen, and `false` when the OS is about to remove it.

✔ `void onExposed()`: This method is called by the BlackBerry OS when a screen is revealed by the removal (through a call to `UiApplication.popScreen()`) of a screen above it in the screen stack.

✔ `void onObscured()`: This method is the opposite of `onExposed()`. The BlackBerry OS calls `onObscured()` when a different screen is pushed on top of your screen.

✔ `void onSave()`: The BlackBerry OS calls this method for your `Screen` subclass when users close a screen where they've made changes: for instance, on a settings screen. You override this method to perform the steps necessary to save whatever changes the user made to your screen.

✔ `boolean keyDown( int, int )`: This method is called by the BlackBerry OS when the user presses a keyboard key while your screen is on display.

Touchscreen devices have a keyboard present only if the selected UI element requires a keyboard.

✔ `boolean keyUp( int, int )`: This method is called by the BlackBerry OS when the user releases a keyboard key while your screen is on display.

User Interface Elements

Your application will present users with information that they need to see and act upon. To do this, you fill your application screens with a variety of text and images, add buttons and editable fields, plus a whole lot more. The BlackBerry library contains more than a few UI elements for your application to employ for communication with the user.

The following is a list of some standard UI elements you'll use frequently:

- ✔ Field (net.rim.device.api.ui.Field): The base user interface class. All the different UI components, such as buttons and labels, inherit their basic functionality from Field. Your application's screens maintain a list of the Field objects that are added to be displayed.

- ✔ BitmapField (net.rim.device.api.ui.component. BitmapField): A class for displaying an image as a bitmap. A BitmapField object can display BMP, JPG, and PNG image types, as well as *Raw ARGB data* (an image as a series of pixels, each pixel's color represented by a 4-byte value of Alpha, Red, Green, and Blue components; Alpha is used to control the transparency of the pixel).

- ✔ ButtonField (net.rim.device.api.ui.component. ButtonField): A class representing a button the user can click to command your application to execute an operation.

- ✔ CheckboxField (net.rim.device.api.ui.component. CheckboxField): A class representing a check box for the user to select an option.

- ✔ ChoiceField (net.rim.device.api.ui.component. ChoiceField): A class representing a set of choices, similar to a drop-down list, from which the user can select one item.

- ✔ DateField (net.rim.device.api.ui.component.DateField): A class that stores a date and time selection for the user.

- ✔ EditField (net.rim.device.api.ui.component.EditField): A class that stores text the user enters.

- ✔ GaugeField (net.rim.device.api.ui.component.GaugeField): A class that displays a horizontal progress bar.

- ✔ LabelField (net.rim.device.api.ui.component.LabelField): A class for displaying static text data, such as labels for text boxes and so on. The text is displayed in the system's main display font; for greater flexibility in text entry and display, use the RichTextField instead.

- ListField (net.rim.device.api.ui.component.ListField): A class for displaying a vertical list of items. Your application can enhance the default functionality of a ListField by providing code to draw the contents of each item in the list.

- PasswordEditField (net.rim.device.api.ui.component. PasswordEditField): A class that allows the user to enter passwords into a text box. Instead of showing the characters the user types, the field shows dots.

- RadioButtonField (net.rim.device.api.ui.component. RadioButtonField): A class that allows the user to make a single selection from a set of radio buttons.

- RichTextField (net.rim.device.api.ui.component. RichTextField): A class that your application can use to display text in a variety of fonts and styles.

- SeparatorField (net.rim.device.api.ui.component. SeparatorField): A class that displays a horizontal line across the width of the component.

- TreeField (net.rim.device.api.ui.component.TreeField): A class that your application can use to display a simple tree structure, similar to the display of a file system hierarchy of folders and documents.

Figure 5-5 shows some of the basic UI elements as they appear on a Black Berry display. These UI elements, plus all the others available as subclasses of net.rim.device.api.ui.Field, represent the components that your application adds to its screens to provide your users a way to communicate with your application, and the means for your application to communicate back.

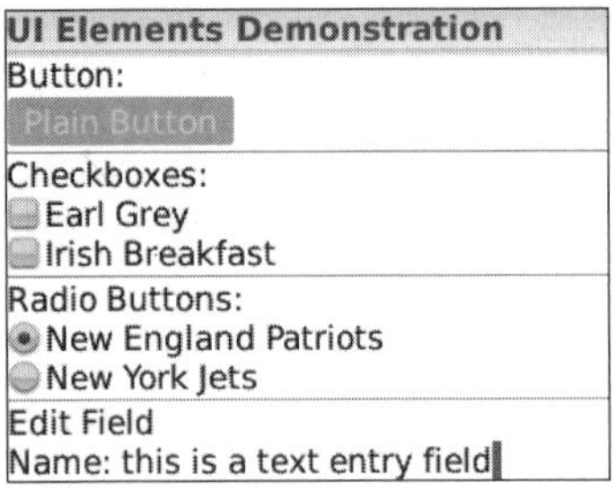

Figure 5-5:
Basic user
interface
elements.

UI Elements Demonstration
Button:
Plain Button
Checkboxes:
▢ Earl Grey
▢ Irish Breakfast
Radio Buttons:
● New England Patriots
○ New York Jets
Edit Field
Name: this is a text entry field

As of this writing, no UI editor exists to allow you to visually implement your screens with all their UI elements. You have to create all your user interfaces *programmatically,* by typing in code to create new screens, button, text fields, and everything else you want your application to display.

User interface callbacks

If your application is simply going to tell users everything you want them to know in one long paragraph, you can do that with one `LabelField` added to a `MainScreen`, filled with all your text. But if you want your application to respond to information the user provides you, your application needs to provide code to support user interactions with items, such as a `ButtonField`. You use callbacks to support user interaction. A *callback* is the code your application adds to buttons and other UI elements so that the button (or other item) will call back your application when the user clicks or presses it.

Callbacks for UI elements are provided through the use of a field change–listener mechanism. Follow these steps to use a callback:

1. **Create a class that implements the BlackBerry `FieldChangeListener` (`net.rim.device.api.ui.FieldChangeListener`) interface.**

   Your application uses this class to support the callback mechanism used by buttons and other UI items.

2. **Fill out the code for the `FieldChangeListener.fieldChanged` (`Field, int`) method.**

   This is the code that executes when the UI element to which this `FieldChangeListener` is assigned undergoes a change, such as a user pressing a button or typing text into an `EditField`.

3. **Create an object of your new `FieldChangeListener` class implementation.**

4. **Assign the object to the appropriate UI element by executing that element's `Field.setChangeListener( FieldChangeListener )` method.**

   This is where the UI element is told to use the code you provided in Step 2 to respond to what the user does with the UI element.

Because callbacks are used often, the preceding approach is sometimes streamlined to take advantage of Java's capability to create classes on the fly. Listing 5-2 shows a `FieldChangeListener` class being created within the code assigning the `FieldChangeListener` to a button.

Listing 5-2: Setting the FieldChangeListener on a Button, on the Fly

```
protected void initializeButtonListener()
{
    ButtonField goButton = new ButtonField( "Go!" );
    goButton.setChangeListener( new FieldChangeListener()
    {
        public  void  fieldChanged( Field infield, int inContext )
        {
            // handle the button click
            Dialog.alert( "Button Click" );
        }
    });
}
```

By using this approach, your application is creating a temporary class —
one that has complete access to the public and protected methods within
the class it is executed within. This means that this temporary `FieldChange`
`Listener` implementation can make calls to the other nonprivate methods
available within the `Screen` class where this method is implemented.

Creating a custom user interface element

Your application isn't limited to using only the UI elements provided by the
BlackBerry library. Anything you can imagine, you can implement as a UI
element and place it on a screen. As long as your custom class is a subclass
of the BlackBerry `Field` class, your application can add it to a screen and
use it as if it were a standard BlackBerry UI element.

The BlackBerry `Field` class (`net.rim.device.api.ui.Field`) is an
abstract class. This means that when you create a custom UI class that
extends `Field`, you must implement two methods for it because the
specification of Field promises that these methods exist, but does not
implement them within `Field` itself. `Field` serves the purpose of providing
a basic set of features and functionality, some of which are already included
in RIM's libraries, two of which must be implemented by subclasses. Here are
the two required methods to be implemented by your custom UI element:

 ✔ `protected void layout( int width, int height )`: This
   method is called by the OS when your application tries to display your
   custom element. Your custom element can use this method to lay out
   any subcomponents it might contain.

 ✔ `protected void paint( net.rim.device.api.ui.`
   `Graphics graphics )`: This method is called for your custom
   element to draw itself on the screen.

Implementing these methods is an absolute requirement: The BlackBerry compiler will fail to compile your custom UI element if you don't provide both methods in your class.

In addition to the two preceding methods, two other methods are implemented by default for the `Field` class, but RIM strongly suggests that your custom UI class override the `Field` implementation with your own. These methods are

- ✔ `protected int getPreferredHeight()`: This method allows your custom implementation to provide a preferred height value. This method is normally called by layout manager objects to ensure that a `Field` subclass on display can get the vertical space it requires.

- ✔ `protected int getPreferredWidth()`: Similar to the previous method, this method provides your custom implementation's preferred width to a layout manager.

Menus

Every BlackBerry application that presents information to users makes use of menus. Unlike those found in a desktop application, BlackBerry menus are separate from the controls and displays within an application's screens. Your users can make your application display a screen's menu by clicking the Menu button. The BlackBerry UI library contains a `Menu` class (`net.rim.device.api.ui.component.Menu`), an instance of which is created by the OS when the user clicks the Menu button. The OS then calls a specific method in the `screen` object to add items to the menu: the `void make Menu(Menu, int)` method. Your application must override this method in all screen classes used by your application. Figure 5-6 shows the menu that appears when the user clicks the Menu button while inside the BlackBerry Browser application.

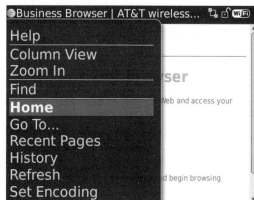

Figure 5-6: The BlackBerry Browser menu.

Understanding the MenuItem class

A BlackBerry menu contains *menu items,* which are the individual commands that a user can select to perform an operation. When an application runs, the screen on display handles the menu interactions, and so that screen's code must set up the menu for the user to see. The items in a menu are represented by instances of the MenuItem class (net.rim.device.api.ui.MenuItem).

For each MenuItem created and added to the screen's menu, the void run() method must be implemented. This method is what the OS executes if the user selects this particular menu item.

The MainScreen class provides a default menu, adding a single menu item, Close, to it. This menu item terminates the application if the user selects it. However, if your application overrides the makeMenu method in your MainScreen subclass, you have to add your own Close menu item, and provide code to handle its selection appropriately.

You can code menu items in two ways:

- ✔ **As a subclass of MenuItem:** This approach is pretty straightforward and useful if your application will reuse a particular menu item on multiple screens, such as a Help menu item. However, this type of menu item usually must be self-contained. Good object-oriented coding practices recommend using this approach.

- ✔ **Inline, when adding a MenuItem to a menu:** This is achieved by creating a MenuItem object and adding methods to it on the fly. If you've done any desktop Java programming, this approach is similar to the usual approach for adding an actionListener object to a button object. Coding a MenuItem inline permits the object created to access any of the methods within the class that creates this object, but restricts usage of the MenuItem to the screen where it was created.

The MenuItem's toString() method can be overridden to support modification of the displayed text while the application is running. Your app can use this feature to display contextual information in a menu item to relate it to a selected item on the user's screen. For instance, if your app manages events in a calendar and displays the different events scheduled on a particular day, when the user selects the Lunch Hour event for deletion and presses the Menu button, your app's MenuItem could update its text to say "Delete Lunch Event?", which would remind the user of the specific item selected.

Creating a menu in a BlackBerry application

The code in Listing 5-3 demonstrates adding menu items to screens so that you can get a feel for how menu items and screens interact.

Listing 5-3: **Code addition to SimpleScreen Class within SimpleScreenApp.java**

```
protected    void    makeMenu( Menu inMenu, int inInstance )
{
   inMenu.add( new MenuItem( "Show Dialog", 10000, 100 )
   {
      public  void    run()
      {
         showDialog();
      }
   });
   super.makeMenu( inMenu, inInstance );
}

protected    void    showDialog()
{
   Dialog.alert( "You clicked the Menu" );
}
```

To implement the preceding code, follow these steps:

1. **In the JDE, open the `SimpleScreenApp.java` module created in the earlier section, "Creating a screen."**

2. **Create several new methods within the `SimpleScreen` class. Add the code snippet in Listing 5-3 within the `SimpleScreen` class.**

3. **Build and run `SimpleScreenApp` (see Chapter 3 for details).**

In the code snippet shown in Listing 5-3, two new methods are added to the MainScreen subclass for the SimpleScreenApp. The first overrides the default makeMenu() method to add a menu item Show Dialog, and then calls the superclass' makeMenu() method to add the default Close menu item. The second method is called when the user selects the Show Dialog menu item.

The added `MenuItem` is created with three parameters:

- ✔ `Show Dialog`: This is the text that the menu item will display.

- ✔ `10000`: This ordering parameter determines where in the menu the item will appear. Lower numbers appear closer to the top of the menu. In addition, a separator bar is added automatically between two `MenuItems` whose ordering values differ by 65536 or more.

- ✔ `100`: This value represents *priority,* which determines which menu item is likely to receive the focus.

You can see an example of menu items and their ordering in Figure 5-7. Lower values of ordering means the menu item is closer to the top of the screen. Lowest value of priority means the menu item gets preselected.

This example comes with five menu items — the first three added by the application's code, and the last two added by the BlackBerry OS. Here's how they were created in code:

- ✔ **The top menu item, 9k Ord, 100 Pri,** was given an ordering value of 9000, and a priority value of 100. Because it has the lowest ordering value of the three menu items, this item is at the top of the menu.

- ✔ **The middle menu item, 10k Ord, 10 Pri,** was given an ordering value of 10000, and a priority of 10. This menu item, therefore, is placed beneath the top menu and above the bottom menu. Because it has the lowest priority value of the three menu items, this item is preselected (the blue highlight color).

- ✔ **The bottom menu, 100k Ord, 100 Pri,** was given an ordering value of 100000 — and because this value is more than 65536 greater than that of the middle menu item, the BlackBerry OS creates a separator line between this item and the one above it. Its priority value is the same as the top menu item.

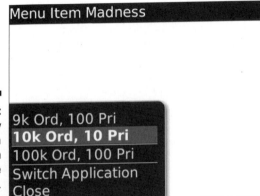

Figure 5-7:
The display
of a
menu with
multiple
menu items.

The three parameters can be adjusted while the application is running by overriding their respective methods within `MenuItem`. Subclassing `MenuItem` makes this easy, but the methods can also be overridden similar to the `run` method created when the instance itself is added to the menu. The three methods are

- ✔ `String toString()` for the menu item text
- ✔ `int getOrdinal()` for the ordering parameter
- ✔ `int getPriority()` for the priority

Responding to User Interaction

Aside from using menus, a BlackBerry user will interact with your application through the use of several mechanisms:

- ✔ **Keyboard:** All text input is performed from the keyboard. This can either be a full keyboard (such as that found on a BlackBerry Curve or Bold) or a condensed one (also known as a SureType keyboard, such as that found on a BlackBerry Pearl). The Storm series of BlackBerry devices can display either, depending on user preference and the device's orientation.

- ✔ **Trackwheel:** The original BlackBerry devices used a wheel on the side to move the *focus* (which item is selected) or scroll the screen. The most recent devices to use the trackwheel are the BlackBerry 7100 and BlackBerry 8700. As of 2007, this selection mechanism has been supplanted by the trackball.

- ✔ **Trackball:** This is the most common selection mechanism, and it permits the user to select UI elements in multiple directions, instead of just one.

- ✔ **Trackpad:** This is the newest input mechanism, very similar to the trackball but with no moving parts.

- ✔ **Touchscreen:** This mechanism is available only on the BlackBerry Storm series of devices. A touchscreen offers users a more direct approach for selecting and manipulating objects displayed on a BlackBerry screen.

Your application can take advantage of how the user interacts with the BlackBerry device by listening for inputs from one of the preceding mechanisms. For instance, you can provide code that will handle the user's pressing the Enter key or the Escape key on the keyboard, or the user pressing the trackwheel or trackball when a custom UI element is in focus.

Laying Out the User Interface

Your BlackBerry app uses screens to display information and interactive UI elements for the user to manipulate. Each piece of the UI that you add to a screen will be drawn according to the rules of the layout manager for that screen. Your app can use the default layout manager that `MainScreen` is initialized with `VerticalFieldManager`. Or you can set a screen to use any of several other layout managers that the BlackBerry OS provides. You can even create one of your own if the stock layout managers don't give you the precise kind of UI your app requires.

Controlling the layout of the user interface

The most important means of controlling the display of your application's information is through the use of a layout manager. A *layout manager* is responsible for determining where a UI element will be positioned on the display. The BlackBerry software library comes with a set of premade layout managers, and the `MainScreen` class uses the `VerticalFieldManager` as its default layout manager. The following list shows the layout manager classes available for BlackBerry applications, and Figure 5-8 shows how they work:

- ✔ `Manager (net.rim.device.api.ui.Manager)`: This is the basic manager class, which provides default functionality for managing UI elements. All layout manager classes inherit from this class. This class is an abstract class like `Field`, which means you can't create an object from this class and must instead create one of its subclasses, or else extend this class with your own custom manager class.

- ✔ `DialogFieldManager (net.rim.device.api.ui.container. DialogFieldManager)`: This field manager is used to lay out Dialog and Status screens. When your app creates a `Dialog` to display information to the user, the BlackBerry OS uses a `DialogFieldManager` to lay out the UI items in the `Dialog` in a specific way. Every `Dialog` comes with an icon image in its upper-left corner, and a text message to the right. Below these two items is where any buttons for controlling the `Dialog` such as OK or Cancel are displayed. And any extra items that your app adds to the `Dialog`, such as a field to enter text, will be placed vertically between the buttons and the first two items.

- ✔ `FlowFieldManager (net.rim.device.api.ui.container. FlowFieldManager)`: This field manager provides functionality to lay out UI elements in a horizontal-then-vertical flow. The first UI element you add to the screen is placed in the upper-left corner, and each subsequent UI element is placed to the right of the previous element until it reaches the right edge of the screen. At that point, UI elements are placed in a new row below the previous one, starting at the left side again.

✔ HorizontalFieldManager (net.rim.device.api.ui. container.HorizontalFieldManager): This field manager lays out UI elements along a single horizontal row.

✔ VerticalFieldManager (net.rim.device.api.ui.container. VerticalFieldManager): This field manager lays out UI elements in a single vertical column.

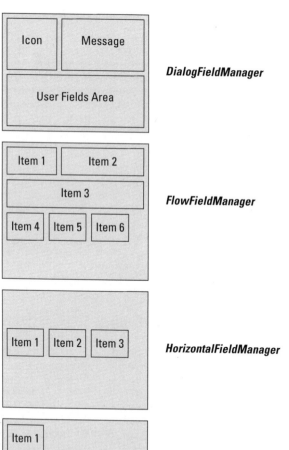

DialogFieldManager

FlowFieldManager

HorizontalFieldManager

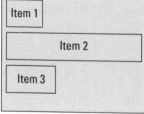

Figure 5-8: How the layout manager classes work.

VerticalFieldManager

Notice that the fully qualified class name of each of the subclasses of `Manager` contains the word `container`. This is an indication that these classes can contain UI elements. All UI elements are subclasses of the BlackBerry library class `Field` (`net.rim.device.api.ui.Field`), which is what layout managers can contain. All layout managers are themselves subclasses of the `Field` class, meaning that a layout manager can contain and be contained within another layout manager, which is extremely useful for making complex display layouts using just the horizontal and vertical layout managers.

A layout manager is essential for applications that need to display on a variety of different screen shapes and sizes. Table 5-1 shows a sample of the different BlackBerry devices and their screen dimensions.

Table 5-1	BlackBerry Device Screen Dimensions	
Device Name	*Screen Width*	*Screen Height*
Pearl (81xx)	240	260
Pearl Flip (82xx)	240	320
Curve (83xx)	320	240
Curve (89xx)	480	360
Bold (9000)	480	320
Storm (95xx) portrait	360	480
Storm (95xx) landscape	480	360
Bold (9700)	480	360

As you can see, your application will encounter a variety of different screen sizes, undoubtedly with more to come in the future as RIM releases new smartphones. To make sure that your application displays its content well on all the devices your users will download (and purchase!) it for, a layout manager becomes a necessity.

Creating a screen with a custom layout manager

Customizing a layout manager is pretty easy: Start with a BlackBerry OS layout manager that almost does what you want, and then create a subclass of it, overriding the methods that you want to control.

The three methods you will want to override to create a custom layout manager are as follows:

- ✔ int getPreferredHeight(): Your customized layout manager reports its desired height to the BlackBerry OS with this method.

- ✔ int getPreferredWidth(): Your customized layout manager reports its desired width to the BlackBerry OS using this method.

- ✔ void sublayout(int maxWidth, int maxHeight): This method is crucial; your customized layout manager performs a sizing and positioning operation on all of its contents in this method.

Listing 5-4 shows the SimpleLayoutManager class that creates a custom layout manager.

Listing 5-4: SimpleLayoutManager Code Snippet

```
class  SimpleLayoutManager extends VerticalFieldManager
{
   public  SimpleLayoutManager()
   {
      super();
   }

   public  int getPreferredWidth()
   {
      int preferredWidth =  Display.getWidth();
      return (preferredWidth);
   }

   protected   void     sublayout( int inMaxWidth, int inMaxHeight )
   {
      int xPos    =   0;
      int yPos    =   0;
      int screenWidth =   Display.getWidth();
      int numberFields    =    this.getFieldCount();
      for (int index=0; index<numberFields; ++index)
      {
         Field   aField =   this.getField( index );
         this.layoutChild( aField, inMaxWidth, inMaxHeight );
         if (0 == index % 2)
         {
            xPos    =   0;
         }
         else
         {
            xPos    =   screenWidth - aField.getPreferredWidth();
         }
         this.setPositionChild( aField, xPos, yPos );
```

(continued)

Listing 5-4 *(continued)*

```
        yPos += aField.getPreferredHeight();
    }
    this.setExtent( inMaxWidth, inMaxHeight );
}
}
```

To use a custom layout manager class, follow these steps:

1. **In the JDE, open the `SimpleScreenApp.java` module.**

2. **Add a new class to the end of the module.**

   The code snippet in Listing 5-4 shows the new `SimpleLayoutManager` class.

3. **Add the following code to import the `Display` class at the top of the module:**

   ```
   import net.rim.device.api.system.Display;
   ```

   This informs the compiler where to find the description of the `Display` class for use in the layout manager.

4. **Rewrite the `initialize` method in the `SimpleScreen` class.**

   The following code snippet shows the instructions that add a `SimpleLayoutManager` as a field contained by the `SimpleScreen`, as well as adding four separate `LabelField` objects that the layout manager will place within the screen.

   ```
   protected   void    initialize()
   {
       this.setTitle( "Simple Screen App" );
       SimpleLayoutManager slm = new SimpleLayoutManager();
       LabelField label0 = new LabelField( "Label Zero" );
       LabelField label1 = new LabelField( "Label One" );
       LabelField label2 = new LabelField( "Label Two" );
       LabelField label3 = new LabelField( "Label Three" );
       slm.add( label0 );
       slm.add( label1 );
       slm.add( label2 );
       slm.add( label3 );
       this.add( slm );
   }
   ```

   The rewritten `initialize` method creates a customized layout manager and adds to it a set of `LabelField` objects. Then it adds the layout manager object to the screen. When the screen is pushed onto the screen stack, its layout method is called, which in turn calls the `sublayout` method of the layout manager.

5. **Build and run `SimpleScreenApp` (see Chapter 3).**

   The screen shown in Figure 5-9 is what you see.

Figure 5-9:
Simple
ScreenApp,
with a
custom-
ized layout
manager
displaying
left-right
labels.

The most important section in the `SimpleLayoutManager` is the `sublayout` method implementation. This is where your custom layout manager dictates how the contents of the screen are going to be displayed. The most interesting line in the code in Listing 5-4 is the line `if (0 == index%2)`. This is where the layout manager decides whether to put a particular child field on the left or on the right. Notice after the execution of `setPositionChild`, the y-position variable is adjusted for the height of the field that was just sized and placed on the screen; this is done to make sure the next field is positioned vertically below the current one. Lastly, the call to `setExtent` must be executed to make sure that the container holding the layout manager (in this case, the `SimpleScreen` object) gives the layout manager its necessary size.

Threaded Operation

A long time ago, computer programs operated *linearly:* one step followed by the next. If a calculation took ten minutes to complete, the user was left tapping a foot, humming some song, waiting for the computer program to return the results. Today, this behavior is no longer acceptable. Applications that go away for longer than a few seconds are wasting a user's time, and are perceived as such. The UI must be responsive to the user's actions, even if something the user enacted takes longer than expected.

BlackBerry applications are encouraged — and in some cases, required — to create threads to maintain their responsiveness to the user's actions while executing a lengthy process. A *thread* is a block of code that executes in parallel with the main application. While the main application is responding to the user's input, a thread can execute in the background to complete a task.

The following sections introduce threads; for more details on threading, see Chapter 7.

Understanding when to use threads

The following types of tasks should be implemented as threads:

- ✓ **Tasks that might take a long time to complete:** A task that must access resources on the Internet through HTTP or other network connection types falls into this category.

- ✓ **Tasks that must update a display repeatedly:** A clock or countdown timer falls into this category.

Both types of tasks usually want to modify the display of information available to users, even if only to inform the user that the task they ordered has completed.

 Certain methods in certain BlackBerry classes will *block:* Their execution will halt your application's progress in whatever thread the method is called. These methods are *required* to be called from within a thread that is not the main application thread. Blocking calls are noted within the API documentation of the call. One example of a blocking call is `Connector.open()` — your app can use this call to send data to and receive data from network services.

This poses a problem. When the user clicks a button onscreen, the application is already in a state where changes to the display can be made and updates appear instantly. However, when a background thread finishes its calculation of the right price to buy XYZ stock shares, updating the display with the new information must occur at the right moment because the application might not be in the proper state for updating the screen.

To handle this situation, the BlackBerry OS provides a set of routines that any thread may call, at any time, to deliver new information from the thread to the display, and have the display updated soon afterward. These routines are available within the `Application` (`net.rim.device.api.system.Application`) class and its subclasses. The routines most often used are

- ✓ `void Application.invokeAndWait( Runnable )`: This routine takes a `Runnable` object as an input parameter, installs it into the application's event queue, and waits until the code in the `Runnable` object has executed before returning. Your app would use this call to update the screen as soon as possible.

- ✓ `void Application.invokeLater( Runnable )`: This routine takes a `Runnable` object as an input parameter, installs it into the application's event queue, and returns without waiting for the code in the `Runnable` object to finish. This is the best method to use when your background thread has finished its lengthy stock-quote calculations and it's time to let the user know at what price she should buy XYZ. The update is not instantaneous, but the user won't notice because she knows the calculations are not instantaneous, either.

✔ Object Application.getEventLock(): This routine retrieves the application's UI event lock. The *event lock* is an object that your code can request whenever you want to ensure that UI changes you intend to make will execute in synchronization with the main event thread. Your application should hold this object for only short periods of time, quickly update the UI while holding the lock, and then release the lock immediately. Your app could use this approach to update the contents of a progress bar to indicate the time remaining for a background process to complete.

Using a thread to update the display from the background

The following code example in Listing 5-5 extends the previous examples in this chapter to update a display.

Listing 5-5: LabelThread Class for Updating the Display from a Background Thread

```
class   LabelThread extends Thread
{
   protected   SimpleLayoutManager m_manager;
   protected   boolean m_continue  =   true;
   public  static  final   String[]   LABEL_STRINGS   =   new String[]
                {"Label 1",
                 "Label One",
                 "Label Uno",
                 "Label Un",
                 "Label Ein",
                 "Label yksi",
                 „Label viens"};
   protected   int m_indexOne =   0;

   public  LabelThread( SimpleLayoutManager inManager )
   {
      m_manager   =   inManager;
   }

   public  synchronized   void   stopThread()
   {
      m_continue  =   false;
   }

   public  void   run()
   {
      while (true == m_continue)
      {
```

(continued)

Listing 5-5 *(continued)*

```
        try
        {
            Thread.sleep( 1000L );
            this.adjustLabelOne();
        }
        catch (InterruptedException iExcept)
        {
            break;
        }
    }
}

protected   void   adjustLabelOne()
{
    if (null != m_manager)
    {
        int stringIndex =   m_indexOne % LABEL_STRINGS.length;
        String  textOne    =   LABEL_STRINGS[stringIndex];
        Field   fieldOne   =   m_manager.getField( 1 );
        if (fieldOne instanceof LabelField)
        {
            final LabelField  labelOne =  (LabelField)fieldOne;
            synchronized (UiApplication.getEventLock())
            {
                labelOne.setText( textOne );
            }
        }
        m_indexOne++;
    }
}
}
```

After some initial setup, the heart of the LabelThread is the adjust
LabelOne method. This method

1. Pulls the second (index 1) Field from the SimpleLayoutManager

2. Picks a text string from the array (bounded by the array's length)

3. After acquiring the event lock from the UiApplication, sets the text

The modification of the text triggers a chain reaction that causes the
SimpleLayoutManager to modify the size, and therefore the position, of the
second LabelField. The stopThread method allows an external agent —
the SimpleScreen in this example — to halt the thread in a manner that is
safe for the thread.

To implement the code in Listing 5-5, follow these steps:

1. **In the JDE, open the `SimpleScreenApp.java` module.**

2. **Add a new class to the end of the module, as shown in Listing 5-5.**

3. **Modify the `makeMenu` method in the `SimpleScreen` class to add two new menu items.**

    The following code shows the original `makeMenu` with the added menu items:

```
protected  void  makeMenu( Menu inMenu, int inInstance )
{
    inMenu.add( new MenuItem( "Show Dialog", 10000, 100 )
    {
      public  void    run()
      {
          showDialog();
      }
    });
    inMenu.add( new MenuItem( "Start Motion", 11000, 100 )
    {
      public  void    run()
      {
          startMotion();
      }
    });
    inMenu.add( new MenuItem( "Stop Motion", 12000, 100 )
    {
      public  void    run()
      {
          stopMotion();
      }
    });
    super.makeMenu( inMenu, inInstance );
}
```

The two menu items simply provide a means for the user to start and stop the thread that modifies the displayed label. The menu items added in this step execute the two methods `startMotion()` and `stopMotion()`. A member variable is added to maintain a reference to the thread created in `startMotion` so that you can stop it inside `stopMotion`.

4. Add a new member variable and the two methods to `SimpleScreen`.

The following code shows the new lines to be added to the `SimpleScreen` class:

```
private LabelThread  m_motionThread;

protected   void    startMotion()
{
    if (null == m_motionThread)
    {
        m_motionThread =   new LabelThread( (SimpleLayoutManager)this.
            getField(0) );
        m_motionThread.start();
    }
}

protected   void    stopMotion()
{
    if (null != m_motionThread)
    {
        m_motionThread.stopThread();
    }
    m_motionThread =   null;
}
```

5. Build and run the application (see Chapter 3).

Unfortunately, I can't show animations in a printed book, so Figure 5-10 just shows the screen in both states. When you run the app, you see the right-hand `Label One` text changing and shifting once every second.

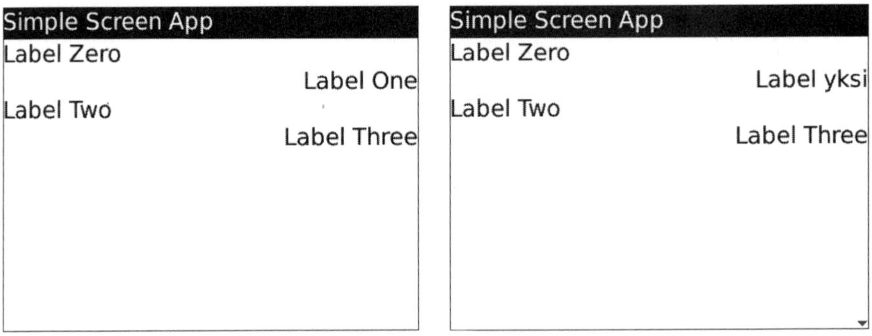

Figure 5-10: The label in the left screen changes to show the label in the right screen.

Simple Screen App
Label Zero
Label One
Label Two
Label Three

Simple Screen App
Label Zero
Label yksi
Label Two
Label Three

The Screen Stack

The BlackBerry OS maintains a screen stack containing your application's screens. To show a screen to the user, your application must push the screen onto the screen stack. This causes the BlackBerry to execute a series of operations that eventually draws the contents of the screen on the user's display. Similarly, to remove a screen from display, your application must pop the screen from the top of the screen stack. The two methods for these two operations are found in the `UiApplication` class, and they look like this:

✔ void pushScreen(Screen)

✔ void popScreen(Screen)

Each screen object can be pushed on the stack only once. Pushing the same screen object onto the stack more than once will cause the BlackBerry OS to throw an exception. If you need to show the same screen more than once, you can push two different screen objects of the same screen subclass onto the stack. Because they are separate pieces of code and data, the BlackBerry OS won't throw an exception.

The most important issue with the screen stack is this:

> When your application pops the last screen off of its screen stack, the application will be terminated.

This means that your application must pay attention to the comings and goings *(pushes and pops)* of screen objects during its operation. It might be perfectly fine for your application to terminate abruptly because the user initiated a course of action that caused the final screen to be removed from the screen stack. Then again, if your application is executing a thread in the background — such as waiting for some data to be returned across a network connection — the connection will be severed because the thread will be terminated when the application ends.

Your application needs to manage its screens wisely. I've found the simplest approach is to always create a new screen and push it onto the screen stack, and then pop the previous screen (if coming from another screen) out from under it. In this way, there's only one screen on the screen stack at a time, and your application will only terminate when your user tells it to close the current screen.

Chapter 6

Storing Your Users' Data

- -

- -

*Y*our users will expect your application to be interactive and respond to every action they make in using it. A worthwhile application must do more than that, though, because users will expect your application to keep track of all the information that they provide. Even if the information your app keeps track of is as simple as where the user left off last time, your users will definitely appreciate your app more if it behaves as a butler, concierge, maitre d' — and that means retaining all the important, relevant, detailed information that your users provide.

This chapter provides you with the guidance necessary for you to quickly understand the various BlackBerry storage models, how to package the data your users expect your application to remember, and how to retrieve it the next time they open your application. You'll also see how to take advantage of backing up the data, and restoring it should a user's device suffer a catastrophe.

The BlackBerry OS has several storage models to choose from, which means you can choose the approach that makes the most sense for your application to follow. For example, your application might use simple file-based storage, recording data either to flash memory or to a removable card. Or your application might use *persistent storage* (for information that lasts long-term) or *runtime storage* (for information retained only while the device is powered on). In this chapter, I demonstrate each storage mechanism and provide details for understanding which model to choose for your data storage needs.

Understanding BlackBerry Storage Models

Current BlackBerry smartphones such as the Storm provide two physical mechanisms for storing application data:

- Flash memory
- MicroSD storage cards

Older BlackBerry smartphones such as the 8700 do not permit storage using removable cards and are thus limited to using only flash memory storage.

The BlackBerry OS extends the physical storage into different models:

- Persistent storage
- Runtime storage
- File storage
- Database storage (for devices running OS version 5.0 or later)

Each storage model has its own advantages and disadvantages, which I explain in the following sections.

Persistent Storage

The persistent storage model is the most convenient of the models that the BlackBerry OS provides. *Persistent storage* is literally that: storage of data that's available from one launch of your application to the next launch of your application, as well as from the moment the device is turned off until it's turned back on again. This is the BlackBerry equivalent of a safe-deposit box: Your users know that whatever information your application puts into the "box" will be there when they need to see it again. After all, your users expect data that gets stored to be available whenever they launch your application, including after a power-off followed by a power-on.

You can see in Figure 6-1 that the application My-Cast Weather returns to showing the weather in San Diego, where it was when I last exited the app.

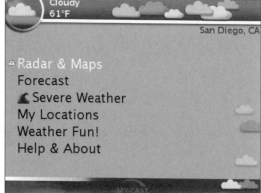

Figure 6-1:
This app uses persistent storage to remember where the user left off.

Persistent storage methods

The BlackBerry persistent storage model depends on both of the following:

✔ PersistentObject (net.rim.device.api.system. PersistentObject)

✔ Persistable (net.rim.device.api.utilPersistable)

PersistentObject is the safe-deposit box that your application uses to store the information your users contribute to your app. Your application will need to use several important pieces of code to store and retrieve information on a BlackBerry:

✔ PersistentObject PersistentStore.getPersistentObject (long ID): Your application uses this method to create a PersistentObject if it doesn't yet exist or to retrieve one that your application created.

✔ Object PersistentObject.getContents(): This is the method that retrieves an object stored persistently: for example, the locations of my favorite places to check on the weather in My-Cast Weather. If the PersistentObject does not yet have any contents, this method will return null.

✔ void PersistentObject.setContents(Object inData): Your application uses this method to set the data that the persistent storage model will contain.

✔ void PersistentObject.commit(): Your application executes this method to cause the BlackBerry OS to copy the contents of the PersistentObject into the persistent storage mechanism.

`Persistable` is an interface that your data objects must implement if your application plans to store the objects instead of just their contents. This interface must be implemented in the class for each object that your application will place in persistent storage. The BlackBerry smartphone OS expects that all objects handed to it to be stored in persistent storage will implement the `Persistable` interface. You can see this implemented for the class `WordLockerCategoryRecord` shown in Listing 6-1.

Listing 6-1:   The Data Class WordLockerCategoryRecord Implements Persistable and Can Be Stored in Persistent Storage

```
import java.util.Date;
import net.rim.device.api.util.Persistable;

public  class WordLockerCategoryRecord implements Persistable
{
    private String m_name;
    private long m_creationTimestamp;

    public WordLockerCategoryRecord( String inCategoryName, Date inCreationDate )
    {
        m_name = inCategoryName;
        m_creationTimestamp = (inCreationDate == null) ? new Date().
                getTime() : inCreationDate.getTime();
    }

}
```

A `WordLockerCategoryRecord` is now a candidate for being placed into persistent storage.

The BlackBerry OS class `PersistentStore` is the first stop on your application's path to storing and/or retrieving any data placed in the persistent storage model. Your application must call the (static) `getPersistentObject` method to access the `PersistentObject` your application will use. Calling this method will either create a `PersistentObject` (if it doesn't exist already) or retrieve an existing one.

Your application must supply a unique, long (64-bit) data value as an input parameter to `PersistentStore.getPersistentObject()`. The simplest way to create such a "key" for your application's persistent stored objects is

1. **In the JDE, with a Java source file or other text file opened for editing, type a unique text identifier.**

    One easy way to do this is to use the main package name for your classes as the unique identifier, such as

    `com.kowalskisoftware.blackberryappdevelopment.MainClassName`

2. **Highlight the unique text identifier.**

3. Right-click the highlighted text.

This brings up a contextual menu.

4. Select Convert *"Highlighted-Text"* to Long.

This replaces the highlighted text with a long value, such as
`0x40f8cf1717f37babL`. You can then copy this value as the identifier
for your persistent storage. This key will always be associated with a
specific `PersistentObject`.

The `PersistentObject` retrieved for your application will store almost
any object that your application can create because every class in Java is a
descendant of `java.lang.Object`, the class that `setContents()` accepts
as a parameter. The following objects can be stored persistently:

- ✔ Basic types (`Boolean`, `Byte`, `Character`, `Integer`, `Long`, `Object`,
  `Short`, `String`, `Vector`, and `Hashtable`)
- ✔ Objects of classes that implement the `Persistable` interface

Container types, such as `java.util.Vector` and `java.util.Hashtable`
objects, will be stored, but only if their contents fall into the preceding
categories.

Serialization is a means by which an object expresses its contents in a form,
usually as a `String`, that can be easily stored. If your application uses custom
data objects to maintain its information, providing a `toString()` method
for the custom data class allows your application to serialize the data in the
object. This can make storage easier because `String` is already set to be
stored persistently. You would also then want to construct objects using the
`String` data retrieved from the persistent storage model, an action known as
deserialization.

Deciding when to save your application's data is up to you. Usually, it's best to
save it as soon as the data changes. You do this by performing a *commit* —
your app executes the method `PersistentObject.commit()` — at the
moment of change; your application will always have the current state of the
user's experience kept in record. However, the performance of your application
may be affected by executing a commit too often. So, you might have to run
some performance tests to determine the optimal frequency at which to save
data for your application.

Your application's persistent data exists in the flash memory on the
BlackBerry smartphone. In order to use it, your app retrieves the data and
makes a copy of it in local memory. If users change the data, they're only
changing the copy in local memory. Your app must then copy that information
back into the persistent storage memory in order to ensure that the user's
additions, modifications, and deletions are remembered when the user
returns to your app. Your app *could* perform the copy-back-to-persistent-
storage every time the user changes something. For an app where only a

small amount of data is changing over time, this would work. However, you will find that as the amount of data your app stores for your users increases, copying each and every change will slow down your app, making it more sluggish over time.

Kinds of information to store in persistent storage

Your application should store every piece of data in persistent storage that your users expect to see the next time they open your application. This includes information such as the following:

- ✔ **Settings:** Suppose your application presents data in textual form. Some users might have difficulty reading the normal text size, so your application could enhance readability by allowing each user to set the size of the text. Your users will expect that the text size they set today will be the same the next time they launch your application, so that size selection is that something your application would need to store, persistently, until they change it again. Any kind of setting that users will modify and expect to be remembered by your application is something that belongs in persistent storage.

- ✔ **History:** Game applications usually record high scores. If your game also allows users to pause midgame and return, your application would need to record where your user left off and then return there when your game is launched again. This is a perfect reason to store this data in persistent storage. And games aren't the only apps that could benefit from recording a user's history. For example, apps like a reader for an e-book and an electronic voice recorder are perfect candidates, too.

- ✔ **User-created data:** Shopping lists, to-do lists, gift lists, holiday card lists — we all have information we want to record. Think of all the sticky notes you've ever written. All this information, recorded electronically and available right in your hand at a moment's notice: all handy stuff to store persistently.

How persistent is persistent storage?

BlackBerry maintains the data stored using persistent storage very long-term: forever, as long as the BlackBerry has some power. The persistent storage model will keep your saved data after your application is closed, and the data will be available when the application is launched again. This data will also be available even when your user turns off the BlackBerry — or worse, forgets to keep the battery charged (there's a small battery in every

BlackBerry that keeps a minimum amount of power just for the memory, so users can forget to charge their smartphone for a few days). And even when your users upgrade their BlackBerry OS to a new and improved version, they will usually temporarily back up the data during the upgrade process. (***Note:*** That depends on how the upgrade occurs; more on that in Chapter 14.)

There is one restriction to persistent data, though: If the *class type* of an object stored using the `PersistentStore` is not known to the OS, the entire `PersistentObject` stored by the application will be removed when the application itself is deleted from the device.

So what does this mean for your application? If your application stores data in an object of a class available only within your application, the `PersistentObject` used to store your application's data will be deleted when your application is deleted.

However, if your application uses a class that's available as part of the BlackBerry OS — for instance, a `java.lang.String` — then the `PersistentObject` used to store the application data will be available to your application even when your app is deleted and then reinstalled. This behavior can be useful, but it can also be dangerous. For example, think about highly sensitive data, such as credit card information or any data that can assist an identity thief. That kind of data should be stored so that deleting your application removes that data as well. Encrypting such data would also make it more difficult to extract, but encryption of data is beyond the scope of this book.

The BlackBerry OS provides classes and examples for encrypting and decrypting data, and you can find all of this information within the HTML documentation files you downloaded when you installed the JDE. Assuming you performed a default installation, you will find the starting point for the HTML documentation at the following location on your Windows PC:

```
C:\Program Files\Research In Motion\BlackBerry JDE 4.5.0\docs\api\index.html
```

Runtime Storage

In addition to persistent storage, the BlackBerry OS offers a less-permanent model for storing data: runtime storage. This storage is *not persistent:* Any data stored using this model will be available only while the device is powered on. Most BlackBerry users, like those of every other mobile device, keep their BlackBerry devices on nearly all the time. (After all, when was the last time you turned off your cell phone completely? Most likely answer: during take-off or landing on an airline flight.)

When a user does turn off a BlackBerry — such as when the OS is updated or an application is installed or removed — runtime storage memory is erased as if nothing had ever been recorded there. For the most part, the persistent storage model is your application's best place to store data.

The runtime storage model is similar to using the company refrigerator at your office: You can put stuff into and take stuff out of it every day of the week, but every Friday, all the contents of the refrigerator are removed and tossed away. So here are some reasons why you would use the runtime storage instead of persistent storage:

- ✔ **E-mail attachment handlers:** Your app can install code that the OS will use to retrieve data from e-mail attachments. However, your app can't ask the OS whether its attachment handler has already been installed — if your app installs a handler each time it's launched, the OS will dutifully add another one to its list. Your app can place a flag inside the runtime store to check whether an attachment handler has already been installed. The OS will remove all attachment handlers when the smartphone is powered off, and will remove the contents of the runtime store as well.

- ✔ **Listeners:** Your app can install code within the OS to be informed of events related to many different processes running on the smartphone. Each time the device is powered off, all the listener objects your app installed will be removed. Your app can use the runtime store to keep track of whether its listeners have been installed, because the runtime store is also erased when the smartphone is off. Your app's runtime store flag will be present only as long as the listeners are installed, and the OS will remove the flag (and everything else) in the runtime store when it removes the listeners.

Runtime storage methods

The BlackBerry OS provides a class, `RuntimeStore`, for you to use when adding and retrieving data using the runtime store. You will find this class similar to that of the persistent store, `PersistentStore`. The `RuntimeStore` object is very easy to work with, and offers just a few simple methods for your app to use:

- ✔ `RuntimeStore RuntimeStore.getRuntimeStore()`: Your application will call this method to access the BlackBerry OS-wide runtime storage object.

- ✔ `Object RuntimeStore.get( long ID )`: Similar to `Persistent Store.getPersistentObject(long)`, your application will provide a unique identifier to retrieve its data object from the runtime store.

- ✔ `void RuntimeStore.put( Object data )`: This method delivers an object containing data into the runtime storage model.

Unlike objects stored in the persistent storage model, custom data objects stored using the runtime storage model do not have to implement Persistable. Any object that your application creates may be added to the RuntimeStore.

Kinds of information to store in runtime storage

In my BlackBerry development experience, I have encountered only one specific situation where runtime storage has proved very beneficial: namely, when knowing that the device had just gone through a power-cycling was necessary.

One project I worked on included a feature that implemented a capability to read e-mail attachments in a special way. This required creating code to act as an e-mail attachment handler. An attachment handler object was created when the application was launched and submitted to the BlackBerry OS to be executed when users performed certain operations.

There was just one problem: Every time the application was launched, an attachment handler object would be added to the BlackBerry OS, even if a prior launch had already done the same thing. There was no way for my application to ask the OS whether such an object had been added at any previous execution of my application. As a result, the user would start to see multiple instances of my attachment handler whenever they clicked an e-mail attachment. If the application had installed five identical attachment handlers, there would be five menu items labeled Import Kowalski Attachment when the user clicked the attachment.

Clearly, this is undesirable behavior. Because resetting the device — powering it off and then on again — cleared the BlackBerry's memory of my attachment handler's existence, the runtime storage model became the perfect place to store knowledge of whether my application had already installed its attachment handler. By storing a flag in the runtime storage area, and checking for the flag's existence when the application starts up, my application could determine whether an e-mail attachment should be created and added into the OS.

The BlackBerry OS also clears out all of the registered listener objects that your app might install. The following is a list of some of the types of listener objects your app can create and install:

- MessageListener: Your app can register to listen for incoming or outgoing messages such as e-mail or SMS.
- PhoneListener: Your app can also listen for when the smartphone makes or receives phone calls.

- ✔ PIMListener: Whenever the user modifies something in their Personal Information Manager (such as the BlackBerry Contacts application), your application can register to receive notification.

- ✔ ProximityListener: Your app can register to be informed of when the user has moved their BlackBerry smartphone within a certain range of a particular GPS location.

Your app should use the runtime store to keep track of whether it has already registered listeners with the OS. The collection of registered listeners is wiped out by the OS when the smartphone is turned off. So is the runtime store. So the runtime store is the perfect place for your application to store a flag indicating that it has created and registered its listeners. If the flag isn't there, that means your app should create and register its listeners. If the flag is there, your app knows it doesn't have to create any more.

File Storage

Current BlackBerry smartphones provide access to greater data storage through the use of MicroSD cards. These cards are available in sizes ranging from 1 to 64GB, and BlackBerry applications can access them to store information persistently. MicroSD cards are useful for storing data such as

- ✔ Audio files
- ✔ Image files
- ✔ Video files

MicroSD cards enable users to move their data physically from one device to another, including backing up the contents of a card to a home PC.

The BlackBerry OS also permits your application to store data as a file in a file system on the device itself, apart from a MicroSD card. Both the device files and the MicroSD card files are accessed through BlackBerry OS file-system methods, including methods that permit your application to create, modify, and find files.

Your app can make use of the file system to store any data it collects that is likely to be rather large. For instance, your app could turn on the smartphone's microphone for the user to record their thoughts orally, and then store the information within an available MicroSD card — audio recordings can become large, and a MicroSD card is a much better place to store this information than flash memory.

File storage methods

The BlackBerry OS uses very few classes and methods to handle file storage. The most important of the file storage classes include

- ✔ Connector (javax.microedition.io.Connector): This class is used to open a connection to a file system location, otherwise known as a *file*. This class is part of the Java Micro Edition (JME) framework.

- ✔ FileConnection (javax.microedition.io.file. FileConnection): This class can be extracted from a Connector object, and provides access to the file in memory. This class specifically provides input and output stream capabilities, to permit read and write access to files in the file system. This class is part of the JME framework.

Kinds of information to store in file system storage

The file storage model is similar to the persistent storage model: Files and data stored inside are maintained across a power-off/power-on cycle on the device. However, the innards of the file are left up to your application to structure — or not — as you see fit. The persistent storage model accepts data as objects, and the file system model requires you to decide how the data must be placed in the file.

The benefit of using file storage is that the files can be moved from one BlackBerry to another via a MicroSD card. A disadvantage is that the file is accessible to any application that knows where to find the file in the file system, and this might require your application to take steps to secure the data stored in the file. Users might not mind if your application's settings values are available to another application; credit card numbers, however, are a different story.

Database Storage

In BlackBerry OS 5.0, the SQLite database system is implemented, and the BlackBerry OS provides classes and methods to create, insert, update, search, and delete database records via standard SQL commands.

Database storage methods

The database framework (`net.rim.device.api.database`) contains the following classes to use in manipulating a database:

- ✔ `DatabaseFactory`: This class is used to create an object that implements the `Database` interface, which your application can use to read information from and add information to a file-based database.

- ✔ `Database`: This class provides access to standard database manipulation tools, including SQL statements and transactions.

- ✔ `Statement`: Your application will create `Statement` objects to act as database queries for reading data from and adding data into a database table.

- ✔ `Cursor`: Your application will use `Cursor` objects to cycle through the rows of a database table.

- ✔ `Row`: A `Row` object represents a single row of a database table, and your application can access the values in the columns of the row.

Kinds of information to store in database storage

The SQLite database engine uses file-based storage of data, so most of the same rules and restrictions for storing your application's data in a file apply to storing it in a database. Database storage provides the structure and syntax of SQL, which can prove more convenient for data storage, retrieval, and modification than streaming data into and out of a file, depending on the amount of data. If you're comfortable using SQL syntax — and especially if your application is going to store large amounts of data — choosing database storage is probably a good choice.

As I mention earlier, database storage is available only on devices that have upgraded to BlackBerry OS 5.0 or higher.

BlackBerry Programming with Storage Models

Time to put your storage system knowledge to use. Because I use BlackBerry JDE 4.5 for this book's examples, I don't demonstrate the database storage model. The BlackBerry smartphone OS 4.5 does not include database storage code. However, using persistent, runtime, and file system storage will work just fine.

The example application implements multiple screens, one each for persistent, runtime, and file storage. Each screen handles its own particular approach to storing data, and provides a `LabelField` indicating what's stored and an `EditField` to allow users to set new data in the storage. Each screen loads data from the appropriate location when the screen is displayed. If no data is available, a default text string is shown. In addition, each screen comes with two menu items:

✔ **Save XXX Data:** Choosing this menu option saves the data entered in the `EditField` into the appropriate storage mechanism.

✔ **Clear XXX Data**: Choosing this menu option clears any stored data by storing a zero-length string.

Listings 6-2 through 6-6 show the entire code for the `StorageTest` application.

Listing 6-2 is the code present in the main application module for the StorageTest application. You will see that this module doesn't really do that much — it just sets up the application when the user launches it. The `main()` method creates a new `StorageTest` application object and tells it to execute its `enterEventDispatcher()` method. The OS takes over at this point, and eventually calls back into the `activate()` method. This method merely creates a `StorageTestScreen` object (implemented in Listing 6-3), and pushes it onto the screen stack.

Listing 6-2:   StorageTest.java (Main Application Module)

```
/*
 * StorageTest.java
 *
 * © Karl G. Kowalski, 2010
 * Confidential and proprietary.
 */

package com.karlgkowalski.blackberryfordummies.storagetest;

import  net.rim.device.api.ui.*;

public  class StorageTest    extends UiApplication
{
    public static void main( String[] inArgs )
    {
        StorageTest st = new StorageTest();
        st.enterEventDispatcher();
    }

    public StorageTest()
    {
    }
```

(continued)

Listing 6-2 *(continued)*

```
public void activate()
{
    this.pushScreen( new StorageTestScreen() );
}
}
```

Listing 6-3 shows what's contained in the `StorageTestScreen` module. This module defines the `StorageTestScreen` class to be a subclass of `MainScreen`, the default BlackBerry OS screen class. This screen contains three buttons, initialized in the `initialize()` method:

- **Persistent:** Clicking this button will execute the method `showPersistent Screen()`. This will display a new screen to demonstrate the use of the persistent store.

- **Runtime:** Clicking this button will execute the method `showRuntime Screen()`. This will display a new screen to demonstrate the use of the runtime store.

- **File:** Clicking this button will execute the method `showFileScreen()`. This will display a new screen to demonstrate the use of the file store.

The methods executed by clicking the above buttons each creates a different screen and displays the screen by pushing it on top of the screen stack. You can see in Listings 6-4 through 6-6 the behavior of the new screens on display.

Screens pushed onto the screen stack are like pancakes piled onto a heap: The last one pushed is on top, and is the only one that your users see. Chapter 5 covers this aspect of BlackBerry programming in greater detail.

Listing 6-3: StorageTestScreen.java (The Main Screen)

```
/*
 * StorageTestScreen.java
 *
 * © Karl G. Kowalski, 2010
 * Confidential and proprietary.
 */

package com.karlgkowalski.blackberryfordummies.storagetest;

import net.rim.device.api.ui.*;
import net.rim.device.api.ui.component.*;
import net.rim.device.api.ui.container.*;

public class StorageTestScreen extends MainScreen
{
    public StorageTestScreen()
    {
        super();
```

```
        this.initialize();
    }

    protected void initialize()
    {
        this.setTitle( "Storage Test") ;
        ButtonField persistentButton    =    new ButtonField( "Persistent" );
        ButtonField runtimeButton       =    new ButtonField( "Runtime" );
        ButtonField fileButton          =    new ButtonField( "File" );
        this.add( persistentButton );
        this.add( runtimeButton );
        this.add( fileButton );
        persistentButton.setChangeListener( new FieldChangeListener()
        {
            public  void    fieldChanged( Field inField, int inContext )
            {
                showPersistentScreen();
            }
        });
        runtimeButton.setChangeListener( new FieldChangeListener()
        {
            public  void    fieldChanged( Field inField, int inContext )
            {
                showRuntimeScreen();
            }
        });
        fileButton.setChangeListener( new FieldChangeListener()
        {
            public  void    fieldChanged( Field inField, int inContext )
            {
                showFileScreen();
            }
        });
    }


    protected   void    showPersistentScreen()
    {
        UiApplication.getUiApplication().pushScreen( new PersistentStoreScreen()
              );
        this.setDirty( false );
    }

    protected    void    showRuntimeScreen()
    {
        UiApplication.getUiApplication().pushScreen( new RuntimeStoreScreen() );
        this.setDirty( false );
    }

    protected    void    showFileScreen()
    {
        UiApplication.getUiApplication().pushScreen( new FileStoreScreen() );
        this.setDirty( false );
    }
}
```

Your dirty flag is showing

The `dirty` flag is a property of every `Screen` object. This flag is set by the BlackBerry OS when the user interacts with a screen, such as entering text, clicking buttons, and so on. If your user selects the default Close menu item and the screen being closed has its `dirty` flag set to `true`, the user will be informed that the screen may need to be saved. Resetting the `dirty` flag in the code in Listing 6-2 prevents this for `StorageTestScreen`.

The next three listings (Listing 6-4 through Listing 6-6) show the implementation of the code for each of the three screens displayed as a result of clicking the buttons in the `StorageTestScreen` display. In Listing 6-4, the implementation of `PersistentStoreScreen` provides two elements, a `LabelField` to display anything currently in the persistent store, and an `EditField` to allow the user to change the contents of the persistent store. If the contents of the `EditField` are modified in any way (such as if the user enters any text into the field), the `setDirty()` method is called. This is because the data in the `EditField` can only be stored in the persistent store if the menu item Save Persistent Data is selected. You can clear the contents of the persistent store through the use of the Clear Persistent Data menu item.

The `getMyPersistentObject()` method is a convenience method, written so that I didn't have to keep typing the same code every time I wanted to retrieve the object stored in the persistent store (this happens when I want to get the data that's been stored, or set the data to be stored). The methods `storeInPersistentStorage()` and `extractTextFromPersistent Storage()` do exactly what their titles claim. Lastly, the `makeMenu()` method adds this screen's menu items to the BlackBerry menu.

When this screen is created, its UI components are initialized to display the contents of the persistent store, if any. By selecting the menu items, the user can either set the persistent store to hold any text entered in the `EditField` component, or clear the contents of the persistent store.

Listing 6-4: PersistentStoreScreen.java (The Screen for Reading Data from and Writing Data into the Persistent Storage Model)

```
/*
 * PersistentStoreScreen.java
 *
 * © Karl G. Kowalski, 2010
 * Confidential and proprietary.
 */

package com.karlgkowalski.blackberryfordummies.storagetest;

import net.rim.device.api.ui.component.*;
```

```
import  net.rim.device.api.ui.container.*;
import  net.rim.device.api.ui.FieldChangeListener;
import  net.rim.device.api.ui.Field;
import  net.rim.device.api.ui.MenuItem;
import  net.rim.device.api.system.PersistentStore;
import  net.rim.device.api.system.PersistentObject;

public  class PersistentStoreScreen extends MainScreen
{
   public  static  final   String DEFAULT_CONTENTS   =  "_nothing_stored_";
   private LabelField  m_fromStorage;
   private EditField   m_toStorage;

   public  PersistentStoreScreen()
   {
      super();
      this.initialize();
   }

   protected  void    initialize()
   {
      this.setTitle( "Persistent Storage" );
      String psString   =   this.extractTextFromPersistentStorage();
      m_fromStorage = new LabelField( "From Persistent Storage: [" + psString +
             "]" );
      m_toStorage =   new EditField( "Store in Persistent Storage: ", "" );
      this.add( m_fromStorage );
      this.add( m_toStorage );
      m_toStorage.setChangeListener( new FieldChangeListener()
      {
         public  void    fieldChanged( Field inField, int inContext )
         {
            setDirty( false );  //  contents must be saved through menu
         }
      });
   }

   public  void    makeMenu( Menu inMenu, int inContext )
   {
      inMenu.add( new MenuItem( "Save Persistent Data", 10000, 100 )
      {
         public  void    run()
         {
            storeInPersistentStorage();
         }
      });
      inMenu.add( new MenuItem( "Clear Persistent Data", 10100, 100 )
      {
         public  void    run()
         {
            PersistentObject    storage =   getMyPersistentObject();
```

(continued)

Listing 6-4 *(continued)*

```
            if (null != storage)
            {
                storage.setContents( DEFAULT_CONTENTS );
                storage.commit();
                Dialog.alert( "Storage reset" );
            }
        }
    });
    super.makeMenu( inMenu, inContext );
}


PersistentObject    getMyPersistentObject()
{
    return (PersistentStore.getPersistentObject( 0xc46aeeaa2592b482L ));
}


protected    void    storeInPersistentStorage()
{
    PersistentObject    storage =    this.getMyPersistentObject();
    if (null != storage)
    {
        storage.setContents( m_toStorage.getText() );
        storage.commit();
        Dialog.alert("Text stored");
    }
}


protected    String    extractTextFromPersistentStorage()
{
    String  psString    =    DEFAULT_CONTENTS;
    PersistentObject    storage =    this.getMyPersistentObject();
    if (null != storage)
    {
        Object  storedContents =    storage.getContents();
        if (null != storedContents)
        {
            psString    =    storedContents.toString();
        }
    }
    return (psString);
}
}
```

In Listing 6-5, you see the code that implements saving and retrieving data
from the runtime store. Notice that this code parallels that in Listing 6-4 —
the only difference is where the data gets stored and retrieved from. Instead
of using a `PersistentStore` object to access the data, the code in Listing
6-5 uses a `RuntimeStore` object.

Listing 6-5:   RuntimeStoreScreen.java (The Screen for Reading Data from and Writing Data into the Runtime Storage Model)

```java
/*
 * RuntimeStoreScreen.java
 *
 * © Karl G. Kowalski, 2010
 * Confidential and proprietary.
 */

package com.karlgkowalski.blackberryfordummies.storagetest;

import  net.rim.device.api.ui.component.*;
import  net.rim.device.api.ui.container.*;
import  net.rim.device.api.system.RuntimeStore;
import  net.rim.device.api.ui.*;

public  class RuntimeStoreScreen    extends MainScreen
{
   private String  DEFAULT_RUNTIME_TEXT   =   "no_runtime_text";
   private LabelField  m_fromRuntimeStore;
   private EditField   m_toRuntimeStore;

   public  RuntimeStoreScreen()
   {
      super();
      this.initialize();
   }

   protected   void   initialize()
   {
      this.setTitle( "Runtime Storage" );
      m_fromRuntimeStore =   new LabelField( "From Runtime Storage: [" +
      this.extractTextFromRuntimeStore() + "]" );
      m_toRuntimeStore   =   new EditField( "Store in Runtime Storage: ", "" );
      this.add( m_fromRuntimeStore );
      this.add( m_toRuntimeStore );
      m_toRuntimeStore.setChangeListener( new FieldChangeListener()
      {
         public  void    fieldChanged( Field inField, int inContext )
         {
            setDirty( false );  //  contents must be saved through menu
         }
      });
   }

   public  void   makeMenu( Menu inMenu, int inContext )
   {
      inMenu.add( new MenuItem( "Save Runtime Data", 10000, 100 )
      {
         public  void   run()
         {
```

(continued)

Listing 6-5 *(continued)*

```
            setRuntimeStorageText( m_toRuntimeStore.getText() );
            Dialog.alert( "Stored text" );
        }
    });
    inMenu.add( new MenuItem( "Clear Runtime Data", 10100, 100 )
    {
        public  void  run()
        {
            setRuntimeStorageText( DEFAULT_RUNTIME_TEXT );
            Dialog.alert( "Storage reset" );
        }
    });
    super.makeMenu( inMenu, inContext );
}

protected  String  extractTextFromRuntimeStore()
{
    String rsString  =  this.getRuntimeStorageText();
    return (rsString);
}

protected  Object  getRuntimeStoreObject()
{
    Object  rsObj  =  null;
    RuntimeStore  rs  =  RuntimeStore.getRuntimeStore();
    if (null != rs)
    {
        rsObj  =  rs.get( 0xe7ccdcf49882229L );
    }
    return (rsObj);
}

protected  void  setRuntimeStorageText( String inText )
{
    RuntimeStore  rs  =  RuntimeStore.getRuntimeStore();
    if (null != rs)
    {
        rs.put( 0xe7ccdcf49882229L, inText );
    }
}

protected  String  getRuntimeStorageText()
{
    String  rsText  =  DEFAULT_RUNTIME_TEXT;
    Object  rsObj  =  this.getRuntimeStoreObject();
    if (null != rsObj)
    {
        rsText  =  rsObj.toString();
    }
    return (rsText);
}
}
```

Lastly, Listing 6-6 shows you how to implement code to store and retrieve data by using the file storage model. Using the file system on a BlackBerry smartphone is more complex than using the persistent or runtime storage models. The OS requires your code to check for any possible problem during some of the methods you will need to execute when opening, modifying, or closing files. The basic operation of the code is similar to that of the runtime and persistent store code: read the data from the file and display it, allow the user to change the data, and store new data into the file when ordered to. You may notice that there's a lot more code involved in retrieving the data from the file and writing data to the file. Using the file system to store data is thus less convenient than using the persistent or runtime storage models for retaining your app's data.

Listing 6-6: FileStoreScreen.java (The Screen for Reading Data From and Writing Data to the File System Storage Model)

```
/*
 * FileStoreScreen.java
 *
 * © Karl G. Kowalski 2010
 * Confidential and proprietary.
 */

package com.karlgkowalski.blackberryfordummies.storagetest;

import  net.rim.device.api.ui.container.*;
import  net.rim.device.api.ui.component.*;
import  net.rim.device.api.ui.*;
import  java.io.*;
import  javax.microedition.io.*;
import  javax.microedition.io.file.*;
import  java.util.*;

public  class FileStoreScreen extends MainScreen
{
private static final String  DEFAULT_FILE_TEXT   =   "_no_file_text_";
private static final String  NO_FILE =  "_no_file_";
private static final String  FILE_URL_START  =   "file:///store/home/user/";
private static final String FILE_STORE_FILENAME = "file_storage_test.txt";

private LabelField m_fromStore;
private EditField m_toStore;

public FileStoreScreen()
{
this.initialize();
}


protectedvoidinitialize()
```

(continued)

Listing 6-6 *(continued)*

```
{
this.setTitle( "File Storage" );
String fileContents= NO_FILE;
fileContents=   this.getFileStoreContents();
m_fromStore=new LabelField( "Text from File Store: [" + fileContents + "]" );
    m_toStore=new EditField( "Store in File: ", "" );
    this.add( m_fromStore );
    this.add( m_toStore );
    m_toStore.setChangeListener( new FieldChangeListener()
    {
      public void  fieldChanged( Field inField, int inContext )
      {
        setDirty( false );
      }
    });
}

protected  String getConnectionString()
{
StringBufferbuffy = new StringBuffer();
buffy.append( FILE_URL_START );
buffy.append( FILE_STORE_FILENAME );
return (buffy.toString());
}

protected  FileConnection getFileConnection( String inConnectionString )
{
  FileConnection conn  =  null;
  try
  {
    conn=(FileConnection)Connector.open( inConnectionString,
          Connector.READ_WRITE );
  }
  catch (Exception except)
  {
    Dialog.alert( "Exception while opening file connection: " +
          except.toString());
  }
  return (conn);
}

protected  String getFileStoreContents()
{
  String  fileContents  =  DEFAULT_FILE_TEXT;
  try
  {
    FileConnection  fileConn=this.getFileConnection(
                     this.getConnectionString() );
    if (null != fileConn && fileConn.exists())
    {
      DataInputStream dis =  fileConn.openDataInputStream();
      int contentLength  =  dis.available();
```

```
            if (contentLength > 0)
            {
                byte[] contentArray  =  new byte[contentLength];
                dis.read( contentArray );
                fileContents  =  new String( contentArray );
            }
        }
        else
        {
            fileContents = NO_FILE;
        }
        fileConn.close();
    }
    catch (IOException ioExcept)
    {
        Dialog.alert( "Exception while loading file contents: "+
                    ioExcept.toString() );
    }
    return (fileContents);
}

protected  void  storeDataInFileStorage( String inData )
{
    try
    {
        FileConnection  fConn  =  (FileConnection)Connector.open(
                            this.getConnectionString() );
        if (false == fConn.exists())
        {
            fConn.create();
            this.writeDataToFile( fConn, inData.getBytes() );
        }
        else
        {
            this.writeDataToFile( fConn, inData.getBytes() );
        }
        Dialog.alert( "Wrote data to file" );
    }
    catch (Exception except)
    {
        Dialog.alert( "exception thrown while storing data:"+except.toString()
            );
    }
}

protected  void  writeDataToFile( FileConnection inFileConn, byte[] inData
        ) throws  IOException
{
    if (null != inFileConn && null != inData)
    {
        DataOutputStream  dos =  inFileConn.openDataOutputStream();
        dos.write( inData );
```

(continued)

Listing 6-6 *(continued)*

```
        dos.flush();
        inFileConn.close();
    }
}

protected  void  storeInFileStorage()
{
    this.storeDataInFileStorage( m_toStore.getText() );
}

protected  void  clearFileStorage()
{
    try
    {
        FileConnection  fileConn= this.getFileConnection(
                            this.getConnectionString());
        if (null != fileConn)
        {
            if (true == fileConn.exists())
            {
                fileConn.delete();
            }
        }
        Dialog.alert( "File storage cleared" );
    }
    catch (IOException ioExcept)
    {
        Dialog.alert( "Exception thrown while clearing file storage: " +
                    ioExcept.toString() );
    }
}

public  void  makeMenu( Menu inMenu, int inContext )
{
    inMenu.add( new MenuItem( "Save File Data", 10000, 100 )
    {
        public  void  run()
        {
            storeInFileStorage();
        }
    });
    inMenu.add( new MenuItem( "Clear File Data", 10100, 100 )
    {
        public  void  run()
        {
            clearFileStorage();
        }
    });
    super.makeMenu( inMenu, inContext );
}
}
```

The BlackBerry OS only allows your app to make a *connection* to the file using
a class called `Connector`. This class requires you to provide a URL to tell the
OS where to find the file you want to access. This URL is of the form

```
file://root_node/file_name
```

The components of this URL are described as follows:

- ✔ `file`: The `Connector` class can make a variety of different types
  of connections. Here, you use `file` to tell `Connector` to create a
  connection to a file stored in the BlackBerry file system.

- ✔ `root_node`: The BlackBerry file system requires a starting point for
  where the file is located. The following two places are acceptable for use
  as the `root_node` of the connection string:

  - `store/home/user`: This starting point tells the BlackBerry
    OS that your app will be looking for and accessing files in the
    BlackBerry smartphone's flash memory.

  - `SDCard`: This starting point tells the BlackBerry OS that your app
    will be looking for and accessing files in the BlackBerry smartphone's
    MicroSD card, if one is installed.

- ✔ `file_name`: This is where you set the name of the specific file your app
  will use to store data.

The important point to note is that your application might need to determine
whether an SD card is installed because the cards are removable. The code
snippet in Listing 6-7 shows one way to figure out whether an SD card is
installed.

Listing 6-7: Finding Out Whether an SD Card Is Installed

```
public boolean  isSDCardInstalled()
{
   boolean sdCardInstalled =   false;
   try
   {
     FileConnection fConn = (FileConnection)Connector.open( "file:///SDCard/",
                      Connector.READ );
     sdCardInstalled = fConn.exists();
   }
   catch (Exception except)
   {
   }
   return (sdCardInstalled);
}
```

This very simple code snippet returns a flag indicating whether the directory exists, which is a good indication of whether the SD card itself is installed in the device.

And that's it. Your application can store and retrieve data from the long-term and short-term storage areas on BlackBerry devices.

Chapter 7

Getting Tied Up in Threads

*Y*our average desktop PC can *multitask* and run several different applications all at the same time, allowing you to browse the Internet, download songs, search for that file whose name starts with Z, all while you play your favorite version of solitaire.

Your BlackBerry smartphone also provides the capability to run multiple applications at the same time. But more importantly, your BlackBerry application can also perform different tasks at the same time. A BlackBerry application that executes different tasks concurrently achieves this by launching different *threads*, each of which represents one task. In this chapter, you read about the threads that the BlackBerry OS provides, and how to exploit them to make your app more accommodating to users' expectations.

Understanding Basic Threads

Time for a crash course in threads. A complete explanation is beyond the scope of this book, but you can readily find quite a few online and written resources available to fill in the gaps.

An *application* is a sequence of instructions delivered to the central processing unit (CPU) of the computer or smartphone the app is to run on. The CPU can execute only one instruction at a time. However, as CPUs have gotten faster and faster, it has become possible for a CPU to operate as if it were executing two or more sets of instructions simultaneously. The OS juggles the different sets of instructions to be executed together, giving each a period of time in which to proceed before interrupting one and starting (or restarting) another. A *thread* is one of those sets of instructions.

Using threads allows developers to perform some tasks in the background of an application while the user is looking at data on display. The user can interact with the UI of an application even while the app is waiting for data to download (a common occurrence with the networked apps of today). This double duty is important because network data retrieval can take a noticeable amount of time. If your app doesn't use threads to perform the data access in the background, your users are left staring at an unchanging display, unable to interact with the app or even the device, until your code returns to interactive execution after the data is or fails to be retrieved. This is not a very pleasant experience for users.

Here are the three thread items that the BlackBerry OS supports:

- ✔ `Thread (java.lang.Thread)`: This is the basic BlackBerry thread class, which implements the `Runnable` interface, described later in this list. You can subclass this class to create objects that the BlackBerry OS executes as independent subprocesses.

- ✔ `TimerTask (java.util.TimerTask)`: Your app uses a `TimerTask` to implement subprocesses that need to be scheduled later, or those that are to be executed repeatedly. You use `TimerTask` objects in conjunction with a `Timer` object (`java.util.Timer`), which manages their execution.

- ✔ `Runnable (java.lang.Runnable)`: This is actually an interface. Your classes can implement the `Runnable` interface and be incorporated into a `Thread` object. You use this interface when you can't or don't want to subclass a `Thread`: for instance, when the class you intend to use as a `Runnable` already extends a different class.

Java does not permit multiple inheritance — that is, one class can't extend two parent classes — but a class can implement multiple interfaces.

Your app uses the preceding classes and the interface for all the operations it needs to perform in the background. The operations, in general, come in two flavors:

- ✔ **Fire and forget.** This is the easiest type of operation to place in a thread. The thread launches, executes some code, and stops. An example of this type of operation would be code that delivers information to a network repository.

✔ **Call me when you're done:** You'll find that this is the type of operation you come across most frequently. Your users direct your application to perform a lengthy operation, after which your app reports back some information about the results of the operation. This type of operation requires that some sort of callback mechanism is in place for the thread to execute when it has finished its processing. An example of this type would be code that searches through a user's Calendar for upcoming birthdays over the next year.

Knowing when to use a thread

You use a thread to perform an operation in only one situation:

When the operation that your app intends to execute will take too much time away from your app paying attention to the user's actions.

BlackBerry users have many things to do. After all, they own a BlackBerry because owning one makes them more efficient in their day. Users read and write e-mail, check their calendars, browse the Web, and maybe even make and receive phone calls. BlackBerry users are always in a rush, have no time to waste, and can't stand to wait. All right, I'm exaggerating, but you get the picture. If your app is holding up everything in its effort to download all the pictures and ads from that hot new restaurant's menu, your user will move on to something else, putting your application into the background.

So, how much time is "too much"? You might not like this answer: It depends. And you might have to wait for feedback from your users before you can determine whether you should put a particular operation into a background thread. I prefer not to leave users waiting, so if something I want my app to do doesn't finish really quickly (a few tenths of a second), that's something I want to put in a separate thread and run in the background.

Here are a few suggestions for particular operations where you will want to consider implementing threaded behavior:

✔ **Network operations:** Accessing the Internet is always a chancy process. You can never tell when the service your app is trying to contact is going to be too busy, leaving your app's connection request in a holding pattern. You should definitely put all code that uses the `Connection` class (`javax.microedition.io.Connection`) into a thread that runs independently of the main event thread. I discuss and demonstrate networking threads in Chapter 9.

✔ **Certain BlackBerry APIs:** Some BlackBerry classes that your app might use — other than networking — will require that your app execute them only in a thread separate from the main event thread. For example, your app may execute `Session.waitForDefaultSession()` when trying to access the default mail service of the BlackBerry OS in order to interact with e-mail. The BlackBerry API documentation points out whether a class or one of its methods is blocking; that is, if calling the method will halt the processor until something external to your app returns data to it. Code that contains a blocking-method call must be placed in a thread separate from the main event thread. In the following code block, you can see a code snippet that must be placed in a `Thread` in order to send an e-mail message. When placed inside a thread, this code will wait for the OS to provide the starting object (`Session`) that allows creating and sending e-mail messages.

```
try
{
  // blocking call
  Session defaultSession = Session.waitForDefaultSession
  if (null != defaultSession)
  {
    Transport emailTransporter = defaultSession.getTransport();
    if (null != emailTransporter)
    {
      Address myAddr = new Address( Address.EMAIL_ADDR, "kgkfordummies@
        gmail.com" );
      Message aMessage = new Message();
      aMessage.addRecipient(Message.RecipientType.TO, myAddr );
        aMessage.setSubject( "This just in..." );
        aMessage.setContent( "Greetings from a remote user!" );
        emailTransporter.send( aMessage );
    }
  }
}
catch (Exception except)
{
  // handle any problem
}
```

✔ **Scheduled operations:** Your app might require a certain event to occur at a specific time, such as a clue being revealed in a detective mystery game or an alarm set to ring after a certain number of minutes. While your app is running, you could code it to periodically check the time and then trigger the event when the time is right. Or else you could create a thread that does nothing but wait for the intervening interval to pass, and then execute at the right moment.

✔ **Repeated operations:** Your app might display a clock that marks progress toward a goal, such as the one shown in Figure 7-1. Your users will expect that clock to be changing its time display, once per second — maybe more frequently if your app marks times for Olympic tryouts, maybe less frequently if your app counts down the shopping days until the next big event or holiday. Regardless of how often your app updates its time display, you need to put the code to update the display inside a thread.

Figure 7-1:
An example
of a prog-
ress clock.

Thread things to worry about

You will find that threads are easy to deal with — as long as you keep them simple. As a rule, I try to keep my threads' main code no longer than one screen's worth of executable statements. The following sections provide a few other rules to keep handy when you're dealing with threads.

Calling back to the thread's origin

One part of your app launches the thread, and because this is usually as a result of user action, the launch occurs within the main event thread. Most likely, your thread has been launched to perform some action in response to a user action that takes too long to perform. In addition, your app's response to the user's action requires a result to be returned to the user when the thread has finished. Because this thread is separated from the main event thread and the rest of your app's code, your thread requires some mechanism to return data back to your app.

The best way to do this is by providing a callback object to the thread, usually in its constructor method. The callback object, usually an interface implemented by the object that creates the thread, provides a means by which your thread can return any results it achieves back to the object that created the thread. You can see in Listing 7-1 the `ThreadCallbackClass` that implements the success and failure methods of the `ThreadCallback` interface.

Listing 7-1: **The Class ThreadCallbackClass Implements the ThreadCallback Interface**

```
public ThreadCallbackClass implements ThreadCallback
{
  public ThreadCallbackClass()
  {
  }

  public void threadSuccess( String inMessage )
  {
    synchronized (UiApplication.getUiApplication().getEventLock())
    {
      Dialog.alert("The thread has completed successfully: " + inMessage );
    }
  }

  public void threadFailure( Exception inException )
  {
    synchronized (UiApplication.getUiApplication().getEventLock())
    {
      Dialog.alert( "The thread encountered a failure: " + inException.
              toString() );
    }
  }
}
```

You can accomplish this by specifying a success method within the interface.

You also want to specify a failure method in the interface because sometimes threads don't always succeed in their tasks.

In Listing 7-2, you see the interface `ThreadCallback`, which the `ThreadCallbackClass` implements. Interfaces are pretty simple, and you use them as placeholders to represent functionality implemented in a separate class. Code that uses an interface's methods, such as shown in Listing 7-3, only knows about the methods that the interface defines.

Listing 7-2: **The ThreadCallback Interface Only Provides Two Methods**

```
public interface ThreadCallback
{
    public void threadSuccess( String inMessage );
    public void threadFailure( Exception inException );
}
```

You can see in Listing 7-3 the `ThreadUsingCallback` class, which is created with a parameter that must implement the `ThreadCallback` interface. A `ThreadUsingCallback` object performs its operation and then calls either the success method or the failure method of the object that represents a `ThreadCallback`. A `ThreadUsingCallback` object extends the `Thread` class, which allows it to perform its operations as a separate subprocess within the main application. A ThreadUsingCallback object must be initialized with an object that implements the ThreadCallback interface. This allows the ThreadUsingCallback object to report its success or failure using the interface's methods

Listing 7-3:   The ThreadUsingCallback Object Reports Success or Failure

```
public ThreadUsingCallback extends Thread
{
  private ThreadCallback m_callback;
  public ThreadUsingCallback( ThreadCallback inCallback )
  {
    m_callback = inCallback;
  }

  public void run()
  {
    try
    {
      // perform operation
      m_callback.threadSuccess( "The Operation has finished" );
    }
    catch (Exception except)
    {
      // something bad happened
      // let the callback know
      m_callback.threadFailure( except );
    }
  }
}
```

Thread count limits

The BlackBerry OS permits only 32 threads per application, so you should really avoid going crazy with them. I tend to permit only one thread at a time, other than the main event thread. So far, I haven't found a need for more than that, although your mileage may vary.

Synchronization

You will find the biggest challenge in keeping your thread's operations synchronized with other code in your app. For example, in an app that launches multiple threads to find the ten best prices for airline flights from Boston to Paris, you'd want to synch the addition of each block of flight data and the display of the summary of all the flights.

You can reduce the likelihood of running into thread synchronization issues by keeping your use of threads to a minimum, as well as keeping the thread code small and simple. However, synchronization problems can still creep in, even if you're careful. You will find that most synchronization problems involve two different threads attempting to modify and use the same resource: a *race condition*. The Java language supplies a resolution to this problem: the synchronized keyword. Assigning this keyword to parts of your code reduces the chances that a race condition occurs. Listing 7-4 shows you two methods, one synchronized (incrementInSync()) and the other not synchronized (incrementUnsync()). The only difference in operation between the two methods is the first one will only operate for one thread executing it at a time. In the second method, the following problem can occur if multiple threads attempt to execute the method:

- ✔ Thread A executes the method incrementUnsync().

- ✔ The CPU starts to perform the sequence of steps to increment the value of the m_unsyncCount variable.

- ✔ However, just before the increment is added, the OS pauses Thread A's execution and allows Thread B to resume its operations.

- ✔ Thread B is also executing the method incrementUnsync().

- ✔ The CPU performs the entire sequence of steps to increment the value of the m_unsyncCount variable. Thread B is completed, and the OS resumes Thread A's execution.

- ✔ Because the resumption of Thread A's operations also resets the values of everything Thread A had in memory, including the value of m_unsyncCount right before Thread A was paused, the value of m_unsyncCount is returned to what it was before Thread B had incremented it. This eliminates Thread B's result, as if it had never happened. If both threads had used incrementInSync() instead of incrementUnsync(), the problem would not have happened because the synchronized keyword ensures that the code inside the method will execute to completion for each thread that uses it and the OS will not pause it during its operation.

Listing 7-4:   The Difference between Synchronized and Unsynchronized Methods

```
int m_syncCount = 0;

public synchronized void incrementInSync()
{
  m_syncCount = m_syncCount + 1;
}

int m_unsyncCount = 0;

public void incrementUnsync()
{
  m_unsyncCount = m_unsyncCount + 1;
}
```

While the example in Listing 7-4 is pretty simplified and its resolution is pretty simple, as your application becomes more complicated, you will encounter more difficulty in tracking down this kind of problem.

Deadlocks

You might encounter situations where one thread is waiting for access to a resource that is locked by another thread, and where the second thread is waiting for a resource that is locked by the first thread. This is a *deadlock:* Neither thread can execute because each is waiting for the other to finish.

The best solution to this problem is to keep your threads' operational code to a minimum: Each thread should have only one task that it should be able to complete independent of the operation of any other thread. Of course, if you choose to have only one thread other than the main event thread, this problem doesn't tend to show up.

Listing 7-5 shows a snippet of code that demonstrates how this can occur. The Sibling class has two methods that are each declared with the synchronized keyword. The code shown after the Sibling class demonstrates the deadlock occurring. When a synchronized method of an object is called, the object itself is considered to be locked. In this snippet, you can see that at some point in time each Sibling object will be locked (because the synchronized method executeActionOnSibling() is being executed), and will be trying to execute a synchronized method (executeAction()) on the other Sibling object (which requires the first Sibling to lock the other). Neither object can obtain the lock on the other, and so the two Thread objects will be forever paused and resumed.

Listing 7-5:   Two Sibling Classes Attempt to Execute Each Other's Methods

```
public class Sibling
{
  public Sibling()
  {
  }

  public synchronized void executeActionOnSibling( Sibling inSib )
  {
    // sleep for a bit, to
    // let the threads catch up
    try
    {
      Thread.sleep( 1500L );
    }
    catch (InterruptedException iEx)
    {
```

(continued)

Listing 7-5 *(continued)*

```
    }
    inSib.executeAction();
  }
  public synchronized void executeAction()
  {
    // perform operations that can take a while
  }
}

// the following is code in some other class
public void lockSiblings()
{
  final Sibling sib1 = new Sibling();
  final Sibling sib2 = new Sibling();

  Runnable runner1 = new Runnable()
  {
    public void run()
    {
      sib1.executeActionOnSibling( sib2 );
    }
  };
  Runnable runner2 = new Runnable()
  {
    public void run()
    {
      sib2.executeActionOnSibling( sib1 );
    }
  }
  Thread one = new Thread( runner1 );
  Thread two = new Thread( runner2 );
  one.start();
  two.start();
}
```

One solution to the deadlock problem is to create a thread-scheduler: A class whose sole purpose is to ensure that only one thread at a time is performing operations in the background. You can see in Listing 7-6 a `ThreadScheduler` that manages `Runnable` objects and launches `SafeThread` objects one at a time. Your code will have to ensure that threads are only ever launched by using the `ThreadScheduler`. The `ThreadScheduler` class holds a collection of `Runnable` objects that each get launched when the previous one is finished.

Listing 7-6: Threads Are Only Launched Using Threadscheduler

```
public class ThreadScheduler
{
  private Vector m_threads = new Vector();
  private boolean m_continue = true;
  private boolean m_paused = false;
```

```
public ThreadScheduler()
{
}

public synchronized void scheduleThread( Runnable inRunner )
{
  m_threads.addElement( inRunner );
}

public void launchScheduler()
{
  Runnable runner = new Runnable()
  {
    public void run()
    {
      while (true == m_continue)
      {
        if (m_threads.size() > 0)
        {
          this.pauseScheduler();
          Runnable runner = (Runnable)m_threads.elementAt( 0 );
          SafeThread aThread = new SafeThread( this, runner );
          aThread.start();
          while (true == m_paused)
          {
            try
            {
              Thread.sleep( 200L );
            }
            catch (InterruptedException iEx)
            {
            }
          }
        }
      }
    }
  };
  Thread schedulerThread = new Thread( runner );
  schedulerThread.start();
}

public synchronized void descheduleFirstThread()
{
  if (m_threads.size() > 0)
  {
    m_threads.removeElementAt( 0 );
  }
  this.wakeScheduler();
}
```

(continued)

Listing 7-6 *(continued)*

```
  public synchronized void pauseScheduler()
  {
    m_paused = true;
  }

  public synchronized void wakeScheduler()
  {
    m_paused = false;
  }
}

class SafeThread extends Thread
{
  private ThreadScheduler m_owner;

  public SafeThread( ThreadScheduler inTS, Runnable inRunner )
  {
    super( inRunner );
    m_owner = inTS;
  }

  public void run()
  {
    super.run(); // call Runnable's method to execute
    m_owner.descheduleFirstThread();
  }
}
```

Hopefully, I haven't scared you away from using threads. A thread is a powerful tool that provides a solution to accomplishing long-running tasks while still giving the user a sense that they are still in control of your app.

Using Threads to Schedule Events

Single-event scheduling is the easiest kind of threading. You use a Timer and a TimerTask subclass to perform the operation you want to schedule for some time in the future. The TimerTask class already implements the Runnable interface, so all you have to do is the following:

1. Create a subclass of TimerTask.

2. Override your subclass's run() method.

   This is where you place the guts of what your scheduled event will do.

3. Create an instance of your subclass.

4. Create an instance of a `Timer`.

5. Execute `Timer.schedule( TimerTask, delayInMilliseconds )`.

That's all that you need to do. Simple, right?

Setting up and executing a TimerTask

The following running example demonstrates how to set up and execute a `TimerTask` with a `Timer` to schedule an event — namely, changing the color of a field — to execute an arbitrary number of seconds into the future (1–99).

1. **Launch the BlackBerry JDE.**

2. **Create a workspace.**

   I call mine `TiedUpInThread` because I use it for all the thread demonstration projects.

3. **Create a project within the workspace.**

   I name mine `ScheduleEvent` and place it in a subfolder of the same name so that I can keep the code of the different projects separated.

4. **Create an application class in the project.**

   I call mine `ScheduledEvent.java`.

5. **Add the code in Listing 7-7 to your application class.**

Listing 7-7: **Application Class Code for ScheduledEvent**

```
package com.karlgkowalski.scheduledevent;

import net.rim.device.api.ui.*;


public class ScheduledEvent   extends UiApplication
{
    public static void  main( String[] inArgs )
    {
        ScheduledEvent  se  =  new ScheduledEvent();
        se.enterEventDispatcher();
    }

    public ScheduledEvent()
    {
    }
```

(continued)

Listing 7-7 *(continued)*

```
public void  activate()
{
   this.pushScreen( new ScheduledEventScreen() );
}
}
```

6. **Create a screen class for your application in the project.**

   I use `ScheduledEventScreen`, as can be seen in the call to `pushScreen` in the application class's `activate()` method.

7. **Add the code in Listing 7-8 to your screen class.**

Listing 7-8:   Code for the ScheduledEvent Screen

```
package com.karlgkowalski.scheduledevent;

import net.rim.device.api.ui.*;
import net.rim.device.api.ui.container.*;
import net.rim.device.api.ui.component.*;

import java.util.*;

public class ScheduledEventScreen   extends MainScreen  implements
            FieldChangeListener
{
   private EditField  m_eventDelay;
   private EventField m_eventField;
   private ButtonField m_scheduleEventButton;
   private ScheduledEventScreenManager m_manager;
   private Timer   m_timer;
   boolean m_isRunning;

   public ScheduledEventScreen()
   {
      super();
      this.initialize();
   }

   private void  initialize()
   {
      m_isRunning =   false;
      m_timer =   new Timer();
      m_manager   =   new ScheduledEventScreenManager();
      this.add( m_manager );
      this.setTitle( "Scheduled Event Screen" );
```

```
m_eventDelay   =   new EditField( "Seconds until event: ", "10", 2,
        EditField.FILTER_NUMERIC );
m_manager.add( m_eventDelay );
m_scheduleEventButton   =   new ButtonField( "Go!" );
m_manager.add( m_scheduleEventButton );
m_scheduleEventButton.setChangeListener( this );
m_eventField   =   new EventField();
m_manager.add( m_eventField );
}

public  void  fieldChanged( Field inField, int inContext )
{
    if (inField == m_scheduleEventButton)
    {
        if (true == m_isRunning)
        {
            m_isRunning =   false;
            m_timer.cancel();
            m_timer = new Timer();
        }
        //  just being sure it's our button
        //  get seconds from edit field
        int secondsToDelay =   10;
        String  secondsString   =   m_eventDelay.getText();
        if (secondsString.length() > 0)
        {
            secondsToDelay = Integer.parseInt( secondsString );
        }
        if (0 == secondsToDelay)
        {
            secondsToDelay = 1;
        }
        long   msToDelay   =   1000L * (long)secondsToDelay;
        EventFieldTask eft =   new EventFieldTask( m_eventField );
        m_timer.schedule( eft, msToDelay );
        m_isRunning = true;
    }
}
}
```

The screen implemented in Listing 7-8 sets up the behavior and operation of the items on display. First, a `Timer` object is created, and the `boolean` is used to indicate whether the timer already running is set. Then an `edit` field is added to allow you to change the delay before the color is changed in the `EventField`. A button is added to execute the scheduled event, and then the `EventField` is added. The button sets the screen to be called when the user clicks it, and that causes the screen's `fieldChanged()` method to be executed.

The `fieldChanged()` method shows what happens when the user clicks the button. If the timer is already running, the application causes it to halt its scheduled events. This is to make sure that any event that gets scheduled takes precedence over anything already in the queue. The `seconds` value stored in the `EditField` is turned into an `integer` value, with a minimum of 1 second and a default of 10 seconds if nothing is entered. The `seconds` value is converted to a `long` (a Java primitive data type, which can represent a value between –9,223,372,036,854,775,808 and +9,223,372,036,854,775,807, inclusive), and then a new `EventFieldTask` is created and scheduled using the timer.

Scheduling events by using the layout manager

The `ScheduledEventScreen` class makes use of a layout manager, so that's the next class to be entered.

1. **Create the screen layout manager class in the project.**

   In my example, the name I choose is `ScheduledEventScreenManager`.

2. **Add the code in Listing 7-9 to your layout manager class to lay out its screen elements.**

Listing 7-9:   Layout Management Code for the ScheduledEventScreen Class

```
package com.karlgkowalski.scheduledevent;

import  net.rim.device.api.ui.*;
import  net.rim.device.api.ui.container.*;
import  net.rim.device.api.ui.component.*;
import  net.rim.device.api.system.Display;

public  class ScheduledEventScreenManager    extends VerticalFieldManager
{
    public  static  final    int TITLE_SEPARATOR_HEIGHT = 4;
    public  ScheduledEventScreenManager()
    {
        super( Manager.NO_HORIZONTAL_SCROLL + Manager.NO_VERTICAL_SCROLL +
                Manager.NO_HORIZONTAL_SCROLLBAR + Manager.NO_VERTICAL_SCROLLBAR );
    }

    public  int getPreferredWidth()
    {
        return (Display.getWidth());
    }

    public  int getPreferredHeight()
```

```
{
   return (Display.getHeight());
}

public void   sublayout( int inWidth, int inHeight )
{
   Font   sysFont =   Font.getDefault();
   int titleBarOffset =   sysFont.getHeight() + TITLE_SEPARATOR_HEIGHT;
   int yPos   =   titleBarOffset;
   int numberFields   =   this.getFieldCount();
   for (int index=0; index<numberFields; ++index)
   {
      Field   aField =   this.getField( index );
      int width   =   aField.getPreferredWidth();
      int height   =   aField.getPreferredHeight();
      int xPos   =   0;
      this.layoutChild( aField, width, height );
      if (aField instanceof ButtonField)
      {
         // want button to be centered
         xPos   =   (inWidth - aField.getWidth())/2;
         // also want available width/height
         width   =   inWidth;
         height   =   inHeight;
      }
      else if (aField instanceof EventField)
      {
         yPos   =   Display.getHeight()/2 + titleBarOffset;
      }
      this.layoutChild( aField, width, height );
      this.setPositionChild( aField, xPos, yPos );
      yPos   +=  aField.getHeight();
   }
   // always remember to set our own display extent
   this.setExtent( Display.getWidth(), this.getPreferredHeight());
}
}
```

The layout manager ensures that the button added to the screen is centered along the horizontal. In addition, it lays out the `Field` subclass `EventField` to place it at the bottom of the screen. (See Figure 7-2.) That's the next class to add.

1. **Create a subclass of `Field` in the project.**

   This class displays a color and its name. My choice is `EventField`. In keeping with the past few classes, I might have named it `ScheduledEventField`, but I think I was getting tired of following a naming convention.

2. **Add the code in Listing 7-10 to your `Field` subclass to display a color and its name, choosing a random color from a predefined set.**

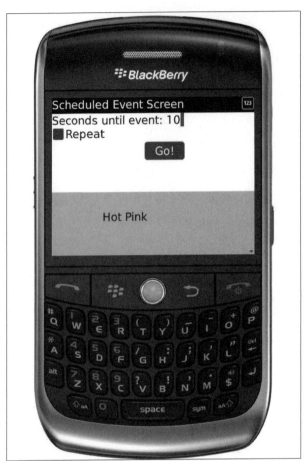

Figure 7-2:
The layout
manager
places the
custom UI
class Event-
Field at the
bottom of
the screen.

Listing 7-10: Code to Display a Color and Its Name

```
package com.karlgkowalski.scheduledevent;

import  net.rim.device.api.ui.*;
import  net.rim.device.api.ui.container.*;
import  net.rim.device.api.ui.component.*;
import  net.rim.device.api.system.Display;

import  java.util.*;


public  class  EventField   extends Field
{
    private Vector  m_colors  =  new Vector();
    private Hashtable  m_colorNames  =  new Hashtable();
```

```
private int m_currentIndex =   0;
private Random  m_random   =  new Random();   //  random number generator

public  EventField()
{
   this.initialize();
}

private void  initialize()
{
   m_colorNames.put( new Integer( Color.BURLYWOOD ), "Burlywood" );
   m_colorNames.put( new Integer( Color.BLUEVIOLET ), "Blue-Violet" );
   m_colorNames.put( new Integer( Color.CHARTREUSE ), "Chartreuse" );
   m_colorNames.put( new Integer( Color.CRIMSON ), "Crimson" );
   m_colorNames.put( new Integer( Color.DARKORANGE ), "Dk. Orange" );
   m_colorNames.put( new Integer( Color.FUCHSIA ), "Fuschia" );
   m_colorNames.put( new Integer( Color.HOTPINK ), "Hot Pink" );
   m_colorNames.put( new Integer( Color.LAWNGREEN ), "Lawn Green" );
   m_colorNames.put( new Integer( Color.SILVER ), "Silver" );
   m_colorNames.put( new Integer( Color.PALEVIOLETRED ), "Pale Violet Red" );
   Enumeration keyEnum =  m_colorNames.keys();
   while (true == keyEnum.hasMoreElements())
   {
      Object  key =   keyEnum.nextElement();
      m_colors.addElement( key );
   }
   m_currentIndex =   this.getRandomIndex();  //  set first index to random
}

public  int getPreferredWidth()
{
   return (Display.getWidth());
}

public  int getPreferredHeight()
{
   Font   defaultFont =   Font.getDefault();
   int titleBarOffset =   defaultFont.getHeight() +
          ScheduledEventScreenManager.TITLE_SEPARATOR_HEIGHT;
   return (Display.getHeight()/2-titleBarOffset);
}

protected  void  layout( int inWidth, int inHeight )
{
   this.setExtent( inWidth, this.getPreferredHeight() );
}

private int getRandomIndex()
{
   int randomIndex =   -1;
   do
```

(continued)

Listing 7-10 *(continued)*

```
        {
            randomIndex =   m_random.nextInt( m_colors.size() );
        }
        while (randomIndex == m_currentIndex);
        return (randomIndex);
    }

    public void   updateField()
    {
        m_currentIndex  =   this.getRandomIndex();
        this.invalidate();
    }

    protected void   paint( Graphics inGraphics )
    {
        Integer colorInteger   =   (Integer)m_colors.elementAt( m_currentIndex );
        inGraphics.setBackgroundColor( colorInteger.intValue() );
        inGraphics.clear(); //  clears entire field background with the background
                color
        inGraphics.setColor( Color.BLACK );
        String colorName   =   m_colorNames.get( colorInteger ).toString();
        int yPos   =   this.getHeight()/2;
        int xPos   =   this.getWidth()/4;
        inGraphics.drawText( colorName, xPos, yPos );
    }
}
```

Your `Field` subclass must implement the `layout( int width, int height )` method. The `Field` class is declared abstract, and the `layout` method is declared but not implemented. The BlackBerry JDE compiler enforces this rule and will holler at you if you forget it.

The most interesting part of the code is the `paint` method. A color, defined by an `Integer` object, is selected from the `Vector` containing all the colors defined for the class. The `Field` background is set to this color, and then the `clear` method is executed, erasing the `Field` by painting the `Field` rectangle with the background color. Then the name of the color, selected from the `Hashtable` using the color `Integer` as a key, is drawn in black.

The `updateField` method, called from the `TimerTask` subclass, does two things:

- ✔ Selects a new *index*, which is a random number less than the maximum colors in the list, as long as it's not equal to the current index
- ✔ Tells the operating system to redraw this `Field`, by calling the `invalidate()` method

Implementing threads

Finally, it's time to implement the threaded portion of the application. This is the subclass of `TimerTask`.

1. **Create a subclass of `TimerTask` in the project.**

   I call this one `EventFieldTask`.

2. **Add the code in Listing 7-11 into the `TimerTask` subclass to tell an `EventField` object to update itself.**

Listing 7-11:   The TimerTask Subclass

```
package com.karlgkowalski.scheduledevent;

import  java.util.TimerTask;

public  class EventFieldTask   extends TimerTask
{
   private EventField  m_eventField;

   public  EventFieldTask( EventField inField )
   {
      m_eventField   =   inField;
   }

   public  void   run()
   {
      if (null != m_eventField)
      {
         //  tell our field to update itself
         m_eventField.updateField();
      }
   }
}
```

You can see that the `EventFieldTask` doesn't really do much at all, and yet it is a fully functional background process. The benefit of using a `TimerTask` to do the background processing is that you don't have to write code that will decide what moment to execute the code in the `run()` method. That is handled by the `Timer` object.

The `EventField` class places the drawing of its contents into its `paint()` method, but the application never calls this method directly. The redrawing occurs as a result of the `invalidate()` method that the `EventField`. `updateField()` method executes, right after a new color is selected. The `invalidate()` method signals the BlackBerry OS that this `EventField` needs to be redrawn whenever the BlackBerry OS has a free moment.

With all these classes implemented, it's now time to see it execute. You build and run the project in the BlackBerry simulator (or a real device, if you also sign the application). You will see an edit field, a button, and a randomly colored `EventField` displayed onscreen when you launch the app from within the simulator, as shown in Figure 7-3.

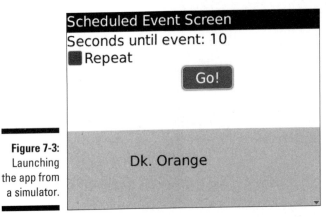

Scheduled Event Screen
Seconds until event: 10
Repeat
Go!

Dk. Orange

Figure 7-3:
Launching
the app from
a simulator.

When you click the button, after a delay of whatever number seconds you entered, the bottom part of the screen will change color and draw the name of the color, as shown in Figure 7-4. (Okay, in this black-and-white book, you have to use your imagination a bit!) If you change the value in the delay field, the change will be delayed by the new amount.

Note: If you have a stopwatch, or even if you count "one-one-thousand, two-one-thousand" up to the delay value entered in the field, you will notice that the *actual* delay is a little bit longer than the number of seconds entered in the field. This has to do with how the BlackBerry OS implements the `Timer` class, but before you go blaming RIM, this behavior is also present in every implementation of Java.

If you implemented your own `Thread` subclass to perform a scheduled operation, your subclass would have to execute the method `Thread.sleep( long delay )`. The input parameter is the number of milliseconds you want the subclass to hibernate, and after that span of time has passed, your `Thread` subclass will awaken and perform the operation you set it to do. However, this approach also exhibits the longer-than-expected delay behavior that the `Timer` shows. For the most part, your users aren't going to notice the difference. But sometimes it's important to get your timing to be exact. The best way to do this is by using the code in Listing 7-12.

Listing 7-12:   Code Snippet for a More Accurate Delay

```
public void run()
{
   long   sleepTime = SLEEP_INTERVAL;
   long   currentTime =   System.currentTimeMillis();
   while (true)
   {
     try
     {
        Thread.sleep( sleepTime );
        long awakeTime = System.currentTimeMillis();
        long timeAsleep = awakeTime - currentTime;
        sleepTime = 2*SLEEP_INTERVAL - timeAsleep;
```

(continued)

Listing 7-12 *(continued)*

```
        currentTime = awakeTime;
        if (...) // conditions for done sleeping
        {
            break;
        }
    }
    catch (Exception except)
    {
    }
  }
}
```

The `Thread` in Listing 7-13 will sleep for a specified `SLEEP_INTERVAL` and then adjust the next interval to account for whether the previous time spent sleeping was greater or lesser than what was desired. Although this work-around won't work perfectly, it does reduce the "drift," which can be considerable if your thread is going to be running for a long time.

Unfortunately, you can't use this code as part of a `TimerTask` approach. The `Timer` object takes care of "sleeping" for the desired amount of time. If you need really accurate time delays or scheduling, you must implement a `Thread` subclass on your own.

Using a Timer for repeated operations

You can also schedule events using a `Timer` to execute at regular intervals. This requires you to use a different `Timer.schedule()` method, adding a parameter that tells the `Timer` how much time to wait before executing the `TimerTask` again. You implement this as a small modification to the application that you just created. All the new code pieces are added to `ScheduledEventScreen.java`.

1. **Add a new member variable to `ScheduledEventScreen`: a `CheckboxField`.**

   This is a `boolean` indicator of whether to repeat. The following line shows the new member variable.

   ```
   private CheckboxField   m_repeats;
   ```

2. **Add the following two lines to the `initialize()` method, right before the creation of the `ButtonField` so that the `CheckboxField` appears above the `ButtonField` in the display.**

   ```
   m_repeats    =    new CheckboxField( "Repeat", false );
   m_manager.add( m_repeats );
   ```

3. Replace this line of code

```
m_timer.schedule( eft, msToDelay );
```

near the end of the **ScheduledEventScreen.fieldChanged()**
method with the code in Listing 7-13.

Listing 7-13: Picking a Schedule Based on the Checkbox Setting

```
if (true == m_repeats.getChecked())
{
    //  use the delay as the repeat period.
    m_timer.scheduleAtFixedRate( eft, msToDelay, msToDelay );
}
else
{
    m_timer.schedule( eft, msToDelay );
}
```

4. Build and run the application.

You can now set the `Timer` to repeat the `EventFieldTask` after another
period of time has passed, equivalent to the delay for the first time. You can
also return to a "one-shot" approach by unchecking the check box and clicking the button again.

I ran into a problem when I first implemented this code. An exception was
being thrown the second time I would click the button, changing from a
repeated schedule back to a one-shot. According to the Java documentation,
after the `Timer.cancel()` method is called, no more tasks can be scheduled:
The `Timer` is *terminated*. The solution was to create a new `Timer`, right after
calling `Timer.cancel()`. Lesson to learn: Always read the documentation
when trying something (relatively) new!

Neither the scheduled event nor repeated scheduled event make use of a callback mechanism. That's next.

Using a Thread to Notify the User of Something Important

As I mention earlier, you want to use a `Thread` subclass to perform operations that are going to take more time than a user is willing to wait. Operations
involving networking fall into this particular category because you can never
tell for sure when a network-based service is going to respond to you.

For example, one application I worked on retrieved time information from a network service to synchronize the app's operation to a particular time. I created a `Thread` subclass that contacted the network time service, interpreted the returned data, and delivered the resulting time value to the application. Because the time-retrieval portion was connecting to the network, the operation of the `Thread` subclass was not synchronized to that of the application, and so I implemented a callback mechanism so that the `Thread` subclass could return the data to the app after it completed its mission.

In the following running example, you see how to provide a callback to a `Thread` subclass and watch it operate. Figure 7-5 shows the steps. Here's the synopsis:

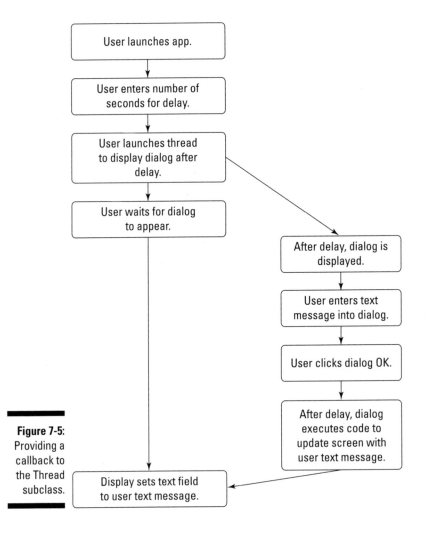

Figure 7-5:
Providing a callback to the Thread subclass.

1. The user launches the application.

2. The user selects a menu item to create a `Thread` subclass and launch it to perform a background operation.

3. After a delay, a dialog box appears.

4. The user provides information to the dialog box and commits or cancels the dialog box.

5. After a delay, the result of the dialog box's operation is reported back to the application.

6. The application displays the results for the user.

Creating the application class to display a notice

Here are the steps:

1. **Create a new project in the same workspace. Call it `NotifyAndReply` and put it in a subfolder of the same name, just to keep things straight.**

2. **Create an application class, `NotifyAndReply.java`, in the project.**

3. **Enter the code in Listing 7-14 into the application class.**

   The application code for this module is pretty much boilerplate: The names have changed, but the execution is still the same. This is basic application class code; you just create an instance of your application and then wait for the event dispatcher to call `activate()` and display the screen.

Listing 7-14: Application Class to Display `NotifyAndReplyScreen`.

```
package com.karlgkowalski.notifyandreply;

import net.rim.device.api.ui.*;

public class NotifyAndReply   extends UiApplication
{
   public static void  main( String[] inArgs )
   {
     NotifyAndReply nar =  new NotifyAndReply();
     nar.enterEventDispatcher();
   }

   public NotifyAndReply()
   {
   }
```

(continued)

Listing 7-14 *(continued)*

```
public void activate()
{
    this.pushScreen( new NotifyAndReplyScreen() );
}
}
```

4. **Create the `interface` class for the callback object.**

   I name this one `NotifyAndReplyOriginator` because the class that implements this is going to be the origin of the `Thread` subclass, and thus the one it needs to call back.

5. **Add the code in Listing 7-15 into the `interface` class that shows the methods that the `Thread` subclass's owner must implement.**

   You'll find this to be pretty simple, I hope!

Listing 7-15: Callback Interface Showing Methods

```
package com.karlgkowalski.notifyandreply;

public interface NotifyAndReplyOriginator
{
    public void notifyAndReplyCommit( String inResult );
    public void notifyAndReplyCancel();
    public void notifyAndReplyInterrupted();
    public long getDelayMS();
}
```

The class implementing the callback must provide four methods. The first three (all starting with `notifyAndReply`) are really the callback methods. These are the methods that the `Thread` calls just before it terminates, indicating that one of three things has happened:

✔ The user clicked the OK button on the displayed dialog box.

✔ The user clicked the Cancel button on the dialog box.

✔ Something else interrupted the flow of operation, probably during the `Thread.sleep()` method call.

The last method, `getDelayMS()`, is called by the `Thread` subclass to get the delay (in milliseconds) from the originator object. This puts the burden of providing that information on the class that is responsible for getting the delay value from the user: the `Screen` subclass.

Using the Screen subclass to get the delay value from the user

Tackling the Screen subclass is next:

1. **Create the subclass NotifyAndReplyScreen.java.**

2. **Add the code in Listing 7-16 into the Screen class.**

   This Screen subclass shows the main application screen for the user to interact with.

Listing 7-16: **The Screen Subclass to Show the Main Application Screen**

```
package com.karlgkowalski.notifyandreply;


import  net.rim.device.api.ui.*;
import  net.rim.device.api.ui.container.*;
import  net.rim.device.api.ui.component.*;

import  java.util.*;

public  class NotifyAndReplyScreen  extends MainScreen  implements
            NotifyAndReplyOriginator
{
   private EditField    m_delay;
   private LabelField  m_response;
   private boolean      m_isExecuting;

   public  NotifyAndReplyScreen()
   {
      this.initialize();
   }

   private void    initialize()
   {
      m_delay =    new EditField( "Delay to display dialog: ", "10", 2,
            EditField.FILTER_NUMERIC );
      m_response  =   new LabelField( "Response: <none>" );
      this.add( m_delay );
      this.add( m_response );
      m_isExecuting = false;
   }

   public  void    makeMenu( Menu inMenu, int inContext )
```

(continued)

Listing 7-16 *(continued)*

```
{
   MenuItem dialogThreadMenuItem = new MenuItem( "", 10000, 10 )
   {
      public void run()
      {
         if (false == m_isExecuting)
         {
            // only want to run if we aren't running already
            startDialogThread();
         }
      }
   };
   inMenu.add( dialogThreadMenuItem );
   inMenu.addSeparator();
   super.makeMenu( inMenu, inContext );
}

private void startDialogThread()
{
   NotifyAndReplyThread narThread = new NotifyAndReplyThread( this );
   m_isExecuting = true;
   narThread.start(); // this calls the Thread's run() method
}

public void notifyAndReplyCommit( String inResult )
{
   m_response.setText( inResult );
   m_isExecuting = false;
   this.invalidate();
}

public void notifyAndReplyCancel()
{
   m_response.setText( "Dialog was cancelled" );
   m_isExecuting = false;
   this.invalidate();
}

public long getDelayMS()
{
   int delay = Integer.parseInt( m_delay.getText() );
   return ((long)delay*1000L);
}

public void notifyAndReplyInterrupted()
{
   m_response.setText( "Thread Interrupted!" );
   m_isExecuting = false;
   this.invalidate();
}
}
```

You can see the Screen subclass being created in the initialize() method, and the startDialogThread() method is where the Thread subclass is created and launched. NotifyAndReplyScreen implements the NotifyAndReplyOriginator interface — it fleshes out the four methods necessary to act as an originator — and that's what gets passed into the Thread subclass constructor.

Delivering the NotifyAndReplyThread class

Finally, deliver the NotifyAndReplyThread class:

1. **Create the Thread subclass, NotifyAndReplyThread.**

2. **Add the code in Listing 7-17 into the NotifyAndReplyThread class.**

   This Thread subclass code does the background work: Namely, delaying before the dialog is displayed, and then delaying after the user clicks OK or Cancel.

Listing 7-17: The Thread Subclass

```
package com.karlgkowalski.notifyandreply;

import net.rim.device.api.ui.*;
import net.rim.device.api.ui.component.*;

public class NotifyAndReplyThread extends Thread
{
    private NotifyAndReplyOriginator  m_originator;
    private EditField  m_responseField;
    private long  m_delayMS;

    public NotifyAndReplyThread( NotifyAndReplyOriginator inOriginator )
    {
        m_originator  =  inOriginator;
        m_delayMS  =  m_originator.getDelayMS();
        if (0 >= m_delayMS)
        {
            m_delayMS = 10000L;
        }
    }

    public void  run()
    {
        if (null != m_originator)
        {
            try
            {
```

(continued)

Listing 7-17 *(continued)*

```
            // wait the requested delay
            Thread.sleep( m_delayMS );
            this.displayDialog();
        }
        catch (InterruptedException iExcept)
        {
            m_originator.notifyAndReplyInterrupted();
        }


    }
}

private void  displayDialog()
{
    // now display the dialog
    final  Dialog aDialog =  new Dialog( Dialog.D_OK_CANCEL, "Enter a text
            response", 0, null, 0L );
    m_responseField =  new EditField( "", "" );
    aDialog.add( m_responseField );
    synchronized (UiApplication.getEventLock())
    {
        UiApplication.getUiApplication().invokeLater( new Runnable()
        {
            public  void  run()
            {
                int result  =  aDialog.doModal();
                if (Dialog.OK == result)
                {
                    handleCommit( m_responseField.getText() );
                }
                else
                {
                    handleCancel();
                }
            }
        });
    }
}

private void  handleCommit( String inResponse )
{
    if (null != m_originator)
    {
        try
        {
            Thread.sleep( m_delayMS );
            m_originator.notifyAndReplyCommit( inResponse );
        }
        catch (InterruptedException iExcept)
        {
```

```
            m_originator.notifyAndReplyInterrupted();
        }
    }
}

private void    handleCancel()
{
    if (null != m_originator)
    {
        m_originator.notifyAndReplyCancel();
    }
}
}
```

The `NotifyAndReplyThread.run()` method implements the background processing. When you're creating your background threads, this is where you implement the work that they will do. In this instance, the thread is simply going to sleep for the time delay that the user specified on the main screen. After the thread wakes up, the `NotifyAndReplyThread.display Dialog()` method is executed. And this is where a most interesting thing happens: a `Runnable` executing in a `Thread`.

`NotifyAndReplyThread` is supposed to display a dialog box that asks the user to enter some information, to be displayed on the main screen when the thread has completed. However, the thread is separate from the main event thread, which means it has no access to the main display operations, where `Screen` subclasses are placed onto the screen stack. Informational dialog boxes — *alerts* — can be launched from any part of your code. But this is an interactive dialog box, which requires something a bit more intensive.

After a `Dialog` object is created and has an `EditField` added to its set of components, the `NotifyAndReplyThread` requests the event lock from the `UiApplication` Singleton instance. This lock is returned as a Java plain `Object`, and this is then synchronized, effectively permitting the thread to act as if it were running within the main event thread. As long as the event lock object is held synchronized, the main application thread will pause while the background thread that requested and synchronized the event lock object performs its tasks. This allows the background thread to make changes to the UI elements on display, and forces the main application thread to respond to those changes when the event lock is released. After it has the event lock, the thread then executes the following:

```
cUiApplication.getUiApplication().invokeLater()
```

This method takes a `Runnable` object — created on the fly, within the call — which implements a `run()` method to display the `Dialog`. The object was created outside the invocation of the `run()` method, and so it is marked as "final" to allow it to be used within the `run()` method.

The preceding complexity is necessary to get around the fact that the `NotifyAndReplyThread` is operating in the background while simultaneously working with the display to show things to the user requires operating in the foreground, otherwise known as the main event thread. If you've ever programmed in Java on a desktop PC, you find a similar arrangement through the use of the `SwingUtilities.invokeLater( Runnable obj )` method.

You can replace the code implemented in the `NotifyAndReplyThread.run()` method with code to satisfy your own app's needs for background operations.

Chapter 9 introduces you to using `Thread` subclasses for handling network communications.

Part III

Developing Enterprise-Class BlackBerry Apps

In this part . . .

The majority of BlackBerry users are tied to their corporate e-mail through a BlackBerry Enterprise Server (BES). As an app developer, you can take advantage of this relationship or be burned by it. This part gives you the details you need in order to understand where the BES can interfere with and even restrict your application, and then how to deal with the challenges. You find out how to take advantage of the features of a BES to enable an administrator to configure your application's use on all the BlackBerry smartphones in the corporate enterprise. And you also see what a networked BlackBerry application is capable of when it can reach the farthest corners of the Internet from the palm of a user's hand.

Chapter 8

Writing Apps for the Enterprise

. . . .

In This Chapter

▶ Introducing the BlackBerry Enterprise Server (BES)

▶ Handling e-mail and e-mail attachments

▶ Paying attention to BES IT policy limitations

▶ Tackling security exceptions

. . . .

*Y*our BlackBerry application will be downloaded by many BlackBerry users. This audience will consist of different types of users, and like it or not, quite a few of them will be using their BlackBerry device as an extension of their work life. These are the Enterprise users, and there are a great many of them — everyone from Mr. Spock to Dr. McCoy.

However, you have to handle these users a little differently than everyone else because to a great degree, an Enterprise user's BlackBerry isn't entirely under his or her control. An Enterprise BlackBerry device connects to an internal corporate network of computers, and the corporate IT security folks need to protect that internal network from the Internet. This means that your BlackBerry application can encounter rules and restrictions imposed upon a user's BlackBerry device — rules and restrictions governed by a BlackBerry Enterprise Server, or BES (pronounced *bezz*).

The BES is a very complex and powerful tool. I don't go over all the details here, but I do make sure you understand the different ways in which the BES can be configured that can have an effect on your application.

In this chapter, I provide background information about the BES and some of its features and functionality. You gain a surface-level understanding of a BES, so you know how your application can be affected by a BES as well as how to take advantage of it.

My intention here isn't to deter you from writing BlackBerry applications for Enterprise customers. Instead, this chapter is meant as a "take heed" post: an information store for you to keep in the back of your mind while you write your BlackBerry applications. Millions of BlackBerry devices and users are out in the world, and the majority of them are connected to a corporate network via a BES. The information provided in this chapter should at least make you aware that your app may have to accommodate the configurations a BES administrator imposes upon the corporate users.

Users can download your app before their devices become Enterprise-activated with a BES, and so your app might suddenly find roadblocks in its way that hadn't been there the day before. Your app will be better positioned to handle this situation now that you're at least aware of the possibility, and hopefully be able to warn your users that the circumstances of its operation have changed. With luck, that won't be a major issue; but the more apps you sell, the more devices you sell them to, the greater the chance that some BES will throw your app a curve ball.

Activating for the Enterprise

Large companies — also called *corporate enterprises* — have lots of computers, all nicely connected with each other. This encourages and enables sharing of information and enhances productivity, which is why large companies set up all this hardware and software, and why they have in-house corporate IT departments to keep things running smoothly. As mobile devices have become more prevalent among the workforce, and as these devices become more powerful and more capable, companies have been adjusting their corporate networks to accommodate these mobile computers.

From a corporate perspective, the BlackBerry is a mobile communications device that can allow a remote user to send and receive e-mail anywhere the user can find a wireless phone signal or a Wi-Fi network connection. This makes the BlackBerry very useful for employees to keep in touch with the rest of their company when they're away from the office. To make the BlackBerry even more useful, a company needs to deploy the BlackBerry Enterprise Server, otherwise known as the BES.

There are two types of BES available from RIM, the standard BlackBerry Enterprise Server, and the BlackBerry Enterprise Server Express. The differences are these:

- ✔ The BES Express is free, so it is more appealing to small businesses and anyone who communicates using BlackBerry smartphones.

- ✔ The BES Express comes with less capability than the full BES, eliminating custom application IT policies and preventing custom data-pushing through the BES Express to applications on the smartphones.

Understanding what the BES does

The BES provides a gateway between the Internet (where the remote BlackBerry users are) and the corporate network (where the proprietary corporate information resides). The connection between the BES and each BlackBerry is encrypted, so data traveling between the BlackBerry device and the corporate network is secure. The BES offers the following capabilities for IT administrators who are going to manage the BlackBerry devices in their corporate enterprises:

- **E-mail access through the device:** This capability is why so many people choose a BlackBerry device: to keep constantly connected to corporate communications. Users send and receive e-mail via their BlackBerry devices. The BES integrates with the corporate e-mail system, and a user's BlackBerry becomes just another mail client. Your application can make use of the e-mail access your users' devices provide, including making sense of e-mail attachments.

- **Calendar maintenance:** In addition to e-mail, users can access their calendars, such as Microsoft Outlook, on their BlackBerry devices. If your application is targeted at the corporate enterprise user, you can take advantage of accessing calendar information.

- **Internet access control:** Corporate Internet usage policies can be enforced on the BlackBerry devices that are activated on the BES. Your application might be unable to connect to certain Web sites on the Internet as a result of this, so you'll have to provide a means of getting around this problem or executing with reduced or zero Internet access. Your app will be prevented from accessing any Web site that corporate policies prevent regular desktop computers from accessing — but your app will have to let your users know of any lack of connection.

- **Push-data delivery:** A BES supports the capability of an external application to push data through its secure connection to a specific BlackBerry. Your application can set itself up to "listen" for incoming data pushes. If you create your app to do so, you will also have to develop a desktop-based application that will connect to a BES and deliver the data to be pushed to your users' BlackBerry devices.

- **Data backup and restore:** The BES supports synchronization of BlackBerry device data and will take "snapshots" of the current set of data on a user's BlackBerry on a regular basis. While the BlackBerry is registered with the BES, the BES will continually update its backup with the contents of the device, keeping the BES database a mirror image of the device's data set. If the device is *wiped* — that is, its user-specific information removed, just as if it had been bought new — when the device is activated with the BES, the backed-up data will be restored to the device. This is especially useful when a user upgrades an old device for a new one, and wants the new device to match what the previous BlackBerry had. Your application can take advantage of data backup to maintain its stored information in a BES for safekeeping.

✔ **Remote wiping:** A BES can wipe any of its registered BlackBerry devices when the device is active on the wireless carrier's network. Generally this is only done when the device is lost, and this is for safety reasons. After all, a BlackBerry device registered with a corporate BES is effectively an open door to the corporate network. Your application will likely not have to worry about this situation; however, any data stored by your application in persistent or runtime storage will be erased. (See Chapter 6 for more information about storage.) Data stored on a removable MicroSD card will be retained.

✔ **Usage-policy enforcement:** The BES can control some of the behavior of the BlackBerry devices that are within its control. The BES calls these *IT policies*. I go over some of these controlled behaviors in the section, "Reading Application IT Policies," later in this chapter.

✔ **Provision of custom application policies:** The BES (with the exception of BlackBerry Enterprise Server Express) can deliver information to BlackBerry devices that's specific to your application. Your app can examine these named policies and extract data associated with them for its own use. If your application is destined to execute in a corporate enterprise, you might want to take advantage of a BES by using its custom application policies to deliver information to your application running on each device the BES controls.

As you can guess, the BES is a very powerful and very complex piece of software. Because most BlackBerry users are part of a corporate enterprise, the odds are high that your application will execute on an Enterprise-activated device. Of course, this also means that if you create an application that provides features intended for a corporate enterprise, you'll have a large customer base to sell into. Your app better be capable of handling all the requirements that an Enterprise-activated device insists upon.

Enterprise activation

When a BlackBerry user pulls a new BlackBerry out of the box, the BlackBerry is ready to talk to the Internet. However, this newly born mobile computing device is not automatically connected to the user's corporate network. The user must *Enterprise-activate* the BlackBerry device. To do this, the user and the BES administrator must collaborate. Two things happen:

1. The administrator must set up the corporate BES to expect the user's BlackBerry's request to activate.

2. The user must direct the BlackBerry to connect to the corporate BES.

The process can take 30–60 minutes, depending on how many pieces of information the BES needs to deliver to the device. As shown in the diagram in Figure 8-1, a BlackBerry device has a long path of communication between it and the corporate network.

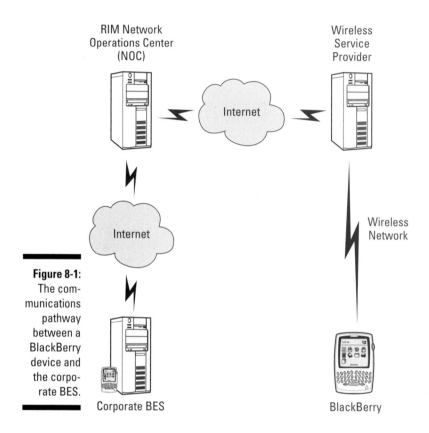

RIM Network Operations Center (NOC)

Wireless Service Provider

Internet

Internet

Wireless Network

Figure 8-1:
The communications pathway between a BlackBerry device and the corporate BES.

Corporate BES

BlackBerry

When the device is activated, the user can access any part of the corporate network from the BlackBerry, just as if the device were a desktop PC connecting via Ethernet cable. Your application can now similarly access the corporate network — if the BES administrator allows noncorporate software to do so.

Interacting with E-Mail

As a networked e-mail device, the BlackBerry will provide access to a user's e-mail. In the corporate BES environment, the BES is connected with the e-mail service that the company provides. A user's e-mail will come into the corporate e-mail service, and the corporate BES will continuously query the corporate e-mail service on behalf of the Enterprise-activated BlackBerry devices. The BES will deliver users' e-mails to their respective BlackBerry devices through its "push" feature.

Your application can access a user's e-mail messages, including any attachments. Your application can even create and transmit e-mail messages on the user's behalf. However, because this kind of automatic behavior (reading, writing, and sending messages) can be exploited by malicious software, the BlackBerry OS will inform the user of what your application is capable of, and will ask the user's permission for your app to behave in this fashion.

This permission request may be taken care of by the BES; the BES administrator can set the BlackBerry device to automatically accept this behavior of your application, or automatically deny it. If your application is meant to operate as an enterprise-class app and is accepted as such by the BES administrators, all is well and good. But if your application is meant for use by individuals, independent of the corporate enterprise, this behavior might fail to operate.

Handling attachments

On a corporate network, employees move many documents amongst themselves by attaching the document to an e-mail message. Because BlackBerry devices are just another e-mail client on the corporate network, they are capable of receiving and manipulating e-mail attachments as well. Spreadsheets, presentations, word processing documents: Standard BlackBerry applications can import and display these sources of information should the BlackBerry user wish to view them.

E-mail attachments can be delivered via the BlackBerry Internet Service (BIS) in addition to a BES, so even non-corporate users can use your app to handle e-mail attachments. A BIS is a simple e-mail service hosted by RIM to provide an e-mail address for the customers of each wireless service provider. For instance, because I'm a BlackBerry-carrying AT&T subscriber, I have an e-mail address at `att.blackberry.net`.

Your application can similarly import and interpret data stored in an e-mail attachment. The process works like this:

1. Your application is installed onto the user's device.

   This step must come before the e-mail arrives on the device. The ordering of this step is critical: If the e-mail arrives before the application is installed or before the attachment handler is installed (see the next step), the BlackBerry OS won't inform your application that an attachment it might be interested in is available.

2. Your application adds an attachment handler to the OS for the types of e-mail attachments your app is interested in.

   This handler will be asked by the OS whether your app wants to accept the contents of an attachment when the user selects one. So if your app expects users to import digital images to create a pocket photo album, your app could make it easy to pull images from e-mails sent to the smartphone.

3. An e-mail message is created.

4. A properly named file is attached to the e-mail message.

   This is another of the important steps of the process. The filename can be any normal desktop PC filename, but the name must start with `x-rimdevice`. The BlackBerry device OS will show the attachment is present even if the filename does not start with `x-rimdevice`, but the data in the attachment will not be delivered to the device without it.

5. The e-mail message is sent to the BlackBerry user's e-mail account.

6. The BES finds the e-mail message when it arrives at the user's e-mail account.

7. The BES delivers the e-mail message to the user's BlackBerry.

8. The e-mail message arrives at the user's BlackBerry.

9. The user opens the e-mail message using the BlackBerry Mail application.

10. The user shifts the selection cursor onto the listed e-mail attachment and clicks the BlackBerry menu button.

    Your application adds a menu item if the attachment is the type of file that your app is interested in.

11. The user selects your app's menu item.

12. Your application imports the contents of the attached file.

Figure 8-2 shows a flowchart illustrating the steps that your app follows in order to deliver an e-mail attachment's contents into your application.

The two key points for e-mail attachment management are that the application must be installed before the e-mail arrives, and the attached file's name must begin with `x-rimdevice`.

The BlackBerry smartphone has to execute some operations behind the scenes for e-mail attachments that your application registers to handle. If your application is not present on the smartphone when the e-mail with your app's attachment arrives, the smartphone OS may not know to ask your app whether it's interested in the attachment. This requirement is documented in the BlackBerry Java API documentation for the interface class `net.rim.blackberry.api.mail.AttachmentHandler`.

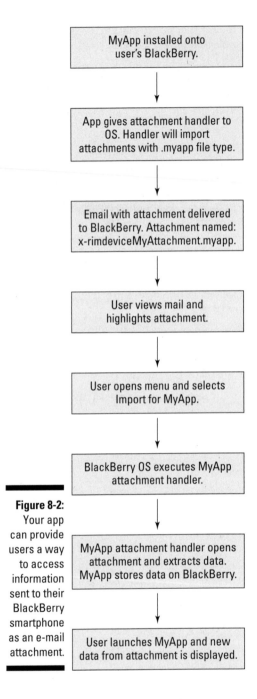

MyApp installed onto
user's BlackBerry.

App gives attachment handler to
OS. Handler will import
attachments with .myapp file type.

Email with attachment delivered
to BlackBerry. Attachment named:
x-rimdeviceMyAttachment.myapp.

User views mail and
highlights attachment.

User opens menu and selects
Import for MyApp.

BlackBerry OS executes MyApp
attachment handler.

MyApp attachment handler opens
attachment and extracts data.
MyApp stores data on BlackBerry.

User launches MyApp and new
data from attachment is displayed.

Figure 8-2:
Your app
can provide
users a way
to access
information
sent to their
BlackBerry
smartphone
as an e-mail
attachment.

The attachment file's name must have *x-rimdevice* as the first letters in its
name, because the smartphone OS will not download the attached file if the
name does not follow this rule. This is to reduce the possibility that a large

e-mail attachment is automatically downloaded against the BlackBerry user's wishes. Unfortunately, your users and therefore your application won't know that the file has not been downloaded until your app tries to pull in the data. In this case, your app will have to inform users that the attachment is empty, and that they should check with whoever sent the e-mail for what went wrong. This is also documented in the BlackBerry Java API documentation for AttachmentHandler.

One application I worked on provided more than a few headaches for customers who have run afoul of these conditions. Your application and its documentation need to clearly explain these requirements to your corporate users. Otherwise, you'll get these headaches, too! One user suggested that my application didn't actually have to be installed before the e-mail attachment had arrived. Upon some investigation, we discovered that the BlackBerry smartphone had received the e-mail with its attachment while a previous version of my application was already installed, and that if the older application were removed and a newer one installed, the prior attachment (downloaded and available for the older app) was still available for the newer app.

Writing an e-mail attachment handler

The code in Listing 8-1 shows what an e-mail attachment handler looks like.

Listing 8-1: A BlackBerry E-Mail Attachment Handler

```
Import net.rim.blackberry.api.mail.*;

public class Uhura implements AttachmentHandler
{
   public Uhura()
   {
   }

   public String menuString()
   {
      return ("Import My Attachment");
   }

   public Boolean supports( String inContentType )
   {
      // check for the right file type extension
      boolean weAreInterested =
         (inContentType.toLowerCase().indexOf( ".mytype" ) >= 0);
      return (weAreInterested);
   }

   public void run( Message inMessage, SupportedAttachmentPart inPart )
```

(continued)

Listing 8-1 *(continued)*

```
{
   if (null != inPart)
   {
      try
      {
         int partSize = inPart.getSize();
         if (partSize > 0)
         {
            byte[] dataArray = (byte[])inPart.getContent();
            // you now have all content in the attachment
         }
         else
         {
            // no content in the part.
         }
      }
      catch (Exception except)
      {
         // something bad happened, didn't get the data
      }
   }
}
```

The attachment handler in the listing does three different things, and these are the methods that the `AttachmentHandler` interface requires:

- ✔ `boolean supports( String )`: Your attachment handler implements this method to tell the BlackBerry Mail application that your application is interested in this type of attachment. The input parameter is a string that incorporates the filename of the attached file. In Listing 8-1, the code checks for whether the string contains the text `.mytype`. This would most likely be the file extension part of the filename. The example converts the incoming string to all-lowercase to rule out any potential case-sensitivity.

- ✔ `String menuString()`: If the BlackBerry Mail application determines that your attachment handler is ready, willing, and able to take on the data in the attachment, your attachment handler will be asked to provide a text string that is inserted into the menu the user has requested be displayed. This method is where you will provide this information.

- ✔ `void run( Message, SupportedAttachmentPart)`: Finally, when the user selects the menu item your attachment handler displays, this is the method that will be executed. The important point to note here is that the data is delivered as an array of type `byte`. You are free to use this stream of bytes in any fashion.

Your application will need to create an attachment handler object, along the basic design shown in Listing 8-1. Creating one is the first step; installing it as part of the device OS is the second step. Listing 8-2 shows how this is done.

Listing 8-2:   Creating and Installing an E-Mail Attachment Handler

```
// need this import statement
import net.rim.blackberry.api.mail.AttachmentHandlerManager;

// add this code to your application class to install an attachment handler
AttachmentHandlerManager ahm = AttachmentHandlerManager.getInstance();
ahm.addAttachmentHandler( new Uhura() );
```

One last issue remains. You will want to install only one attachment handler while the device is active. This makes installing an attachment handler slightly more complicated than just executing the code snippet in Listing 8-2. If this code snippet is executed more than once, another attachment handler will be added for each execution, and the attachment handler object that you created in every previous execution will still be part of the device OS. So how do you ensure that only one is ever installed while the device is on? Simple: Use the runtime storage mechanism, which I explain in Chapter 6.

The runtime store is purged every time the device is powered on, making it a great place to keep track of whether you've done something in a previous launch of your app. The runtime store is one of several different places your app can use to hold on to data for later use. In this instance, your app will use the runtime store to inform your app for whether it should install its e-mail attachment handler. If your application wants to install an e-mail attachment handler, you should implement the following:

✔ In your application's `main()` method, check the runtime storage for the existence of an attachment handler object. This can be as simple as a `Boolean` object, or even just a `String`, used as a flag. You're interested only in the presence or absence of some specific object, such as a `String` (perhaps some text you can use while making sure your app works perfectly) or a simple Integer object — it really doesn't matter, as long as your app treats its absence in the runtime store to mean your e-mail attachment handler was not installed, and its presence to mean your app doesn't need to add another handler.

✔ If the flag exists in the runtime storage, your app doesn't need to do anything more.

✔ If the flag doesn't exist, you create and install the attachment handler object, as shown in Listing 8-2. And don't forget to create the flag and add it to the runtime storage so your app won't do this a second time. The code snippet Listing 8-3 shows how to check the runtime store to see whether your flag object exists. First the code sets the variable `flagIsPresent` to `false`, and then the `RuntimeStore` object is retrieved from the OS — there is only one. If the `RuntimeStore` object is present, the code tries to retrieve anything that might be stored under the key value (the `long` data type `MY_APP_RUNTIME_STORE_KEY`, which can be any 64-bit value, unique to your app). If there's something there, the variable `flagIsPresent` is set to `true`.

Listing 8-3:   Snippet of Code to Check for a Flag in the Runtime Store

```
private static final long MY_APP_RUNTIME_STORE_KEY = 0xe7ccdcf49882229L;

public boolean isFlagPresent()
{
   boolean commanderDataIsHere = false;
   RuntimeStore rs = RuntimeStore.getRuntimeStore();
   if (null != rs)
   {
      if (null != rs.get( MY_APP_RUNTIME_STORE_KEY))
      {
         commanderDataIsHere = true;
      }
   }
   return (commanderDataIsHere);
}
```

Listing 8-4 shows you how to place an object into a runtime store. Like the code in Listing 8-3, this snippet retrieves the `RuntimeStore` object from the OS. Assuming it's not `null`, the code then executes the `put()` method and places a `string` value into `RuntimeStore` using the same key that the code in Listing 8-3 used.

Listing 8-4:   Snippet of Code to Set a Flag in the Runtime Store

```
private static final long MY_APP_RUNTIME_STORE_KEY = 0xe7ccdcf49882229L;
public void setRuntimeStoreFlag()
{
   RuntimeStore rs = RuntimeStore.getRuntimeStore();
   if (null != rs)
   {
      rs.put( MY_APP_RUNTIME_STORE_KEY, "warpFactorTen" );
   }
}
```

That's all you need do to access and process e-mail attachments.

Standard BES IT Policies

The BES comes with a standard set of IT policies already defined and ready to be imposed upon all the BlackBerry devices that have gone through Enterprise-activation. These policies encompass a wide range of different categories for controlling users' Blackberry devices for the corporate enterprise. As a developer, you want your app to take advantage of all the features of a BlackBerry smartphone that can make your users' lives easier. However, sometimes corporate policies for how users use their BlackBerry smartphones can interfere with your app's attempts to exercise BlackBerry functionality to its fullest — and the corporate enterprise is going to win.

The following is a list of some of the IT policies that a BES administrator can set that may affect your application's behavior when installed on a BlackBerry:

- **Allow External Connections:** This IT policy can disable external network connections. This is likely the most important IT policy that can hamper your application if your app is going to try to talk to a network resource outside the corporate network. For instance, some corporate enterprises use a Web site filtering system to ensure corporate users aren't wasting time with sites that provide online gambling. If your app checks the current lottery numbers at `www.lottery.com`, the corporate BES policy might prevent your app's operation.

- **Allow Internal Connections:** This IT policy determines whether network connections are permitted inside the corporate network. The BES administrator might disable internal network connections to prevent the possibility that malicious software on a BlackBerry would attack the corporate network. Your application would be concerned about this policy being enabled if you were delivering an enterprise application intending to communicate with resources in the corporate network.

- **Allow Access to the Interprocess Communications API:** Although it doesn't sound threatening, this IT policy, if enabled, can deny your application access to the device's persistent store mechanism (which you can read about in Chapter 6).

- **Allow Access to the Media API:** This IT policy allows or prevents your application to run or create multimedia files on a BlackBerry device.

- **Allow Access to the Phone API:** All the phone APIs — which allow your application to make calls, or access call logs — are controlled by this policy.

- **Allow Access to the PIM API:** Your app's capability to pull out information from the user's personal information, such as contacts, is controlled by this IT policy.

- **Allowed Access to the Wi-Fi API:** This IT policy determines whether a BlackBerry device can use a Wi-Fi connection for data transmission. Your application might not depend on Wi-Fi use specifically, but you might need to inform users if your application is going to attempt to download a large amount of data via the wireless network, giving them a chance to opt out.

- **Disable Bluetooth:** This IT policy can prevent the use of Bluetooth communications.

- **Disable Photo Camera:** If your app makes use of the built-in camera, this IT policy can foil your attempts to take pictures using the BlackBerry.

- **Disable GPS:** Some BlackBerry devices contain GPS hardware and software to determine the geographic location of the device. This IT policy can disable the device's capability to make this determination; therefore, your application might be prevented from performing location-based services.

✔ **Disable All Wireless Synchronization:** BlackBerry devices normally synchronize their data with a BES on a regular basis. This IT policy will disable that backup data operation, and your application will be unable to rely on data being backed up to the BES. When developing your app to take advantage of automatic BES data backups, you must keep in mind that a BES administrator might prevent this operation.

✔ **Disable External Memory:** Some BlackBerry devices allow external memory cards to be added, providing greater storage capacity, especially for media files such as video and audio. If your application plans to access these memory cards, this IT policy can disable that access.

A great many more IT policies are available for BES administrators to configure, so I don't list them all because it would take too many pages and most won't affect an app's operation. The ones in the preceding list can have a direct effect on your application's capability to operate as planned.

Reading Application IT Policies

The BES provides a means by which an administrator can configure your application for application-specific settings. BES IT policies are name-value pairs defined at the BES by the administrator and then assigned to one or more BlackBerry devices. Your application can retrieve IT policies that are present on a user's BlackBerry device, but your app must know the name of the policy, as set by the administrator, to get the value.

The BlackBerry Enterprise Server Express does not permit custom application IT policies, so administrators on that type of BES can't configure your application for their users.

The following value types are available as IT policy values:

✔ `Boolean (boolean)`

✔ `Byte (byte)`

✔ `Byte Array (byte[])`

✔ `Integer (int)`

✔ `String`

The most useful of these is `String` because you can convert from a `String` to any other type (assuming you know what's in it). The other types are more constrained, but the BES will then enforce their individual nature for the value part of the IT policy being defined. An administrator creating an `Integer` name-value pair will find that only integers can be used as input for the value.

IT policies are only available for a user whose BlackBerry is managed by a BES. Your application can look for the specific IT policy name your app wants to read, but you must be prepared to handle those cases where the IT policy has not been set, or does not exist. The BlackBerry class responsible for retrieving IT policy data is (not surprisingly)

```
ITPolicy (net.rim.device.api.itpolicy.ITPolicy)
```

It has a number of methods, and the basic ones are listed here:

- ✔ `static boolean getBoolean( String, boolean )`: Returns a `boolean` value for the IT policy named in the `String` parameter. The second parameter is the value used if the named policy does not exist.

- ✔ `static byte getByte( String )`: Returns a `byte` value for the IT policy named in the `String` parameter. The null byte (`'\0'`) is returned if the named policy does not exist.

- ✔ `static byte[] getByteArray( String )`: Returns a `byte` array for the IT policy named in the `String` parameter. A value of `null` is returned if the named policy does not exist.

- ✔ `static int getInteger( String, int )`: Returns an integer for the IT policy named in the `String` parameter. The second parameter is the value used if the named policy does not exist.

- ✔ `static String getString( String )`: Returns a `String` for the IT policy named in the `String` parameter. The value of `null` is returned if the named policy does not exist.

Using these methods, your application can retrieve data set up by the BES administrator specifically for your application.

Dealing with BES Security

One of the most important issues that will arise when your application is running on a BES-controlled BlackBerry is when it tries to do something that the BES administrator does not allow. The simplest of these is network access: The IT department may implement a set of policies that limits whether and how applications running on its users' BlackBerry devices can make network connections to online resources. The real problem with this issue is that your application might not be informed that its network access is limited until your app makes an attempt to download from or upload to a Web-based resource.

In Figure 8-3, you see a dialog box that will come up when your application is installed on a BlackBerry and your application is set to attempt to make a network connection — or, as in this case, attempt to start a server to listen for incoming HTTP-Push connections.

At this point, one of two things can occur:

- ✔ The user clicks Yes, and your app is allowed to proceed. The device will never again ask the user to permit your application to perform its operation.

- ✔ The user clicks No, and your app is prevented from performing the operation that triggered this message. In addition, the device will never again ask the user to permit your application to execute this code. Your app is effectively prevented, until and unless the user resets the permissions.

This is the normal behavior of the device, all by itself. But when a BES is involved, things get a little more complicated. The BES administrator can configure all users' BlackBerry devices to either deny or allow applications permission to perform potentially dangerous operations. If configured by the BES, the user will never see a dialog box from the device asking to grant permission to your application to do its work.

Your application will have to handle this possibility. The only way to do that in code is to wrap all your network-connection calls with a `try-catch` block and check for exceptions being thrown, of any type — and fail, gracefully. In addition, you should inform users prior to their purchasing your app from the BlackBerry App World that your application makes use of restricted APIs, and that they should take this into account before purchasing your application. Although this tack might turn some potential buyers away from your application, this is much safer than leading them astray after purchase.

Chapter 9

Networking Your BlackBerry App

*B*lackBerry devices are connected to the Internet all day long, from sunrise to sundown to sunrise again, every day of every week, every week of every month, every month of every year. All right, that's an exaggeration. But that's what you should assume when your app is on a BlackBerry — and your app should take advantage of this.

After all, today's world is internetworked: Every computer that wants to communicate is able to do so with every other computer that wants to. And that paradigm has shifted to the mobile computer world, down to the level of smartphones. Your BlackBerry app will run on a powerful handheld network platform, capable of firing a tractor-beam to drag in data for your users. And your users will expect nothing less.

For example, I created an app that uses the BlackBerry's networking capability to do several things, all of which illustrate what I mean:

✔ **Access the Help page:** Rather than place the instructions on how to use the app within the app itself, I put together a simple Web page that users can view from the comfort of the BlackBerry Browser. The app itself takes care of launching the browser to access the URL users will need to see the details of using my app, The Word Locker.

✔ **Set up password retrieval:** Users who misplace or forget their passwords need some way of retrieving them. In order to permit users to retrieve unknown passwords, The Word Locker provides a process through which users can identify themselves to the Web site, which can assist them in resetting passwords.

✔ **Resetting the password:** I lost track of how often I forgot very important passwords. The Word Locker anticipates this, and its Web site contains a storage system that accepts the information the user provides through the app, and if the information is correct, enables the app to allow the user to provide a new password without destroying the data.

In this chapter, using my app as example, I show you how to connect your app to a Web site and any other network data repository. Your apps will be able to pull data from sources on the Internet, and push data up to wherever you want it to go.

Using a Well-Connected BlackBerry

BlackBerry devices are smartphones, so they're connected to a wireless service provider such as AT&T, Sprint, T-Mobile, Verizon, or one of many others (at least as long as the bill is paid). Some BlackBerry devices can connect using Wi-Fi over a wireless router, and the numbers of these are increasing, keeping pace with the arrival of more Wi-Fi hotspots. Your users will very nearly always be connected to the Internet, and your app should make use of this fact in every way that you can imagine.

Users believe they are always connected to a networked world, so you should take advantage of that belief to deliver features that expand and enhance your app's goals with this belief at the core.

The communication channels available to your application on a BlackBerry are these:

✔ **Wireless service:** This is the wireless provider's network, using 3G and now 4G network technology to speed data between the phone and the Internet.

✔ **Wi-Fi:** Hotspots in hotel rooms, restaurants, coffee shops, commuter trains, and now even airplanes make access to the Internet an expected feature. In fact, the exceptional situation is for there to *not* be Wi-Fi access.

✔ **Bluetooth:** This technology started as a simple means for users to wirelessly connect headphones to their smartphones for hands-free operation. But your app can use Bluetooth communications to talk to another copy of your app running on a nearby BlackBerry device. This could lead to some interesting social networking apps.

As you can read in Appendix B, a BlackBerry might have its communications capability governed by rules set on a BlackBerry Enterprise Server (BES). This possible limitation can cause some of the communications channels that your app wants to use to be unavailable.

Checking for service

Your app can ask the BlackBerry smartphone about the kinds of communication channels that your app can use before your app makes any attempt to use them. This will enable your app to act responsibly, and your users won't be left with an app that seems to be nonfunctional when they try to download something — like high scores — from your Web site.

The BlackBerry OS provides two classes

- RadioInfo (net.rim.device.api.system.RadioInfo)
- WLANInfo (net.rim.device.api.system.WLANInfo)

to deliver information about a variety of different aspects of wireless communication:

- **Network type:** Your app can determine whether communications are occurring through the wireless service provider or Wi-Fi connection.

- **Radio state:** You should definitely check this value, which will let you know whether network communication is possible.

- **Whether data service is available:** The BlackBerry "data service" is a feature that enables a BlackBerry to communicate via TCP/IP networking through the wireless service provider. Service providers sell data plans to their BlackBerry users, so this value will indicate whether the BlackBerry your app is running on can make network or socket connections.

- **The current carrier network name:** Your app might not use this for its normal operations but for debugging on multiple devices with the multitude of carriers, knowing this information might assist when tracking down and isolating problems.

The preceding information is for network communications, such as Wi-Fi and the carrier wireless networks only. Bluetooth information is available through two Bluetooth classes:

- BluetoothSerialPort (net.rim.device.api.bluetooth. BluetoothSerialPort): You use objects from this class to read and write information across a Bluetooth connection.

- BluetoothSerialPortInfo (net.rim.device.api.bluetooth. BluetoothSerialPortInfo): You use objects in this class to provide more detailed information about Bluetooth connections.

The code in Listing 9-1 shows how to determine whether and which types of communications are available on a user's BlackBerry:

Listing 9-1:   Determining Communications Capability from within Your App

```
public boolean isWirelessOn()
{
    int radioState = RadioInfo.getState();
    return (radioState==RadioInfo.STATE_ON);
}


public boolean isWiFi()
{
boolean isWiFi = false;

    int networkType=RadioInfo.getNetworkType();
boolean validNet=(networkType==RadioInfo.NETWORK_802_11);
    boolean wifiOn=(RadioInfo.getActiveWAFs() & RadioInfo.WAF_WLAN)!=0;
    boolean wifiConnected= (WALNInfo.getWLANState()==WLANInfo.WLAN_STATE_
            CONNECTED);
    boolean isWiFi = validNet & wifiOn & wifiConnected;
    return (isWiFi);
}


public boolean isNetwork()
{
    int networkType = RadioInfo.getNetworkType();
    return (networkType!=RadioInfo.NETWORK_802_11);
}


public boolean hasBluetooth()
{
    return (BluetoothSerialPort.isSupported());
}
```

Choosing what service to use

You should analyze what your app is going to do with the information it collects from your users. This question should lead you to ask several others:

✔ **Does my app need to retrieve data from a Web site on the Internet?**
   This requires a network channel.

✔ **Does my app need to deliver data to a Web site on the Internet?**
   Similar to retrieving data from a Web site, this requires using a network channel.

✔ **Is my app going to receive data from a BlackBerry Enterprise Server (BES) via HTTP-Push?** This will require a network channel, but different from communicating with a Web site: You have to set up a "listener" within your app for a BES to contact to deliver data.

✔ **Does my app communicate with other nearby BlackBerry users?** The Bluetooth short-range communications channel is your best choice for this. However, a combination of GPS (Global Positioning System) and a network channel (if both services are available) could extend the distance beyond what Bluetooth allows.

Communicating with Services on the Internet

Your app connects to a service on the Internet by following these generalized steps (see Figure 9-1):

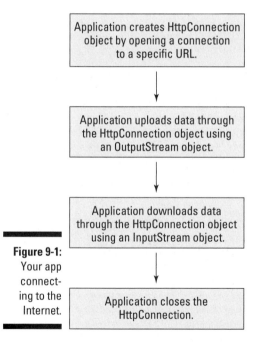

Application creates HttpConnection object by opening a connection to a specific URL.

Application uploads data through the HttpConnection object using an OutputStream object.

Application downloads data through the HttpConnection object using an InputStream object.

Application closes the HttpConnection.

Figure 9-1: Your app connecting to the Internet.

1. Your app opens a connection to the resource, defined by a URL.

   This connection is an HttpConnection object (or perhaps an HttpsConnection object), and your app might have to provide additional parameters to open the connection successfully.

2. Using the connection, your app delivers data *(upload)* to the service running at the URL and expecting incoming data.

This delivery is done through the use of an `OutputStream` object (`java.io.OutputStream`).

3. Using the connection, your app retrieves data *(download)* from the service (which may be as simple as a file containing the data).

   This retrieval is done through the use of an `InputStream` object (`java.io.InputStream`).

4. Your app closes the connection.

This is the standard approach to communication between a client application (such as your app running on a networked BlackBerry device) and a service (such as a Web site). Before I dive into the code examples to demonstrate how a BlackBerry app trades data with a network service, an introduction into packaging your data is appropriate.

Structuring your data

You will find it important and useful to structure your data because software behaves best when everything is orderly. Your application is either going to deliver data to a network service or retrieve data from one. For all the different data resources on the Internet available to your app, the data is going to possess some kind of structure. If your app is going to deliver or retrieve data in conjunction with a service under your control, you will be responsible for defining what that structure is. If your app is trading data with a service you don't control, you will have to determine what the data's structure must be.

My preferred form of data trading involves using XML (eXtensible Markup Language). You can find a great many good resources and tutorials about XML on the Internet, as well as several good books in the *For Dummies* series. My app uses XML to package the data delivered to the Web service and receives data from the service packaged as XML. The BlackBerry OS provides built-in functions to handle XML data that make reading and writing XML data blocks very easy.

My app, The Word Locker, stores users' notes in their smartphones. The user can access these notes only by entering the password. The Word Locker app provides a means to reset the password without deleting the notes. This process, if the user chooses to use it, requires the user to enter answers to selected security questions. The answers are then encoded and stored at `www.thewordlocker.com`.

The code in Listing 9-2 shows what the XML data that my app delivers to the Web service for initializing the security questions looks like.

Listing 9-2:   XML Data Delivered to a Web Service Running at thewordlocker.com

```
<?xml version="1.0" encoding="UTF-8" ?>
<thewordlocker version="1.0">
   <passwordResetInit>
      <query id="1">1913005938794</query>
      <query id="2">2967726624309986171</query>
      <query id="3">8439910125</query>
   </passwordResetInit>
</thewordlocker>
```

Here are the important points to remember about the preceding XML data:

- ✔ The first line must always be the XML identifier. Nothing else can be first.

- ✔ The `thewordlocker` tag (line 2) is the document tag. The `version` attribute is an identifier that tells the service what version of the XML data structure is being used by the client application. This lets the Web service know what to expect in the XML data that follows, in case the Web service is updated.

- ✔ The `passwordResetInit` tag is used to tell the service that the service should initialize the data for a future password-reset request.

- ✔ The `query` tag is used to provide specific identifying information to the service, to match that presented when a future password-reset request is made. The data within the tag is a compressed form of information the user provides within the application.

Because my app and the service are communicating with each other, each transmission of data between the app and the service will initiate a response from the receiver. This is to ensure that the data was received. The service's response to the XML data delivered in Listing 9-2 can be seen in Listing 9-3.

Listing 9-3:   The Response My App Will Receive after Transmitting the Data to the Service

```
<?xml version="1.0" encoding="UTF-8" ?>
<thewordlockerService version="1.0">
   <passwordResetInitOK/>
</thewordlockerService>
```

The response is very simple and easy to understand — just what you'd expect. If something bad had happened at the service's end of things, the service would respond with something different.

When users have forgotten the password to access their notes, they will initiate a password-reset operation. To do this, the user must enter information into the screen to answer selected security questions. After the user has entered the answers, the app transmits the data to the Web service using the XML data, shown in Listing 9-4.

Listing 9-4: The Word Locker App Delivers the Security Question Answers to the Service

```xml
<?xml version="1.0" encoding="UTF-8" ?>
<thewordlocker version="1.0">
   <passwordReset>
      <query id="1">1913005938794</query>
      <query id="2">2967726624309986171</query>
      <query id="3">8439910125</query>
   </passwordReset>
</thewordlocker>
```

Finally, Listing 9-5 shows the response sent by the Web service to my app when the information entered by the user and transmitted to the service is correct.

Listing 9-5: The XML Response Sent to The Word Locker When the Answers to the Security Questions Are Correct

```xml
<?xml version="1.0" encoding="UTF-8" ?>
<thewordlockerService version="1.0">
   <passwordResetOK/>
</thewordlockerService>
```

Very simple, and very easy for my app to read and interpret. When The Word Locker receives this response, the user will be allowed to create a new password without losing any data.

After you decide upon a structure for the blocks of data you want to move around, or after you determine how to interpret the blocks of data your app will be receiving from a service not under your control, you're ready to set up your application to connect to the service and deliver or retrieve data.

Your application will have to handle one more important issue, though, which I address in the following section.

Behaving like a well-mannered application

You will find that writing code to communicate with network services can be straightforward and easy. That's on your side of the process, which might lead you to innocently assume that network communications just work.

Unfortunately, the real world of communicating across the Internet is sometimes a bit unpredictable. Any number of problems can occur while your app is trying to make a network connection. Because of this, and because of the nature of the BlackBerry code that your app will execute to connect to a network service, your app's network communications code is required to operate from within a thread of execution that is separate from the main application thread. Chapter 7 covers how threads work in BlackBerry applications, but because this issue is important for networking, I take a few paragraphs to explain some of the code you see in the examples.

Your application runs as a process in the BlackBerry OS on the smartphone. Each process can have several different threads of execution: sequences of application code that execute independently. The BlackBerry smartphone's processor executes only one command at a time, but the commands for one thread can be paused while the processor starts executing the commands of a different thread. The BlackBerry OS does a great job of managing all that operation; you don't need to add anything special to your application to manage these low-level details.

However, certain operations your application can execute will *block,* which means that the processor is halted while it waits for something to happen. The BlackBerry OS won't allow the main event thread to become blocked, and this is the code in the BlackBerry `Application` object (`net.rim.device.api.system.Application`) that handles messages that come from the operating system and from the user.

The reason for this is simple: The BlackBerry user expects the device to be responsive to use, and if your application halts itself while waiting for incoming data or for a connection attempt to succeed (or fail!), this interferes with the user experience.

In addition, the BlackBerry OS maintains an event queue for each running application, which is limited in size. If your application halts the code that manages the event queue, the OS will pick up on this situation and terminate your app. Network communications operations generally take perceptible amounts of time to achieve either success or failure, and certain of these operations will block. To accommodate this behavior, your app must take a few precautions, as shown in Figure 9-2:

- ✔ Place all code that communicates with the network into a separate thread of operation.
- ✔ Provide a means for the thread to call back into your application's code.

    Usually, your application is going to want to find out whether the network communication operation in its own thread has succeeded or failed, so your thread code needs to provide a mechanism for transmitting that information, plus any information that's been retrieved from the network service, back into the main body of the application.

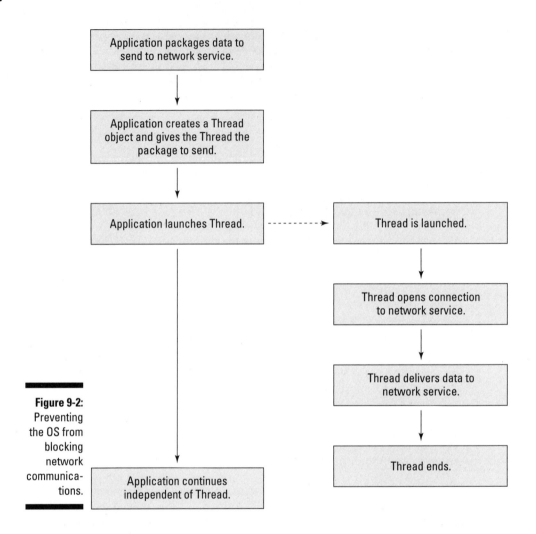

Figure 9-2:
Preventing
the OS from
blocking
network
communica-
tions.

The code examples in the next sections demonstrate using threads to assist in performing network communications.

Coding to send data to a network service

You're ready to create code that sends data to a network service. Your app accesses that service through a URL, and your app connects to that URL and uploads the data to it. Listing 9-6 shows the structure of a Java interface class that provides the callback mechanism for the network data retrieval thread. You can see the `interface` class provided to the thread so that the successful result of the data delivery, or an exception, can be delivered to the application.

A *callback* is a piece of code intended to be executed by a thread outside the main application thread of execution, which delivers information back to the main application thread. Much like an actor who performs in an audition and waits for the producers to call him back, the main application is waiting for the thread to call back with the results of its operations.

Listing 9-6:   The Interface Class Provided to the Thread

```
package com.karlgkowalski.wordlocker.util;

public interface WordLockerNetworkResponse
{
    public void passwordResetInitialized();
    public void passwordResetInitFailure( Exception inFailure );
    public void executePasswordReset();
    public void passwordResetFailure( Exception inFailure );
}
```

The `interface` class is pretty simple to understand, which makes explaining it easy:

✔ The thread calls `passwordResetInitialized()` or `executePasswordReset()` if the operation succeeds. One method is required for each of the two types of communications request (uploading the data to initialize a future password reset, and uploading the data to request a password reset).

✔ The thread calls either `passwordResetInitFailure()` or `passwordResetFailure()` if the operation fails. The parameter passed into each of those routines is the exception that caused the failure.

My application includes a class that implements this interface, and an instance of that class is handed to the thread classes that will communicate with the Web service to initialize or request a password reset.

The Word Locker app provides users with the opportunity to reset passwords without losing their notes, but only if they initialize the Web service with the answers to security questions they select. You can see the code in Listing 9-7 that acts as a repository in the app to package the answers the users provide. The `SecurityQuestionResponse` class also creates the XML delivered to the Web service.

Listing 9-7:   The SecurityQuestionResponse Class Implementation

```
package com.karlgkowalski.wordlocker.util;

import net.rim.device.api.system.DeviceInfo;
```

(continued)

Listing 9-7 *(continued)*

```
public class SecurityQuestionResponse
{
    private String m_q1;
    private String m_q2;

    public SecurityQuestionResponse( String inQ1, String inQ2 )
    {
        m_q1 = inQ1;
        m_q2 = inQ2;
    }

    public String getXml()
    {
        StringBuffer buffy = new StringBuffer();
        buffy.append( "<?xml version=\"1.0\" encoding=\"UTF-8\" ?>" );
        buffy.append( "<thewordlocker version=\"1.0\">" );
        buffy.append( "    <passwordResetInit>" );
        buffy.append( "        <query id=\"1\">"+m_q1+"</query>" );
        buffy.append( "        <query id=\"2\">"+m_q2+"</query>" );
        buffy.append( "        <query id=\"3\">"+this.getDeviceId()+"</query>" );
        buffy.append( "    </passwordResetInit>" );
        buffy.append( "</thewordlocker>" );
        return (buffy.toString());
    }

    private String getDeviceId()
    {
        int deviceId = DeviceInfo.getDeviceId();
        String deviceIdString = Integer.toHexString().toUpperCase();
        return (deviceIdString);
    }
}
```

Listing 9-8 demonstrates the basic code needed to perform the delivery of the `SecurityQuestionResponse` data to the Web service, and Figure 9-3 shows the progression:

1. The user selects security questions and enters the answers on the screen.

2. The application packages the information and launches a thread to deliver the information to the Web service.

3. The application waits for a response from the Web service but allows the user to continue using the app.

4. The thread opens a connection to the Web service.

5. The thread delivers an XML form of security question answers to the Web service by writing the data through an `OutputStream` that it gets from the connection.

6. The thread executes the `flush()` method of the `OutputStream`.

   This ensures that the data has all been delivered to the Web service before the next step.

7. The thread opens an `InputStream` from the connection and reads the success or failure response from the Web Service.

8. The thread informs the application about success or failure.

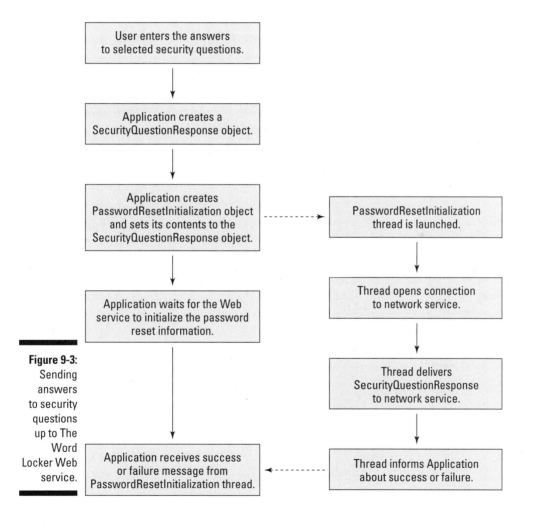

Figure 9-3:
Sending answers to security questions up to The Word Locker Web service.

Listing 9-8:   Transmitting the Security Question Responses to The Word Locker Web Service

```
/*
 * PasswordNetworkReset.java
 *
 * © Karl G. Kowalski, 2010
 * Confidential and proprietary.
 */

package com.karlgkowalski.wordlocker.util;

import javax.microedition.io.Connector;
import javax.microedition.io.HttpConnection;
import java.io.*;
import org.w3c.dom.*;
import net.rim.device.api.xml.parsers.*;

public class PasswordNetworkReset extends Thread
{
    private SecurityQuestionResponse m_data;
    private WordLockerNetworkResponse m_responder;

    public static final String WORDLOCKER_PASSWORDRESETSERVICE_URL =   "http://
            www.thewordlocker.com/passwordresetservice.asmx";
    public static final String  WORDLOCKER_PASSWORDRESETINITOK_TAG  =
            "passwordResetInitOK";
    public static final String  WORDLOCKER_PASSWORDRESETOK_TAG  =
            "passwordResetOK";
    public static final String  WORDLOCKER_FAILUREMESSAGE_ATTRIBUTENAME =
            "message";

    public PasswordNetworkReset( WordLockerNetworkResponse inResponder,
            SecurityQuestionResponse inSqr )
    {
        m_data = inSqr;
        m_responder = inResponder;
    }

    public void run()
    {
        boolean keepGoing = true;
        int attemptsRemaining = 3;
        while (true == keepGoing)
        {
            boolean connectionSuccess = false;
            try
            {
                attemptsRemaining--; // reduce count
                HttpConnection conn =   (HttpConnection)Connector.open( WORDLOCKER_
                    PASSWORDRESETSERVICE_URL );
                connectionSuccess = true; // got past attempt to open
                // set the proper HTTP request method
```

```
conn.setRequestMethod( HttpConnection.POST );
//create an output stream to upload data
OutputStream oStream = conn.openOutputStream();
//
oStream.write( m_data.getXml().getBytes() );
oStream.flush();
// create an input stream to show the result
DataInputStream diStream   =   new DataInputStream( conn.
  openInputStream() );
int availableBytes   =   diStream.available();
ByteArrayOutputStream   baos   =   new ByteArrayOutputStream();
// loop until no more bytes to read
while (0 < availableBytes)
{
   byte[]  wsResponse  =   new byte[availableBytes];
   diStream.read( wsResponse );
   // add incoming bytes to buffer
   baos.write( wsResponse );
   // find out how many more there are
   availableBytes   =   diStream.available();
}
// all bytes are now available in the baos
// time to check the response
// since the response is in XML, create an
// XML Document object to see it
DocumentBuilderFactory  dbf =   DocumentBuilderFactory.newInstance();
DocumentBuilder db  =   dbf.newDocumentBuilder();
// change the array of bytes just retrieved
// into an input stream
Document   doc =   db.parse( new ByteArrayInputStream( baos.
  toByteArray() ) );
// now check the response
this.checkResponseDocument( doc );
}
catch (Exception except)
{
   if (false == connectionSuccess)
   {
      // if an exception occurred in the
      // Connector.open() call, accommodate
      // the possibility that a subsequent
      // attempt might succeed (workaround for
      // issues discovered on a BlackBerry
      // Storm2 with a 5.0 OS where the call
      // to open failed the first attempt but
      // succeeded the second)
      if (0 == attemptsRemaining)
      {
         keepGoing   =   false;
         this.handleException( except );
      }
   }
```

(continued)

Listing 9-8 *(continued)*

```
            else
            {
                this.handleException( except );
            }
        }
    }
}

private void    checkResponseDocument( Document inDoc )
{
    if (null != inDoc)
    {
        if (true == m_data.isInitializer())
        {
            NodeList    initResponseNodes   =   inDoc.getElementsByTagName(
                WORDLOCKER_PASSWORDRESETINITOK_TAG );
            if (initResponseNodes.getLength() > 0)
            {
                // report success
                m_responder.passwordResetInitialized();
            }
            else
            {
                // failure
                this.handleAttemptFailure( initResponseNodes );
            }
        }
        else
        {
            NodeList    responseNodes   =   inDoc.getElementsByTagName(
                WORDLOCKER_PASSWORDRESETOK_TAG );
            if (responseNodes.getLength() > 0)
            {
                // report success
                m_responder.executePasswordReset();
            }
            else
            {
                // failure
                this.handleAttemptFailure( responseNodes );
            }
        }
    }
}

private void    handleAttemptFailure( NodeList inResponseNodes )
{
    Node    responseNode    =   inResponseNodes.item( 0 );
    // attributes should contain failure message
```

```
        if (responseNode instanceof Element)
        {
            Element responseElement =  (Element)responseNode;
            NamedNodeMap  attributes  =  responseElement.getAttributes();
            Node   messageAttributeNode  =  attributes.getNamedItem(
                WORDLOCKER_FAILUREMESSAGE_ATTRIBUTENAME );
            if (null != messageAttributeNode)
            {
                // retrieve the text of the failure message
                String  message =  messageAttributeNode.getNodeValue();
                Exception  except  =  new Exception( message );
                this.handleException( except );
            }
        }
    }

    private void   handleException( Exception inExcept )
    {
        if (true == m_data.isInitializer())
        {
            m_responder.passwordResetInitFailure( inExcept );
        }
        else
        {
            m_responder.passwordResetFailure( inExcept );
        }
    }
}
```

The `PasswordNetworkReset` class is created with two parameters: the object that implements the `WordLockerNetworkResponse` callback methods, which is called when the network communications have succeeded or failed; and the `SecurityQuestionResponse` object. Everyone hopes for success, but failures happen — but now you are prepared for it.

The code in Listing 9-8 demonstrates the basic approach for uploading information to a Web service and downloading the response. You can see that the Web service is contacted through the use of the URL `http://www.thewordlocker.com/passwordresetservice.asmx`. The `PasswordNetworkReset` thread object uses the `Connector.open()` method to make the network connection and open it. The object that is returned is cast to an `HttpConnection` type, which is a class that supports the methods used by the thread to transmit data to the Web service as part of an HTTP-POST transmission. The Web service returns its data into the connection, which the thread retrieves using the `Connector.getInputStream()` method. This stream is then provided to an XML document builder class that builds an in-memory XML document of the data coming in. The `Document` object that is created from the stream is then parsed to find the response of the Web service to the original request:

✔ The initialization request was successful. The body of the `Document` contains the `<passwordResetInitOK>` tag.

✔ The initialization request failed. The body of the `Document` contains an XML block that looks like `<passwordResetInitFailure message="failure reason">`.

✔ The password reset request was successful. The body of the `Document` contains the `<passwordResetOK>` tag.

✔ The password reset request failed. The body of the `Document` contains an XML block that looks like `<passwordResetFailure message="failure reason">`.

The successful end of this code results in the thread executing the appropriate success callback method provided by the object representing the `WordLockerNetworkResponse`. If anything goes wrong, the appropriate failure callback method of the `WordLockerNetworkResponse` object will be executed, and the reason for the failure will be provided in the form of an `Exception` object.

You may notice something interesting near the beginning of the `run()` method. I have set a pair of `boolean` data values, one called `keepGoing` and one called `connectionSuccess`. The first of these is a value used by a `while` loop, which causes the code to keep trying to connect to the network service. The second is initialized to `false`, and immediately after the `Connector.open()` call it gets set to `true`. The reason for this is that if the `Connector.open()` call throws an exception for any reason, then `connectionSuccess` will be `false` within the `catch` block. Inside the `catch` block, the code will return to the beginning of the `while` loop to make the connection attempt again, up to a total of three separate attempts. This is to guard against a particular situation that occurs on certain BlackBerry smartphones running certain versions of the BlackBerry OS. I discovered that occasionally the `Connector.open()` method would fail and throw an exception the very first time it was executed, but would succeed the second time it was executed. The code implemented above is a workaround for this issue. Although the issue appeared only on one smartphone running a specific version of the OS, it was easier to implement a try-it-again approach than to check for which OS version and which smartphone the app was executing on.

What you should remember from this are the following tips:

✔ Sometimes your app has to implement code to get around unexpected issues in the BlackBerry OS.

✔ Because the issue described previously was not apparent when testing the code on a simulator, you really do need to test your app on a real smartphone.

Making use of HTTP connections

As shown in Listing 9-8, if your app is going to be connecting to a Web server, using an `HttpConnection` enables your app to provide, as well as make use of, more detailed information regarding the connection. An `HttpConnection` object provides more methods for accessing HTTP header fields of a Web resource, some of which are

✔ `setRequestMethod(String)`: A Web server can respond to several different request methods. If you don't modify this, the default method used is `GET`. In The Word Locker's password reset communication I have set the request method to `HttpConnection.POST`, which is defined within the `HttpConnection` class.

✔ `int getLength()`: Your app can determine the length of the data to be delivered by the online resource. This value is retrieved from the `content-length` header field.

✔ `int getResponseCode()`: Your app will likely be most interested in calling this method because it returns the HTTP response code of the connection request. You can find a list of the available HTTP response codes online at `www.w3.org/Protocols/rfc2616/rfc2616-sec10.html`. You can also find a set of constants defined in the documentation of the `HttpConnection` class (`javax.microedition.io.HttpConnection`). The two most common are

  • *200:* This response code means: Okay, everything worked as expected.

  • *404:* This response code means: Nothing found at the URL (no file or service).

✔ `long getLastModified()`: This method returns the value of the `last-modified` header field. Your app can check this field to determine whether the information retrieved from the online resource is newer than the last set of data you retrieved.

All these methods are available for use as soon as the call to `Connector.open()` is executed and returns an `HttpConnection` object.

Making use of HTTPS connections

Sometimes Web services use a level of security that encrypts the transmission of information between a client application and the service. This type of connection uses an `HttpsConnection` object instead of an `HttpConnection` object. If the URL your app will use starts with `https://` instead of `http://`, you will want to cast the object you receive from `Connector.open()` as an `HttpsConnection`.

Your app may need to use an `HttpsConnection` when communicating a secure Web service, such as a bank or financial institution — the kind of communication that your users and the services your app is connecting to expect to be protected from any prying eyes. For example, if your app connects to a user's stock market account over the Web, use the `HttpsConnection` class: The stock market service will very likely require it. If you've set up your own Web service to provide stock information to your app's users and your app allows users to make trading decisions, users will expect that those orders are secure when your app communicates them to your Web service: This requires that your app communicates with your service using `HttpsConnection`.

Using `HttpsConnection` in place of an `HttpConnection` adds another new method not available in `HttpConnection`: `SecurityInfo getSecurity Info()`.

The object returned (`javax.microedition.io.SecurityInfo`) contains information related to the encryption protocol used to protect the communications, and can also be used to retrieve the certificate used by the Web service. Your app might need to access the certificate in order to verify that the service is owned and operated by the proper authority.

When your app executes `Connector.open()` for an HTTPS URL, the BlackBerry device will perform some verification of the credentials that the network service presents to the BlackBerry OS when the connection is attempted. BlackBerry smartphones come with some certificates preinstalled, and these are used to validate any new certificate that is presented. If the BlackBerry can't validate the service's certificate, the OS might interrupt the process and ask the user to accept or deny the attempt. If your user refuses to allow the connection to proceed, your application's attempt to connect with the service will fail.

Setting Up a Push Listener

The preceding example shows how your application running on a BlackBerry can communicate with network resources, such as Web pages and even scripts on Web servers. If your application is for a corporate enterprise environment and is intended to run on a BlackBerry connected to a BES, another network communication opportunity is available: running a process that waits for an incoming HTTP-Push connection from the BES.

HTTP-Push is the protocol that the BES and the BlackBerry Internet Service (BIS) use to deliver information to BlackBerry devices. BlackBerry users don't have to continually check for whether they've received new e-mail messages; the BES or the BIS simply pushes the messages out to their devices.

The BES also provides a feature that allows administrators to deliver data to applications running on specific devices using the same HTTP-Push mechanism, as shown in Figure 9-4. The process works like this:

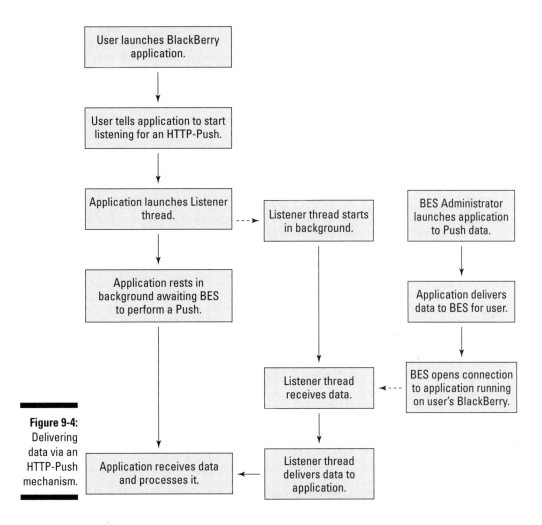

Figure 9-4: Delivering data via an HTTP-Push mechanism.

1. The user launches the app on the BlackBerry device.

2. The user initiates a push listener from within the app.

3. The BES administrator executes an application on a desktop machine.

   This application is something you would have to write for your users in addition to the application running on the BlackBerry device itself.

4. The desktop application connects with the BES and delivers a destination and a package of data for delivery to the user's device.

5. The BES queues the delivery of the data and eventually transmits it to the device.

6. The push listener on the device receives the information and processes it.

This operation requires more effort than simply connecting to a Web-based resource via a URL. In a BES-based environment, this process delivers information much more securely through the connection between the BES and the device. Note that the connection is one way: The push works from the BES to the device.

The BIS does not provide HTTP-Push features. This is a BES-only process.

On the BlackBerry device, your application effectively becomes a *server*, which means that your app waits for the BES to open a communications connection to your app. Of course, this means that your app will block while waiting for an incoming connection, and so the push-listener process must be launched as a thread separate from the main execution thread of your app. This also requires that your app is up and running until the BES makes the connection. When a user exits your application, the device will terminate all running threads. This means that your app will have to be careful when a user attempts to close your app, and prevent the app from getting killed. Luckily, there's a safe way to do this:

```
void Application.requestBackground()
```

Executing this method will cause the BlackBerry OS to place your app into the background. Effectively, this hides your application from the user, and the user will believe the app has exited. The app will receive no interaction from the user, but the thread containing the push listener will still be able to receive incoming connections.

The code snippet in Listing 9-9 demonstrates the run method of a thread that sets up a push listener and waits for incoming HTTP-Push connections from a BES:

Listing 9-9: The Setup of a Push Listener inside a Thread

```
public void run()
{
    try
    {
        synchronized(this)
        {
            StreamConnectionNotifier notify = (StreamConnectionNotifier)Connector.
                open( "http://:1234" + ";deviceside=false" );
            StreamConnection conn = notify.acceptAndOpen();
            InputStream dataStream = conn.openInputStream();
```

```
        DataBuffer db = new DataBuffer();
        byte[] dataBlock = new byte[1024];
        int dSize = 0;
        while (-1 != (dSize = dataStream.read(dataBlock)))
        {
            db.write( dataBlock, 0, dSize);
        }
        dataStream.close();
        conn.close();
        notify.close();
    }
}
catch (Exception except)
{
    // handle issues
}
}
```

The code in Listing 9-9 sets up a push listener that will block at the `accept AndOpen()` call, waiting for the BES to open a connection. This connection is at a specific port number, which must be between 1 and 65535, but several port numbers are not available:

✔ 80

✔ 443

✔ 7874

✔ 8080

Your app won't know before trying to use a particular port number whether that port isn't already in use — someone else's app may already be using it. Figure 9-5 shows you information about the `IOPortAlreadyBound Exception` exception that is thrown if two separate pieces of code try to start listening on the same port.

Figure 9-5: Your app receives this exception if it tries to listen on a port other code is using.

Port Tester

net.rim.device.api.io.
IOPortAlreadyBound
Exception: Port
[1234] is unavailable

OK

Your code enters the `catch` block in Listing 9-9 if the port your app tries to use is already in use. Because 65,000+ ports are available, there's only a small chance you'll run into a conflict. But because setting up a listener port is crucial for receiving HTTP-Push data from a BES, and because both the BES application and the BlackBerry app have to use the same port value, this is definitely something you will have to determine before you deliver your final product. In addition, running a listener thread in your app should be done only infrequently, so you're not using a particular port more than absolutely necessary.

The code in Listing 9-9 uses port 1234. After the connection is made, the execution of this code will continue, opening an input stream and setting up a buffer to hold the data. A byte array is created to hold 1,024 bytes, and the code execution loops while reading the stream of data 1,024 bytes at a time. When all is done, the `DataBuffer` object will contain all the bytes that were read in from the BES. Your app can then interpret this data and use it.

From the BES administrator side of things, a different application is required: namely, one that can connect to the HTTP-Push feature on the BES, as illustrated in Figure 9-6. The process for performing this is as follows:

1. The administrator collects information about the BES — specifically, the network location of the BES (IP address, host name, and so on).

2. The desktop application connects to the BES using a URL, and delivers the data as part of a `POST` request.

3. The administrator collects the data to be delivered to a user. This data is delivered via `HTTP-POST` to the BES.

4. The administrator determines the recipient to whose BlackBerry the data is to be delivered.

   This can either be the device's PIN (an 8-hexadecimal digit number, unique for each BlackBerry device), or the user's *enterprise* e-mail address (the e-mail address that the BES uses to identify the user).

5. The administrator executes the desktop application and provides all the preceding information to the application.

6. The desktop application opens an `HTTP-POST` connection to the BES at the IP address or host name provided.

   Included in the URL are the port number that the push listener in your application is listening to and also the recipient's PIN or e-mail address.

7. The desktop application writes the data to be delivered to the output stream of the connection.

8. The BES returns a status of `200` if everything succeeds (this is the HTTP response code for "everything is okay").

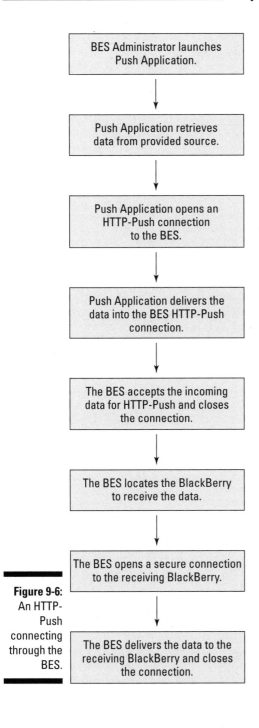

Figure 9-6:
An HTTP-Push connecting through the BES.

The code in Listing 9-10 shows an example method used in a desktop application to deliver data to a BES for it to push to a device.

Listing 9-10:   Connecting to a BES and Delivering Data for the BES to Push to a Device

```
public void executePush( String inHost, int inAppPort, String inUser, String
            inData)
{
   try
   {
      URL connUrl = new URL( "http", inHost, 8080, "/push?DESTINATION=
               "+inUser+"&PORT="+inAppPort+"&REQUESTURI=localhost" );
      HttpURLConnection conn=(HttpURLConnection)connUrl.openConnection();
      conn.setDoInput( true );
      conn.setDoOutput( true );
      conn.setRequestMethod( "POST" );
      OutputStream oStream = conn.getOutputStream();
      oStream.write( inData.getBytes() );
      oStream.flush();
      oStream.close();
      int contentLength = conn.getContentLength();
      if (contentLength > 0)
      {
         // check the response
      }
   }
   catch (Exception except)
   {
      // handle errors
   }
}
```

And that's all there is to BES push and BlackBerry push listening.

Recent changes within the BlackBerry Push services allow for BIS users to create push applications on their own with no BES required. The only caveat to this is that the free services are rather limited (8kb of data pushed through BIS) and applications must be approved. However, you can sign up for the BlackBerry ISV program and gain more access to the services — though the services aren't free. More information can be found at http://na.blackberry.com/eng/developers/javaappdev/pushapi.jsp#tab_tab_features.

Part IV
Finishing and Debugging Your App

The 5th Wave   By Rich Tennant

"I've tried every other way of debugging it. Let's just throw the chicken bones and see what happens."

In this part . . .

After you put together all the pieces of your BlackBerry application, you need to make sure that it runs with no surprises. In this part, you find out what it takes to move your application from a BlackBerry simulator onto a real BlackBerry device, and all the joys and challenges you might encounter. Developing software on your desktop PC for a virtual device is nice and safe, but here, you find out just what it's like to use your app as your users do. You also experience the thrill of hunting down and taming any pesky bugs that infiltrate your code. This is where you polish your app and smooth off its rougher edges.

And finally, your app is ready to upload to the App World. This part contains the steps you follow to organize all the various files and information you need to submit your app to RIM's reviewers for delivery to the BlackBerry App World.

Chapter 10

Running Your Code on a Real Device

*Y*our application is written, the JDE compiles and builds it with no errors, and it runs perfectly well in the BlackBerry simulators. Now the true test arrives: Does your app work on a real device?

The tests you've run so far using BlackBerry simulators demonstrate that your app will run without error. Deploying your app to a real BlackBerry smartphone is a simple procedure, and your app should run as easily on a real BlackBerry as it does on a simulated one. But there can be some not-so-obvious differences between running your app on a simulator in an environment where everything is controlled, and running your app on a physical smartphone whose behavior is somewhat less than perfect.

This chapter explains how to move your app from your desktop computer to your BlackBerry to test it. This is one of the most important parts of BlackBerry application development. Your users have real, physical BlackBerry smartphones. Just like Ford and GM test their autos not only at closed proving grounds but also on real city streets, you need to bring your app to a real BlackBerry before you're done with developing it. And RIM will definitely test it on a real smartphone when you submit your app for distribution through the BlackBerry App World.

Moving from Simulator to Device

Before you test your app on a BlackBerry, be aware that some of the BlackBerry OS classes that your application uses might require your application to be signed by using signing keys that you purchase from RIM. Signing your app is a very simple process — you use a tool that comes with the BlackBerry JDE you downloaded (see Chapter 2). As a result of signing your app, the BlackBerry smartphone OS will recognize that your app has been authorized by RIM to execute on the smartphone. This is a simple mechanism for BlackBerry users to know that RIM has approved your application. I go over the process of signing later in this chapter in the "Signing up to do signing" section.

You sign your app because RIM has restricted the use of certain code in the BlackBerry OS to apps that have been signed. Many of the classes available in the BlackBerry OS don't require your application to be signed to use them, and your application can do many useful and interesting things without needing to be signed. However, your application can do much more that is useful and interesting with those BlackBerry classes that require you to sign your app. For instance, here's a list of some features you might want to use in your application that require signing your code for execution on a real device:

- ✔ **Storing data in persistent or runtime storage**
- ✔ **Launching the BlackBerry Browser to view a Web site**
- ✔ **Creating, sending, and viewing e-mail and attachments**
- ✔ **Using the RIM encryption libraries**
- ✔ **Connecting to servers on the Internet**

After your application is signed, you are ready to install it on a device using *Desktop Manager,* which is the desktop PC application that comes with a BlackBerry smartphone to help users manage their BlackBerry and all the content they put on it. Chapter 14 gives more details about the BlackBerry Desktop Manager.

Signing up to do signing

To sign your applications, you need to register with RIM and pay a $20 fee to acquire three files you then use to generate your signing keys.

Follow these steps to register and download the signing files:

1. **Using a Web browser, navigate to `https://www.blackberry.com/ SignedKeys`.**

2. **Fill out all required information (name, address, credit card information, and e-mail address).**

3. **Enter a Registration PIN.**

   This is the most important step. Your PIN is a ten-digit number that you choose and provide to RIM in the appropriate field. I selected a combination of two area codes, and the ages of two members of my family.

   Keep a record of your PIN in a safe place. You need it later on when you are installing the files RIM will e-mail to you. RIM will also send you through the postal service a piece of paper confirming your purchase and with the PIN printed on it, but you will get this piece of paper sometime after RIM e-mails you the files to install.

   RIM will e-mail three files to the account you specify in the registration. These files contain the data necessary to set up the Signature tool you use to get your code signed. Each of the three files covers a separate set of restricted code in the BlackBerry OS.

   - *The file* `client-RBB-1234567890.csi` *covers some of the BlackBerry Application APIs (1234567890 is a number that RIM uses to identify your registration, and will be the same for each of the files).* You can use these APIs to give your app control over the BlackBerry Browser app.

   - *The file* `client-RCR-1234567890.csi` *covers some of the BlackBerry Cryptography APIs.* If your app performs any cryptographic functions, such as using a password to encrypt and decrypt sensitive data such as credit card numbers, you need to use these APIs. Using these APIs may cause issues with submitting your app to the App World because some governments dislike the idea of encrypted data running around outside the government's control. I go over this in Chapter 12.

   - *The file* `client-RRT-1234567890.csi` *covers some of the BlackBerry Runtime APIs.* You would use these APIs to access certain hardware features of the BlackBerry smartphone, such as GPS services.

4. **Double-click each file and follow the instructions to install them.**

   You need the PIN you registered with RIM when you purchased the signing keys in order to set up the Signature tool. After you've used your PIN in the installation of the keys RIM sent you, you no longer need it. However, the most important part of the setup process is that you need to supply a password that you use for as long as you have these keys. This is the only password you use when signing your apps with the Signature tool, so be sure to keep this in a safe place. After you install the data from the three files and the Signature tool is set up, you're ready to sign your application's code modules so your application will be permitted to execute on a real device!

Signing apps on multiple machines

Your signing keys, used to perform part of the app-signing process, are stored in a specific place on your computer after you install them. If you plan to do all your application builds on that one machine, you're all set.

However, over the years that I have been developing software, putting all my eggs (keys) in one basket (machine) sounds like an invitation to serious problems should something ever go wrong with that machine. At the very least, I want to be able to perform signing from a separate machine as well as my main build machine. That way, the chance that both machines will fail at the last possible second before I try to sign my application seems to be small compared with the chance that the one machine I can sign from will. So you might find it useful to copy the keys stored for the Signature tool to at least one other machine, or to back up the files on a CD or DVD.

You need to copy two files from the machine where you installed the Signature tool. On your Windows development machine, these files can be found at `C:\Program Files\Research In Motion\BlackBerry JDE 4.5.0\bin`. The two files are

- ✔ `sigtool.db`: This file contains information that the Signature tool uses to connect to the RIM signing servers for the three different signatures.

- ✔ `sigtool.csk`: This contains the public and private key information that the Signature tool uses to generate the data used as part of the signature of your app (this data is what the Signature tool transmits to RIM, which RIM then signs itself and sends back to the Signature Tool to add it to your app's code).

Under no circumstances should you modify the contents of these files. I keep copies of mine safe, on a CD-ROM, just in case my computer experiences a failure that corrupts its hard drive.

After you install the Java Development Environment (JDE) onto another machine, do the following:

1. **Copy these two files to the exact same place on the new machine.**

2. **Launch the Signature tool.**

   Read how to launch the Signature tool in the upcoming section, "Signing Your Application."

You might be required to create keys used to store the information in the DB and CSK files again, but both sets of Signature tool data (on the old and new machines) will execute a BlackBerry application signing process successfully.

This process is also useful for teams of multiple developers. Each developer is enabled to sign BlackBerry applications using their own workstation.

The Build Process, Revisited

As indicated in Chapter 3, the BlackBerry JDE performs a variety of tasks when it builds your application. The following files are created as a result of performing a build. (Here, `Application` is a placeholder for the actual name of your application.)

- `Application.cod`: This is the *code module* file: the compiled and linked program that will be installed and run — after being signed — on a BlackBerry device

- `Application.csl`: This file, used by the Signature tool, contains information about what kind of signatures is needed. This file tells the Signature tool which signatures are required, if any.

- `Application.cso`: Like the CSL file, this file is used by the Signature tool, in this case to determine which signatures are optional. You will always use the Signature Tool to sign your application's COD files, and so you don't need to pay too much attention to whether a signature is optional — just let the Signature tool do its job, and everything will work.

- `Application.debug`: This file is used during debugging, providing information that the JDE debugger uses.

- `Application.jad`: This is the Java Application Descriptor file, which allows your application to be hosted on a Web server for users to download it.

- `Application.jar`: This file is an intermediate container for your application's compiled Java classes, prior to their being packaged as a COD file.

- `Application.rapc`: This file contains some information that will be folded into the JAD file.

The Signature tool makes use of the COD, CSO, and CSL files.

Signing Your Application

You can launch the Signature tool in several ways:

- **From within the JDE:** This is the simplest way, seeing as how as you'll be spending most of your time developing the application using the JDE.

- **From the Start menu:** If you installed the JDE Components package, you can launch the Signature tool from the Start Menu by choosing Start⇨ Research In Motion⇨BlackBerry JDE Component Package 4.5.0⇨ Signature Tool.

✔ **From the command line:** The Signature tool can be found within the BIN directory in your BlackBerry JDE directory. At the command prompt, enter **java –jar SignatureTool.jar**.

I always launch the Signature tool from the command line. To save time navigating the file system to find the files I want to sign, I create a little batch script file:

```
java -jar "C:\Program Files\Research In Motion\BlackBerry
JDE 4.5.0\bin\SignatureTool.jar"
```

I save this in a file called `sign_app.bat` in the same directory as the app I want to sign. When I execute this script, the Signature tool is already at the right directory in the file system, with the files I want to sign ready to be opened. The nice thing is that I can reuse it by copying it to any directory where I have files that need to be signed.

The signing process goes as follows:

1. **Launch the Signature tool, using one of the methods described in the preceding bullet list.**

   Figure 10-1 shows the Open dialog box. The Signature tool wants to sign a file!

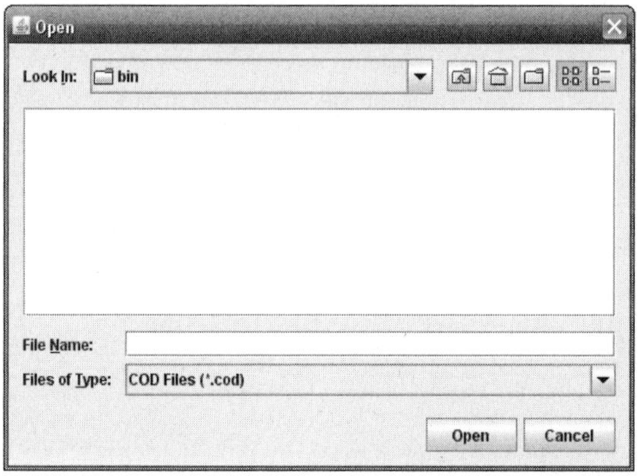

Figure 10-1:
The startup
screen
for the
Signature
tool.

2. **Navigate to find the COD file that the JDE built for your application.**

   This example uses the `StorageTest` application created in Chapter 6.

3. Select the COD file and then click OK.

Figure 10-2 shows the elements of your COD file that the Signature tool will need to sign.

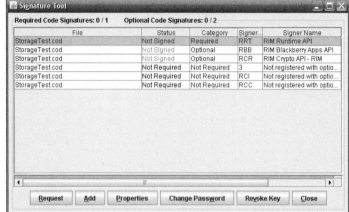

Figure 10-2:
The Signature tool's view of your unsigned COD file.

4. Click the Request button.

You're prompted for the password you supplied during the setup of the Signature tool. This is the password you entered into the Signature tool while setting it up with the three files RIM e-mailed to you — *not* the PIN you entered when you filled out the Web form to purchase the signing keys.

5. Enter your password in the Password text box and then click OK.

The items in the Status column will be updated as the Signature tool requests RIM to sign the COD module(s).

The result is a signed COD file. Figure 10-3 shows the message that the Signature tool displays when the signing request has been successful, and Figure 10-4 shows the screen with Signed in the Status column for each signature.

Figure 10-3:
The Success message.

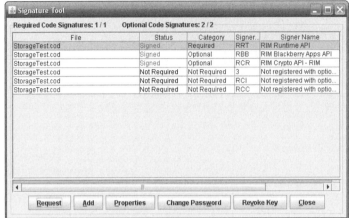

Figure 10-4:
The
Signature
tool's view
of your
successfully
signed app.

6. **Click the Close button to end the signature process.**

   Your application is now signed and ready to be loaded onto a real device.

Understanding what the signing process does

If your application makes use of any of the restricted classes in the BlackBerry OS, the OS will look for the required signatures within the COD file loaded on the device.

RIM restricts your application's use of certain classes, mainly to reduce the chance that a malicious application developer could do something unpleasant. While RIM's approach doesn't prevent such behavior, it does provide RIM with some capability to track down anyone who tries to abuse the use of the restricted classes. Some examples of the restricted classes are:

- ✔ **Message class:** Your app can access the smartphone's set of e-mail messages through a series of restricted classes, of which Message is the final result. I use my mobile device to send e-mail messages to my business associates when we're generating new ideas for new products; I would definitely be unhappy if those messages fell into a competitor's hands.

- ✔ **Phone class:** Your app can set up code to keep track of the smartphone when making and receiving calls. Similar to my e-mail privacy, I'd prefer to keep my phone usage to myself.

✓ **Cryptographic classes:** A large number of cryptographic classes are in the BlackBerry OS, and your app can use them to store information in an encrypted form to be decrypted later. Originally, the cryptographic libraries in the BlackBerry OS were the property of a third party, and so your app would have to use a separate signing key obtained by license from that third party in order to make use of these classes. Recently, RIM purchased that company and made the cryptographic classes available without a separate license. However, you must still sign your app to use these classes.

When you request your COD file to be signed using the Signature tool, after providing the correct password, the Signature tool creates a hash value of your application's code and then transmits that value to RIM's signing service. A *hash value* is a calculation of the numeric value of all the bytes of data in your COD file. The algorithm used to calculate the hash value is supposed to generate a unique value such that a small difference between two COD files will produce significantly different hash values — the objective is that the set of bytes in two different COD files will always produce two different hash values. This is what the BlackBerry smartphone OS uses to make sure that your application — the collection of bytes in the COD file — was the one that was actually signed by RIM.

The signing service — hosted by and at RIM — signs the hash value that the Signature tool delivered, incorporating information regarding your business organization through the keys that you purchased from RIM. The signed value is then returned to the Signature tool, which then incorporates the signature into your COD file. A separate signature might be required for different parts of the BlackBerry OS; in the example earlier in this chapter, one signature was required and two were optional, and all three were performed and added to the `StorageTest.cod` file.

By default, the simulators that come with the JDE, as well as any simulators downloaded separately from RIM, don't require COD modules to be signed. However, the simulators can be executed with a setting that does require COD modules to be signed, which makes them a better simulation of a real device.

Finding out if your signing succeeded or failed

The e-mail address that you used when you purchased code-signing keys will receive an e-mail from the RIM signing service for each signature it generates when you use the Signature tool. I recommend creating a folder to hold these e-mails and setting up a filter to automatically place them in that folder. That way, more important e-mails don't get lost amid dozens of messages from RIM.

The message in the e-mail is one of the following types:

- ✔ **A signing was successful.** In this (optimal) kind of message, you'll note that it indicates which signing was performed (required, optional, and so on), as well as how many signing attempts you have left. The number you start with is 2,147,483,648 and that gives you approximately 68 years of signatures at one every second. I haven't yet found out what happens when you run out.

- ✔ **A signing failed.** This can happen for a variety of reasons. Most commonly, the password was entered incorrectly. As I mention previously, failure also happens because of network problems or because RIM's service is temporarily down.

Deploying Your Application onto a Real Device Using Desktop Manager

Here's one more step before your application is ready to be loaded onto a real device. A separate file, which does not get created by the build process, must be created for Desktop Manager. The file is the ALX file (Application Loader XML) and has the file extension .alx. This file contains information about your application for Desktop Manager and the BlackBerry OS to understand.

You create an ALX file as follows:

1. **Open your project in the JDE.**

   I'll use the StorageTest project in this sequence of steps.

2. **Right-click the project element, and then choose Generate ALX File from the contextual menu that appears.**

   Figure 10-5 shows what you should see just before selecting the menu item.

   The ALX file will be created in the folder containing the COD file.

   The contents of the ALX file are generated from the project properties that are set for the application. To edit the project properties

   a. *Right-click the project element and then choose Properties from the contextual menu that appears. Alternatively, you can press Alt+Enter.*

   The Properties dialog box appears.

   b. *Select the General tab to see or modify some of the content that will be placed in the ALX file.*

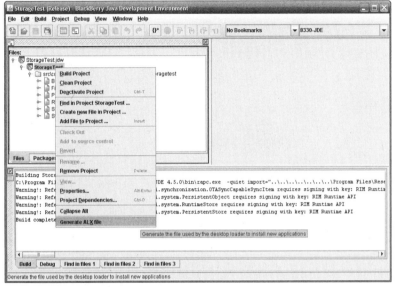

Figure 10-5:
Select the
menu item
to generate
an ALX file.

The most important project property, especially regarding the ALX file, is the application version number.

The application version number — a.b.c — is what Desktop Manager will use to determine whether to replace a version of your application already on a device with a newer one.

After you have the ALX file generated and the COD file signed, Desktop Manager is the tool you use to deploy your application to a device. Here's how you do that:

1. **Launch Desktop Manager by choosing Start⇨All Programs⇨BlackBerry⇨Desktop Mananger.**

   You should have already installed it when you unpacked your device. Figure 10-6 shows the startup screen for Desktop Manager version 4.6.

2. **Connect your BlackBerry to your computer with the USB cable.**

   DM picks up on the fact that you connected your BlackBerry and displays the BlackBerry device PIN.

3. **Click the Application Loader icon.**

   This switches to the Application Loader screen, as shown in Figure 10-7.

4. **Click the Start button.**

   The DM connects to the device. Both DM and the device flash their screens until DM figures out what applications are already on the device, and lists them, as shown in Figure 10-8.

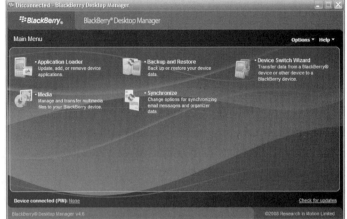

Figure 10-6:
Starting
up the
BlackBerry
Desktop
Manager.

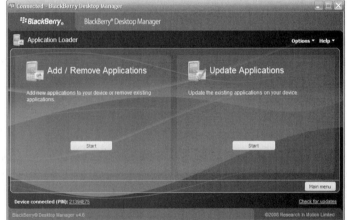

Figure 10-7:
Load an
applica-
tion on the
Application
Loader
screen.

5. **Click the Browse button, and in the dialog box that appears, navigate to your application's ALX file.**

6. **Click Open.**

The DM processes the data and decides whether to include your application in the list of applications to be deployed to the device. This is one place where problems can occur. Desktop Manager might refuse to accept your application, with the message Unable to find any applications for the device. This results from a situation where there is a mismatch between Desktop Manager and the particular device connected to your PC.

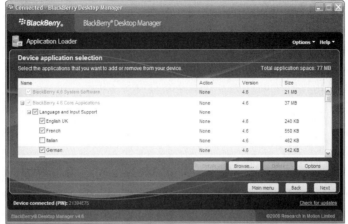

To fix this problem, you must do one of two things:

- *Update the version of Desktop Manager to match the version of BlackBerry device OS on the device.* Desktop Manager has a version number, such as 4.6, that matches the BlackBerry OS version number on the device.

  Note: In general, software written for one Blackberry OS version number will run on a BlackBerry OS with the same or higher version number. This is not always 100 percent true, but it is almost always true.

- *Install the BlackBerry OS onto your PC that matches the OS on the BlackBerry device.* Don't worry. You're not replacing Windows on your desktop PC; you're providing a copy of the BlackBerry device OS to Desktop Manager so that it learns how to "speak" appropriately to your device.

Desktop Manager displays a list of items with check boxes next to them, indicating which items are marked for deployment to the device. In addition, the Action column indicates what Desktop Manager will do with the marked items. Unchecked items will be removed from the device if they are installed; their Action value will be Remove. Checked items are added to the device if they're not installed; their Action value will be Install. Everything else will have an Action value of None, indicating no action will be taken.

7. Click Next.

This displays a summary window, indicating the actions that Desktop Manager will take with your next click.

8. Click Finish.

Your app is installed onto your device, and Desktop Manager displays `Update complete` and `The loading operation was successful.`

You have now successfully deployed your app through a USB cable and onto a real device. Now it's time to see what it looks like.

Running Your Application

I assume that you're familiar with launching applications on a BlackBerry, so here I will focus on finding the application you just installed. You can find your app in one of two places, depending on what BlackBerry device you have and what BlackBerry OS is installed:

- ✔ **Downloads folder:** Because your app is not standard equipment, the Desktop Manager delivers it into the Downloads folder. This happens on devices running OS 4.6 or later, such as the BlackBerry Storm or Tour.

- ✔ **Applications folder:** Devices running OS 4.5 or earlier have an Applications folder, and you'll find your application hiding there. These devices include the BlackBerry Pearl and 8800.

After you find your app, you're all set to launch it.

Because you've coded the application perfectly, tracked down all the bugs with the simulator, and successfully signed and deployed your app, you'll find no issues running it on your BlackBerry. You'll also find it behaves exactly like it did on the simulators, but you might notice a few discrepancies between the app running on a simulator and running on a device:

- ✔ **Performance is slower.** Your desktop PC running a BlackBerry simulator generally runs faster than the actual BlackBerry device, unless you're using a really slow PC.

- ✔ **Graphics are different.** Your desktop PC's resolution (unless you're a graphics professional with really high-end equipment) is a lot worse than your BlackBerry screen's resolution. This means that pixels on the BlackBerry screen are smaller than they are on your monitor; the simulator's display makes things look larger, and the device's screen shows them smaller.

You might want to experiment with your user interface elements to determine what works and what doesn't. Creating an intuitive user interface is still more an art than a science. You can find some user interface design assistance from RIM at `http://docs.blackberry.com/en/developers/deliverables/6625/`.

Chapter 11

Debugging Your Application

*I*n an application developer's fantasy world, applications would always be perfect the moment you wrote the last line of code, the JDE built the COD module, the ALX file was buffed and shined, the signatures were glued on, and Desktop Manager streamed the resulting bytes down into a perfectly working BlackBerry device.

In the real world, however, applications don't always execute correctly. Sometimes they don't even build correctly — the dream gets cut short before you even need to use the Signature tool. So you need to find a way to fix things.

Using the Debugger is very easy. Debugging, however, is a long and painful process. Your application is only ever as complete as its most challenging user — and the more users you deliver to, the more challenges they will subject your application to. You can lock down the more obvious defects in your application through judicious use of the Debugger and the tools available in the JDE.

In this chapter, I show you how to use the JDE Debugger, and how to use the BlackBerry Event Logger to track down the bugs and fix them.

Understanding Where Errors Occur

Luckily, the JDE provides tools you can use to analyze your application while you're coding it, while it's running in the simulator, and even while it's running on a device. And as you develop more BlackBerry applications, you will discover that you find errors during all three phases. Here's a look at what defects in your code can cause for each phase:

✔ **While you're writing code:** Face it. Everyone makes typing mistakes. Sometimes they're easy to spot; sometimes they're not. The BlackBerry JDE is unforgiving about typing mistakes, though, and will refuse to build your application unless it's satisfied that all the words are spelled correctly. That includes all the elements of your classes, their methods, and their variables.

The BlackBerry JDE uses the standard version of Java to compile your source code, albeit with a subset of its libraries. Just like the standard Java compiler, the BlackBerry JDE might spew several lines of errors when only one part of your code is really broken. You should always start your review of coding errors from the first one that the JDE shows you because fixing this first might resolve all the other error messages the JDE displays.

✔ **While you're using the simulator:** The BlackBerry simulator will catch a great many runtime errors. In Java, when something really bad happens while a program is running, the Java Virtual Machine throws an exception. This is a special situation, one that your code might or might not be ready to handle. For instance, attempting to call a method of an object before it has been created will cause the Java Virtual Machine to throw a `NullPointerException`. The JDE Debugger halts the execution of the application if this exception is not caught by your application's code. At that point, the JDE provides substantial information regarding what was attempted and what part of your code is misbehaving.

Some BlackBerry OS classes and methods require your code to anticipate exceptions that might be thrown, and others might throw exceptions even without requiring your code to prepare for the possibility. And sometimes, bad things still get through despite the best of intentions.

✔ **While you're running the app on a BlackBerry:** Running your application many times on the simulator might shake out a great many runtime errors, but you still need to execute your application a number of times on a real device. This provides more, and even significantly different, types of errors that your application will need to handle. These problems tend to be caused more by logic errors: places in your code where the BlackBerry is happy to do precisely what you told it, but you told it to do the wrong thing. Unfortunately, the BlackBerry can't intuit what you meant for it to do, and so it just goes ahead and does its best to succeed at completing the orders you gave it.

The BlackBerry JDE displays any coding errors you made when you tell it to build your application. You'll also see it showing warning messages about stuff the compiler wants you to know. In the top part of Figure 11-1, you can read about three separate errors, which all come from a typing mistake in an earlier line — the code in that section depends on a variable called `ordinal`, which was defined earlier as an integer except back in the definition I spelled it as `ordnal`. The bottom of Figure 11-1 shows you some warnings. Many of these can be ignored — for instance, the compiler will tell you about each code module that must be signed because your code is using BlackBerry classes that only signed applications are allowed to use, and I'm pretty certain you're planning to sign your app when it's built, regardless.

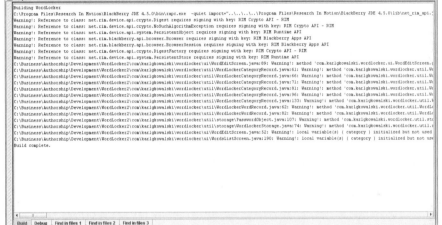

Figure 11-1:
Coding errors and warning messages show you something is wrong.

The BlackBerry JDE also comes with its Debugger, which is a tool that executes your code on a simulator and allows you to see precisely where in your source code bad things are happening. The Debugger won't execute if your code doesn't build, so coding errors must be fixed first. However, because runtime errors can be found only while your code is running, you will find the BlackBerry Debugger to be an invaluable tool for tracking down just what's going wrong. And you can also debug your application running on a real device while looking at the source code it's executing from within the JDE.

Using the JDE Debugger

As I mention earlier, you can debug your application while it runs in a simulator within the JDE. Every time you launch a simulator from the JDE, you are running its Debugger. The lowest pane of the JDE window has a

Debug tab that becomes the active tab when you launch the simulator, and shows informative messages as the simulator starts up. See Figure 11-2.

Figure 11-2:
The JDE
Debugger
buttons.

Debug tab is active.

The Debugger comes with buttons for standard debugging operations:

- **Go (F5):** The Debugger continues from where it was stopped, first executing the line it has stopped upon.

- **Break Now:** The Debugger halts execution, wherever the app currently is, just as if it had hit a breakpoint. There is no function key assigned to this operation — so you can't accidentally hit it. Because the application is mostly running BlackBerry code while your app is running, clicking the Break Now button almost always halts the code while it's executing something inside the BlackBerry OS. You see the result shown in Figure 11-3. I use Break Now to halt my application when I believe my code is doing something incorrect, or the application is not responding.

✔ **Step Over (F10):** The Debugger executes the line it stopped on, and then stops at the next statement or breakpoint. (Read more about breakpoints in the following section.)

✔ **Step Into (F11):** If the Debugger stops on a line of code that's a method call, Step Into tells the Debugger to go to and stop at the first line within the method. Note that this is useful only for methods within your code, and not code provided by the BlackBerry OS.

✔ **Step Out (Shift+F11):** The Debugger executes every line of code from the point at which it stopped, until it exits the method in which it stopped.

✔ **Run to Cursor (Ctrl+F11):** The Debugger executes every line of code from the point at which it stopped, and stops at the line where you place the editing cursor. I use this if I don't know precisely where an error is hiding. I set a breakpoint at the beginning of a block of code where I suspect the problem lies, and then place the cursor further ahead in the code, and click this button. If the Debugger gets to the cursor's location, then I know the problem is somewhere else.

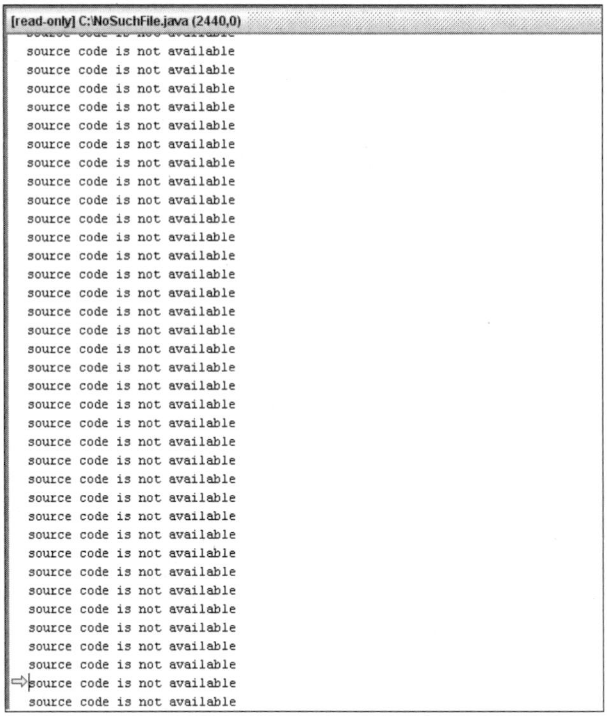

Figure 11-3:
The JDE Debugger after clicking the Break Now button, showing that no source code is available for you to see.

[read-only] C:\NoSuchFile.java (2440,0)
```
source code is not available
source code is not available
source code is not available
source code is not available
source code is not available
source code is not available
source code is not available
source code is not available
source code is not available
source code is not available
source code is not available
source code is not available
source code is not available
source code is not available
source code is not available
source code is not available
source code is not available
source code is not available
source code is not available
source code is not available
source code is not available
source code is not available
source code is not available
source code is not available
source code is not available
source code is not available
source code is not available
source code is not available
source code is not available
source code is not available
source code is not available
source code is not available
source code is not available
source code is not available
```

Setting, deleting, and disabling breakpoints

A *breakpoint* is a location where the JDE places a flag that the simulator will detect, telling it to halt just before it tries to execute that line of code. You can use breakpoints to stop the operation of your application before it does something wrong. For instance, if your application is storing data within the persistent store (see Chapter 6 for details on the BlackBerry persistent storage) but doesn't seem to retrieve the correct data, you could set a pair of breakpoints: one in the code that stores the data, and one in the code that extracts it. With your app stopped at either breakpoint, you can step through each code statement and check the data at each step to make sure everything is as it should be. If your app is doing something wrong, some part of the data at one of the steps won't be what you expect. At that moment, you can track down the source of the error.

Setting a breakpoint within your application is simple:

1. **Open a source code file in the JDE.**

2. **Move the cursor onto the line of code where you wish to set a breakpoint and then press F9.**

   You can also right-click the line of code and choose Set Breakpoint at Cursor from the shortcut menu that appears.

   The breakpoint appears on the far left of the line of code as a large red dot, as shown in Figure 11-4.

Breakpoint

Figure 11-4:
An active
breakpoint.

When the application executes, the Debugger halts the simulator at the indicated line of code. The application now waits for you to tell the simulator how to proceed. Normally, you set a breakpoint to check the data in use by the application where the Debugger has stopped it — you can check every piece of data in the method being executed, and in the member variables of the class this method is part of. So if your app has halted in the `initialize()` method of a screen that is about to be displayed, you can review all the text that the screen is going to show to make sure that the buttons the user is supposed to see have all been created and added to the screen.

When you no longer need the breakpoints you set, you'll want to remove them. After all, when you've fixed the code that was misbehaving, there's no need to keep stopping to see whether it behaves like it's supposed to. To remove a breakpoint, right-click the breakpoint and choose Delete Breakpoint at Cursor from the shortcut menu; alternatively, click the line containing the breakpoint and press F9.

You can also disable breakpoints. Disabling a breakpoint means the debugger will no longer stop at the breakpoint when your code executes, but the breakpoint is still indicated (gray instead of red) on the screen. This allows you to temporarily remove the effects of a breakpoint but doesn't completely erase it, making it easy to remember where you left the breakpoint. To disable a breakpoint, right-click and choose Disable Breakpoint at Cursor.

Executing your application with the JDE Debugger

To start your application with the JDE Debugger and the JDE simulator, do the following:

1. **Press F5.**

   This builds your application (if necessary) and launches the simulator.

2. **Using the simulator, navigate to your application and launch it.**

That's all there is to it. The Debugger is connected to your application and monitors its progress. If you have set any breakpoints, the debugger halts when one is reached, and the JDE displays an arrow pointing to the line of code where it stopped. Figure 11-5 shows you the JDE stopped within my application, right before the app shows its first screen.

The simulator is a separate application. When a breakpoint is reached and the Debugger stops your application, the simulator will appear to be unresponsive. You have to bring the JDE main window to the front. Windows flashes the JDE item on the taskbar to indicate that the JDE wants your attention.

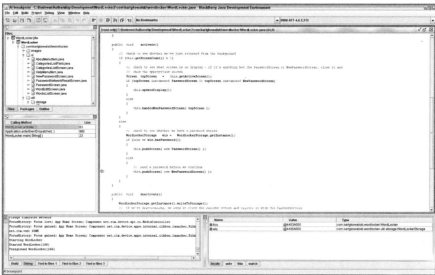

Figure 11-5:
The
Debugger
stopped
right before
the New
Password
Screen
object is
pushed onto
the screen
stack.

Using the BlackBerry Event Logger

My favorite form of debugging desktop applications involves printing text to a screen, or better still, a file. I call this "`printf`-debugging," after the C-language print-to-standard–output function, `printf`. It's very retro, from a time before integrated development environments (IDEs), before source-level debuggers (yes, I'm old enough to remember those years). It's also very reliable, and it works with just about every programming language or development platform.

The BlackBerry compiler will accept the standard Java form of `printf`, `System.out.println()`, but this will work only on a simulator through the JDE. Luckily, the BlackBerry OS provides a mechanism to do the same thing: the BlackBerry Event Logger (`net.rim.device.api.system.EventLogger`). In this section, you discover how your application can deliver messages into the BlackBerry event log, as well as how to retrieve them.

Your application can place text and other types of messages in the BlackBerry event log. Your application thus can provide operational feedback to you while you're developing your code, so you can keep track of what's going on while the application is running and get a list of all the important information your application comes across. This assists your debugging efforts when you need to know precisely where something is going awry, especially if a problem occurs when a user is running your application.

The BlackBerry OS itself uses the event log, but the OS events are rather cryptic and difficult to interpret. However, every time your application catches a *throwable* Java object, a message is automatically sent to the event log by the OS. And if an *exception* is thrown that your code does not catch, the OS writes a stack trace of that exception to the event log.

Setting up your application to use the Event Logger

The `EventLogger` class provides only static methods. You don't have to create an `EventLogger` object: You simply execute the method you want, whenever you want. You must register your application with the Event Logger before you can start logging messages to the event log.

Here are the steps to follow to register your application and then send data into the event log:

1. **In your code, create a unique application identifier.**

   The simplest way to do this is as you did for accessing the persistent storage model, covered in Chapter 6:

   a. Open the application's main class file in the JDE.

   *b. Type the fully qualified class name (for example, **com.karlgkowalski. storagetest.StorageTest**).*

   c. Select the entire fully qualified class name.

   d. Right-click and choose Convert Your Application Class Name to Long from the shortcut menu.

   The JDE converts the text string in place to a long integer.

2. **Early in your application's execution, register the unique identifier and your application's name with the Event Logger by entering the following code:**

   ```
   EventLogger.register( your-app-id, "your-app-name", EventLogger.VIEWER_
           STRING );
   ```

   This statement links your application's name with the event log whenever your application's unique identifier is used to log an event. In addition, the `VIEWER_STRING` log type tells the BlackBerry event log that it should present information coming from your application as a string of text. This is the best choice.

3. **Execute `EventLogger.logEvent()` where you want to write information into the event log:**

   ```
   String logMessage = "message for event log";
   EventLogger.logEvent( your-app-id, logMessage.getBytes() );
   ```

That's all there is to sending events to the BlackBerry event log.

Your application can't read events from the event log. It can only write events into the log.

Viewing and extracting the event log

The BlackBerry event log can be read at any time on the device itself. To view the event log on the device, hold down the Alt key and type **lglg.** (For a touchscreen device using BlackBerry OS 5.0 or later, show the SureType keyboard, hold the Alt key until it locks, and then type **,5,5.**)

Your device displays a screen much like the one shown in Figure 11-6.

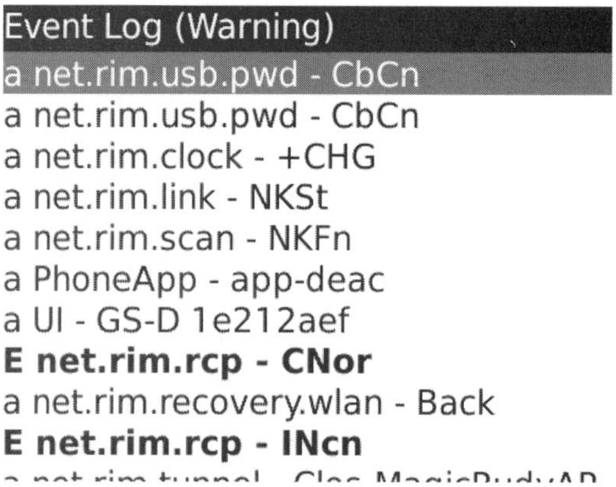

Event Log (Warning)
a net.rim.usb.pwd - CbCn
a net.rim.usb.pwd - CbCn
a net.rim.clock - +CHG
a net.rim.link - NKSt
a net.rim.scan - NKFn
a PhoneApp - app-deac
a UI - GS-D 1e212aef
E net.rim.rcp - CNor
a net.rim.recovery.wlan - Back
E net.rim.rcp - INcn
a net rim tunnel Clas MagicBudyAP

Figure 11-6:
A
BlackBerry
event log
displayed on
a device.

Viewing the event log using the device is somewhat challenging because of the device's screen size and because you can only look at the contents of one message at a time. However, you can avoid reading the log on the device in a couple ways:

✔ **Copy the day's contents and paste them into an e-mail.** While viewing the log on the device, press the Menu button and select Copy Day's Contents. Figure 11-7 shows you a dialog box that asks whether you want all messages or just a subset — I recommend choosing All. Selecting this item copies the log messages for that day into the BlackBerry's copy buffer, and you can then switch to the Messages app and paste the text into an e-mail message. (I usually send the message to my e-mail address so I can view it on my PC.)

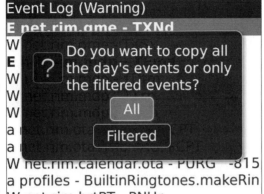

Figure 11-7:
Choose All
to copy the
entire
day's log
messages.

> ✔ **Download the entire event log to your PC.** I have found this to be the
> approach I use the most because I can search the contents of the entire
> log (or as much as the device has retained) at my leisure.

To download the event log to your PC, follow these steps:

    1. Connect your device to your PC with a USB cable.

    *2. Launch a command line window and navigate to the JDE's bin
      directory.*

    If you installed the JDE using the default location, that should be
    here:

```
C:\Program Files\Research In Motion\BlackBerry JDE 4.5.0\bin
```

    3. Type the following into the command line prompt:

```
javaloader -u eventlog > logfilename.txt
```

    You now have a file `logfilename.txt` in the current directory on
    your PC that contains all the contents of the event log from your
    BlackBerry device.

I prefer to name my downloaded log files using a combination of date, time,
and BlackBerry device, such as `20100213_1738_8900.txt`. This gives me
enough information to be able to differentiate log files from different devices
and dates.

For example, the text in Listing 11-1 shows some event log statements
generated for one of the example applications, `ScheduledEvent`, found in
Chapter 7. These statements were at the end of a thousand-line log file
downloaded from a BlackBerry running the application. The first, second,
and last messages came from the application; the third message was generated
by the BlackBerry OS. In each message are the following items:

- ✔ guid: This is the numeric value that the application initializes the EventLogger with, to uniquely identify the application.

- ✔ time: The date and time the event was logged.

- ✔ severity: The value representing the severity of the event that was logged. You can set this value as desired for each log statement your app sends to the EventLogger, but I recommend using the default value (0).

- ✔ type: This is the type of EventLogger message, defined when the EventLogger is initialized by your application. I recommend initializing the EventLogger with EventLogger.VIEWER_STRING as done in the steps to set up the EventLogger earlier in this section.

- ✔ app: This is the name of the application, set when the EventLogger is initialized.

- ✔ data: This is the information delivered using the EventLogger. logEvent() method. This is where you can see the text delivered in the three messages logged by ScheduledEvent.

In the last message, you can see the text displaying some data retrieved from the ScheduledEventScreen class in its fieldChanged() method (note that this text is part of the data delivered to the EventLogger, and is something the application code provides).

Listing 11-1:   BlackBerry Event Log from the ScheduledEvent Application

```
guid:0x96D9820232F61853 time: Thu Jul 15 21:48:18 2010  severity:0 type:2
            app:ScheduledEventApp data:Event Logger start message
guid:0x96D9820232F61853 time: Thu Jul 15 21:48:18 2010  severity:0
            type:2 app:ScheduledEventApp data:Finished initializing
            ScheduledEventScreen
guid:0x34B0DF76DFC172F2 time: Thu Jul 15 21:48:29 2010  severity:0 type:2
            app:net.rim.simapp data:ABRT
guid:0x96D9820232F61853 time: Thu Jul 15 21:48:39 2010  severity:0 type:2
            app:ScheduledEventApp data:ScheduledEventScreen.fieldChanged>
            secondsToDelay[7] repeats[true]
```

The event log will also contain a record of exceptions that your application runs into. Listing 11-2 shows what a NullPointerException being thrown in the ScheduledEvent application would look like in the event log. Note that this exception was intentionally created by the application.

Listing 11-2:   Exceptions Your App Encounters while Executing

```
guid:0x9C3CD62E3320B498 time: Thu Jul 15 22:41:42 2010  severity:1 type:3
               app:Java Exception data:
   NullPointerException
   ScheduledEvent constructor threw me!
   ScheduledEvent
      ScheduledEvent
      <init>
      0x303
   ScheduledEvent
      ScheduledEvent
      main
      0x2AD
```

The standard elements are all there, but after those pieces, some more information comes about the NullPointerException and where in the application it occurred. The last ten lines of the exception listing are broken down like this:

✔ **Line 1:** NullPointerException. This is the type of the exception that the application ran into. You should know that this means the application attempted to execute a method on an object when the object had not yet been created.

✔ **Line 2:** ScheduledEvent constructor threw me! This text is the message that was added to the NullPointerException when it was created.

✔ **Lines 3–6:** These four lines indicate four items:

   • *The application where the exception occurred:* ScheduledEvent

   • *The class where the exception occurred:* ScheduledEvent

   • *The method where the exception occurred:* <init>, which in this case indicates the ScheduledEvent constructor

   • *The offset (in bytes as a hexadecimal value) from the beginning of the method where the exception occurred:* 0x303

✔ **Lines 7–10:** Similar to the previous four lines, these show information about what part of the application made the call into the code at the previous four lines. This represents the sequence of method calls that the OS keeps track of, where one method executes code in another method, which executes code in yet another method, and so on.

A `NullPointerException` is the most common exception your app will encounter — it happens because your app tries to use an object that hasn't been created. The BlackBerry compiler won't issue a warning or an error while it creates your application if you don't set up a `try/catch` block around all the possible places in your code where a `NullPointerException` might occur.

Although I prefer to use event logging as my main debugging approach, this method does have limitations. The primary drawback of this method is performance. If you write information to the event log at every step of your app's execution, you slow down the device. Therefore, I use event logging to narrow the scope of examining my application's behavior, ideally drilling down to one method in one class, where I can then heavily log events and inspect just that one area of my application. This does prolong the experience, as you create log statements, execute, review the log, and repeat until you discover the misbehaving piece of code.

Keeping Track of Bugs

You will spend a great deal of your time writing your application. And although it would be fantastic to write completely bug-free code, your application will eventually run afoul of someone doing something, somewhere, that causes a malfunction. Perhaps the worst that will happen is your app just crashes and refuses to run. Then again, perhaps your bug will be more subtle, only executing every third Tuesday at midnight but only during a full moon — and taking out the entire accumulated data at that precise moment, leaving your users really upset, and you unable to reliably reproduce the error.

You don't need a full-featured, bug-tracking database to support small development efforts. However, the sooner you start taking development seriously, the sooner you will find yourself delivering high-quality apps. Serious development efforts require equally serious bug-maintenance efforts. And while you might find it easier to just list all the "known issues" with your application in a plain vanilla text file, at some point, you will find it worth the effort to formally write up all issues you or your users encounter in a more-structured repository.

Unfortunately, most bug-tracking software systems require a database server for storing and searching through all the issues you will record. In addition, some of the free systems require using a Web server to support a Web-based front end to the database. This means that you will have to get your hands dirty to keep track of your bugs. Only a little dirty, though, because the free database and Web servers are pretty easy to maintain if you use them only for bug tracking. And you shouldn't provide access to them from outside your connection to the Internet, which can reduce the chances of a security vulnerability that could compromise your system.

Getting serious about tracking bugs

The most important action you can take to keep track of your application's bugs is to write down everything. This may sound simple, but you will find that it can be very difficult to actually accomplish when you're running your app and something unexpected happens. The simple bugs are easy to reproduce, and generally are the result of one particular set of circumstances that occurred at the last possible moment before your app did something that caused a bad thing to happen. This is what makes them easy to resolve.

You will find that the more-challenging bugs are subtle, and depend upon a sequence of events — some user-initiated, some not — that occurs in the right order. You might not pick up on all the elements of the sequence, or the proper order, when the bug causes the operation of your app to go wrong. Usually, you see only the end result, and lose track of all the steps that transpired (seemingly correctly) on the way to that end result. Of course, the subtle bugs typically show up only when you're trying to solve or see something else, and your focus is on something *other* than the problem that shows up. But, hey! No one said this was going to be easy.

Here's a list of the information you will want to keep track of when you find an "anomaly" in your code:

- **Steps to reproduce:** Recording the steps to reproduce an issue gives you two critical pieces of data: what it takes to cause the problem, and how to know when the problem has been resolved.

- **Device type:** Luckily, only RIM makes BlackBerry devices, so you don't have to worry about problems from differences among various manufacturers. However, you do still have to consider the potential differences between the various devices. Does it have a trackball or a trackpad? A real keyboard or (on a touchscreen) a virtual one?

- **Device operating system.** Each BlackBerry has its own version of device OS, different from that of other device types and wireless service providers. When RIM changes the OS enough to renumber the device OS, sometimes an app that used to work no longer does.

This information will help you define what aspects of your app a bug is interfering with. Because there are so many different ways an application can go wrong, you will want to establish the limitations of the device plus your app to "fence in" the behavior of the bug. The following is a list of circumstances that bring bugs into existence:

- **Improper initialization of variables:** This is probably the biggest cause of all bugs, and happens more frequently than any other cause. In a Java class, a member variable can be initialized in any method of the class. You will see that my classes generally have an `initialize` method, used to set up the values of the member variables for an instance created of that class. However, that doesn't prevent initializing the member variables in some other method, which gets executed at some other point in time. You can restrict access to internal member variables through the disciplined use of `getter` and `setter` methods, and by making all your member variables have `private` or `protected` access control.

✔ **Improper timing of threads:** You can avoid this error by avoiding the use of all threads, all the time! Still, you will see this happen eventually. This situation occurs when your app has multiple threads running at the same time, and you haven't prepared for the possibility that the first one to finish is not the one you expected.

✔ **Unhandled exceptions:** This particular type of bug can be challenging to track down. You should always keep the following idea in mind: An exception can be thrown at you without any warning. Although the BlackBerry APIs clearly specify when a class' methods can throw an exception during their operation — and the compiler will not let you escape without setting up your code to handle one of these — sometimes exceptions are thrown that are *not specified* by the APIs. You can't predict these, which means you will be exceptionally frustrated when you come across one. However, you'll still have to figure them out.

Using a bug-tracking program

Using a bug-tracking solution solves the problem of keeping track of everything that goes wrong, which also enables you to trace progress in fixing things. In addition, sooner or later, users are actually going to use your app — and this means that they'll start finding more bugs for you. Users are a lot like unpaid Quality Assurance engineers: They will exercise your application in ways you never thought possible.

So far, my favorite bug-tracking solution is Bugzilla (`www.bugzilla.org`). It's fairly easy to get it up and running, but as I mention previously, you need to install both a database server and a Web server to make use of it. Bugzilla depends on the Web server to deliver the forms and reports to you, and uses the database server to store all the information regarding the bug tracking it does. You can find documentation for setting up all three pieces on the Bugzilla Web site. I like Bugzilla because it's free and because it's fun to use and supported by expert developers who like to keep it that way. However, Bugzilla is an open source effort, which means getting support for it can be a little challenging. The Bugzilla support Web page (`www.bugzilla.org/support`) provides a link to some Bugzilla consultants you can contact for paid support of issues you encounter. Or you can search through the Bugzilla newsgroup (`news://news.mozilla.org/mozilla.support.bugzilla`) to find answers to questions others have asked in the past, and even ask your own.

You can get away without using a bug-tracking system for a while, but the more prolific you are, the more apps you develop, and the more users you sell to — meaning, you're going to have to get organized on this. For a small shop, your development machine itself will suffice to provide a running Apache Web server, database, and Bugzilla deployment.

Implementing a solution ahead of time and disciplining yourself to use it correctly is an investment in the future, which will reward you in the end.

Chapter 12

Submitting to the BlackBerry App World

*Y*our app is finished. You ran it through multiple simulators, multiple times. Maybe you even tested it in multiple languages (say, French, German, Spanish, and Italian). You also installed it onto a real BlackBerry to make sure the app runs as perfectly there as it does on a simulator because, after all — especially for corporate apps — a real BlackBerry behaves noticeably different from its simulator. Your app is now ready for the BlackBerry App World, though, so it's time to get it there.

In this chapter, I submit the app I wrote called The Word Locker to the BlackBerry App World. Every smartphone I've used has an application for taking notes that comes with the phone. This turns your smartphone into an electronic notepad — flashes of genius will hit you from time to time, and because your smartphone is always nearby, you can jot down these notes quickly and save them. The BlackBerry smartphone comes with Memo Pad. The Word Locker takes this a step further by providing a level of security — no one can see the notes you create without entering the correct password.

This chapter shows you how to get your app into the App World, taking you through the final steps for bringing your app out to users whose lives will be greatly enhanced as a result of your efforts.

Getting Ready to Submit Your App

Before you can submit your app to the App World, you must be a vendor. In Figure 12-1, you can see the entry point for App World Vendors, which is the starting point for you to become one. The URL for the portal is https://appworld.blackberry.com/isvportal. (Chapter 2 walks you through that process.) After you receive an acknowledgment e-mail from RIM indicating that your request to become an official vendor has been approved, you can submit your first app. Submitting your application to the App World is a little more involved than just uploading the COD file, though: You also have to provide *metadata* (information about the application you're delivering) to help users understand your app and decide whether to download it.

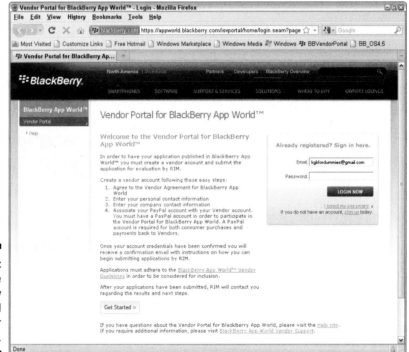

Figure 12-1:
Entering the
BlackBerry
App World
Vendor
Portal.

You can find more information about submitting applications and managing your vendor data at

```
http://docs.blackberry.com/en/developers/deliverables/15522/BlackBerry_App_
        World_storefront-Administration_Guide--1086301-0409112053-
        001-2.0-US.pdf
```

Have all the required information in the following list ready to go before you start the process of submitting your app to the App World. This will make the process go more smoothly and faster. (***Note:*** The App World Vendor Portal site has a habit of timing out after a few minutes of inactivity, so if you can get out of the gate with all your information and files ready to go, you can avoid wasting time re-entering required items that didn't get saved.)

Here's what metadata and files (some of which is optional) you need to have ready when you submit your app to the App World:

✔ **Application name:** This is the name you implemented and built with the Java Development Environment (JDE). Most important is the restriction against using special characters such as ™ or ®. RIM recommends using only ASCII characters. (This means you should only use characters in your app's name that can be typed directly from your PC's keyboard, excluding function keys. Pretty much anything alphanumeric will be okay.)

✔ **Application icon or logo:** You need to provide an icon or logo as a PNG (Portable Network Graphics) file for the App World to use to display and identify your application to BlackBerry users. The file must be sized at 480 x 480 pixels. See Figure 12-2 for some example logos.

Figure 12-2:
Application
icons.

✔ **Category:** RIM provides 20 categories of applications through the App World, so you need to decide upfront where your app belongs. ***Note:*** You can select only one category for your app. The current set of categories are

Business	Education	Entertainment	Finance
Games	Health & Wellness	IM & Social Networking	Maps & Navigation
Music & Audio	News	Photo & Video	Productivity
Reference & eBooks	Shopping	Sports & Recreation	Test Center
Themes	Travel	Utilities	Weather

You can find the current number of apps available for each of the categories by navigating to the BlackBerry App World site. The first App World Web page you come to shows the available categories, but not the number of apps in each. To find this information, simply click any of the categories, and the current count of apps in those categories will appear. In each category, the app count for each subcategory (if any) is also displayed. The top three most populous app categories are Themes, Games, and Reference & eBooks. The least populous app categories are Weather, Shopping, and Education. Your app will appear with all the other apps in your chosen category, which means it will be fighting to catch the eyes of the App World visitors looking for an app like yours. A weather or shopping app will have less competition than a game or a theme, but don't let that stop you from writing your app.

✔ **License type:** RIM provides three different license types that you can choose from to allow users to download your application:

- *Free:* Users download your app, and neither you nor RIM make any money off the transaction. This is clearly not going to turn you into a millionaire. I submitted The Word Locker as a Free app because it was fairly simple in its design and has no frills. One reason I did this was to generate feedback from users to help guide me in improving the app — and an improved Word Locker may be submitted as a Paid app.

- *Paid:* Users download your app only after making a payment, which is split between you (70 percent) and RIM (30 percent). To charge users to download your app, you have to have signed all of the license agreements during the process where you registered to become an App World Vendor. (Chapter 2 covers the vendor registration process.) If your app is submitted as a Paid app, you will also have to choose a license model, covered next.

- *Try & Buy:* This license type allows users to download a version of your app with limited functionality for free, and then purchase the full version after they get hooked. Note that you may have to provide two separate COD files for this license type, depending on which license model you choose for your license.

✔ **License model:** You have to choose a license model if your app's license type is either Paid or Try & Buy. RIM provides the following license models to choose from:

- *Static:* This is the simplest license model. No other information is required. RIM handles all the details. For Try & Buy, this license model requires you to submit two separate COD files: one is your Try app with limited functionality, and the other is the full-featured Buy app.

- *Single:* This license model requires you to supply a single license key that is used to unlock the application.

- *Pool:* This license model is similar to the Single model, except that you provide RIM a collection of different serial numbers that unlock the application. RIM delivers a different serial number to each user.

- *Dynamic:* This license model means that the App Store server makes an HTTP connection to a URL — which you must also provide during the submission process — when it is time to generate a license key. The Web site at the URL must generate a dynamic license key based on your own algorithm. You can find more detailed information about this at

  `http://na.blackberry.com/eng/developers/appworld/Dynamic_License_Flow.pdf`

✔ **Application description:** The description is your place to tell users what your app does to make their lives better. Your application description is your primary marketing tool, so you want to make sure you cover the basic details of what your application does in a way that gives users a vision of how using your app will be beneficial. You are limited to 2,000 characters, though, so write concisely and compellingly. Here's an example of good and bad application descriptions:

- *Bad:* The Word Locker application stores your notes, and only someone who has the password can see them.

- *Good:* Your notes are safe from prying eyes with The Word Locker. Enter a password, and you can store any text you like, knowing only you can see your notes.

✔ **Wireless service providers:** RIM sells BlackBerry smartphones through a wide variety of service providers. Generally, you want to deliver your app to as many providers (and therefore customers) as you can, but if you want to give only one provider's users exclusive access to your app, this is where you so indicate that. (I haven't found any good reason for excluding the customers of a particular wireless service provider.)

✔ **Country/Region:** You can limit your app to specific countries to which the App World delivers. Again, the fewer restrictions you place on the sale of your app, the more you will sell. One reason you may choose to limit which countries your app is available for purchase could be related to export control restrictions. For instance, The Word Locker required an export control classification number that indicates the fact that some cryptographic code is executed (to hide the password). Restricting the country to USA-only would mean less export control because the product would not be available outside the United States. Of course, I would be limiting my sales because of this restriction. You can select from the following:

- *Available in All Countries:* This selection allows App World to offer your app in all the countries where App World is available.

- *Available Only in the Countries Selected Below:* Selecting this option reveals a list of all the countries in the world, and you select those countries where App World will allow users to download your app. Note that although all countries are listed, the App World is not necessarily available everywhere.

- *Available in All Countries Except for the Ones Selected Below:* This selection is the opposite of the previous bullet. You select those countries where you do *not* want App World to allow users to download your app.

✔ **Releases:** Your app must have at least one release version number, although for the Try & Buy license type, you need two: one for the trial version and one for the full release. You can use any numbering scheme you prefer, but most BlackBerry applications generally follow the dotted-triplet format (for example, version 4.2.1).

✔ **File bundles:** You provide a collection of information about your application, including the COD file(s) that make up your app. In addition, you can set up different versions of your app to be provided to different BlackBerry devices. For example, you might have optimized a version of your app for certain devices, such as the BlackBerry Storm, to take advantage of its capability to do both landscape and portrait orientations. You can upload the different COD files for each separate device at this stage of the submission process.

✔ **Screenshots (optional):** You can provide screenshots from your app. The App World allows up to 50 screenshots, each of which can be up to 640 x 640 pixels. GIF, JPG, and PNG image types are accepted. You will want to show off screens from your app to give potential buyers some visuals of your app in use.

Deciding on a price for your app

The pricing tiers for BlackBerry applications are as follows:

✔ **Free**

Users don't pay to download your application.

✔ **$2.99–$19.99,** in increments of $1

✔ **$19.99–$99.99,** in increments of $10

✔ **$99.99–$599.99,** in increments of $50

✔ **$599.99–$999.99,** in increments of $100

I chose to set The Word Locker price as Free because it is a fairly simple app with very few frills. I have already thought of features that I will probably add in a future version — for instance, the capability to back up the set of data to a PC using Desktop Manager. I have an idea for another app already, and if I can get it implemented, I will definitely charge something for it because I believe there's a market for this particular app idea, and the price will be low enough (less than $10) that a BlackBerry user who makes use of this app will be happy to pay a small fee for it.

You can search through the App World for apps similar to yours and discover what other developers are asking for their apps. A quick look over the App World Catalog shows that the most populous categories have about 10 percent of their apps for free, and the lesser categories have about 50 percent of their apps for free. As of this writing, the most expensive game app was $14.99, and the most expensive business app was $199.99.

Paying for the submission

When you submit your application for RIM to review and finally deliver to the App World, RIM will charge you $20 for the effort. This fee comes from the $200 you pay when you register to become a vendor at the BlackBerry App World, which in essence means that you have a total of ten submissions already paid for in advance. If you use them up, you'll have to purchase another set of ten submissions for another $200. RIM is also happy to take your money at any point, so you can purchase as many submissions as you have money to pay. The important points to remember about this are

- ✔ Each time you submit an application to be reviewed, it will cost one submission ($20).

- ✔ If your application is rejected by RIM, submitting a revised application will again cost one submission.

- ✔ If you submit multiple versions of the same application to be reviewed, with each version submitted for a different BlackBerry model, the combined set of application versions counts as one submission.

Understanding What RIM Looks for in Your App

The BlackBerry App World allows one-stop shopping for BlackBerry users to find and download software to make their BlackBerry smartphones more useful. RIM wants to sell more smartphones, of course, and so RIM wants users to enjoy the experience of not only being able to find quality applications in their App World, but also the experience of the applications themselves. Accordingly, your application must meet RIM's expectations of quality and consistency. Although I'm not privy to all the details of what RIM does and does not look for, here are a few do's and don'ts to keep in mind:

- ✔ **Your app should not crash the user's BlackBerry smartphone.** This is something that holds true on just about every machine or operating system. Users abhor and eschew apps that crash or terminate abruptly. RIM will run your app on the BlackBerry smartphones you designate as being able to run your app. So your app must not crash.

✔ **Your app should comply with the BlackBerry App World Vendor Guidelines.** You can find the guidelines by going to the Vendor Portal site at `https://appworld.blackberry.com/isvportal` and clicking the BlackBerry App World Vendor Guidelines link.

✔ **Your app should be careful about memory usage.** BlackBerry smartphones may have a couple of hundred megabytes of *operational memory* (memory your app will use to manipulate information while running), but that's total memory, used by the OS and any other running applications. For example, if you're planning an app that creates animation in the palm of a user's hand, be sure that your app is very stingy when it comes to creating objects. You want your app to "play nice" with the limited resources.

✔ **Your app should be careful about communicating over the wireless network.** A lot of users pay for every byte that gets moved up to or down from the network, so your app should inform the user of the potential for large amounts of data being uploaded or downloaded, and give them the option of living without that particular feature.

✔ **Be careful with your application description.** Remember that the App World is a public place, with no parental oversight restrictions, and your app's description will be read by a wide variety of people. RIM will want all the aspects of your app displayed at the App World to make the user's experience of using the App World to reflect well upon RIM and the App World in general. RIM will probably consider your application description worthy of review although it's not clear that RIM will reject an application and require another submission payment just because your wording is not "politically correct." One of the reasons I mention this is that although this has not occurred in my experience with the App World, I have seen this happen while submitting an application to another online marketplace for a different smartphone. The description my colleagues and I put together included the app's name in just about every sentence, and the reviewer felt that this was a little too much. So, we removed about one-half of the usages of the app name, and within a day or two, the app was available for download.

After RIM reviews your application submission and accepts it, you will be able to "light it up" and mark it ready to be downloaded at the App World. On average, the time between submitting your app and RIM completing the review is about one business week. After your app is accepted, it takes about 24 hours from the time you post your application for sale at the App World until it becomes available for users to download. I cover this in the next section.

Submitting Your App to the BlackBerry App World

This section covers the steps of delivering all the data you collected, plus your BlackBerry application to the BlackBerry App World, for review by RIM and eventual successful downloads by your prospective users. Ready?

1. **Do a clean build of your app from the JDE (see Chapter 3).**

   This step makes sure that your code compiles and builds correctly — and, most importantly, that nothing has inadvertently gone wrong since the last time you built it.

2. **Sign your COD file (refer to Chapter 10).**

   Without the signature, your app won't run on a real device, and RIM doesn't sign your submitted COD files for you.

3. **Point your browser to `https://appworld.blackberry.com/ isvportal`.**

   Refer to Figure 12-1 to see the Vendor Portal page.

4. **Log in, using the username and password you selected when you registered to become a vendor.**

   Figure 12-3 shows the successful login page.

Figure 12-3: A successful vendor login.

5. **Click the Manage Applications link.**

   This brings you to the Manage Applications page, which shows a list of all the apps you've submitted and their status. For the first app you submit, this page will be pretty empty.

6. **Click the Add Application button.**

   Figure 12-4 shows the result. Your next step is to tell RIM about any Export Control information you have regarding your application. Because RIM will sell your application in foreign countries, certain procedures must be followed to ensure that you're not trying to deliver high-value technology without permission.

7. **Fill out the Export Control information and then click Next.**

   The Export Control information you provide to RIM is used to determine whether RIM can sell your application in a country other than that of its origin. The U.S. government wants to be sure that the software you ship to customers outside the US meets the export control regulations. For example, a mobile app that provides access to a user's eBay account can be exported because it won't be doing anything more than a Web browser can already do. However, the U.S. government has decided to restrict foreigners' access to some types of applications. For instance, an application that uses strong encryption to store data entered by a user on their BlackBerry would make it difficult for the agents of a law enforcement agency to retrieve the data in a timely manner. My app The Word Locker ran slightly afoul of this part of the App World submission, and I had to determine how my app was to be classified under the U.S. export control regulations. Because my app didn't use encryption but did use part of the BlackBerry cryptographic libraries, RIM wanted to know precisely how the app should be classified so that it would not be punished for selling something outside the U.S. borders that the U.S. government classifies as not to be exported. You can find out more about U.S. export classifications at www.bis.doc.gov.

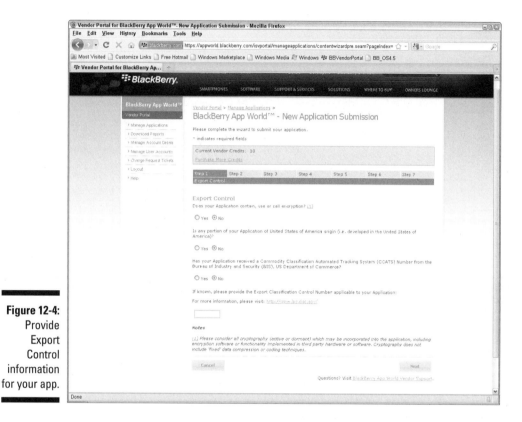

The Enter Main Application Data screen appears, as shown in Figure 12-5.

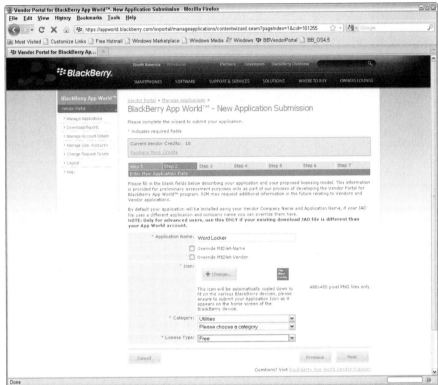

Figure 12-5:
Tell the App
World about
your app on
this page.

8. **Enter the requested application data and then click Next:**

   • *Application Name:* Enter your application's name in the text box.
     Note: You can't use copyright or trademark symbols in the
     application's name, as mentioned in the section, "Getting Ready
     to Submit Your App." The two check boxes below the Application
     Name field should be left unchecked.

   • *Icon:* Click the Add button and select the 480 x 480 image you
     want to be used for display through the App World on the various
     BlackBerry devices. ***Note:*** This is not necessarily the same file as
     that used within the application for display on the device Home
     screen; the two images should be nearly identical in appearance,
     however.

   • *Category:* Select the category that your app best fits from this
     drop-down list.

   • *Sub-category:* If your Category selection reveals another drop-down
     list, select the subcategory that your app best fits.

- *License Type:* Select the type of license from the drop-down list. Refer to the earlier section, "Getting Ready to Submit Your App" for more about the License Type.

After you click Next, the Add Languages and Descriptions of Your Application page appears, as shown in Figure 12-6.

9. **Select the language(s) that your app supports, enter a description of your app in the Application Description(s) text field, and then click Next.**

The Distribution Restrictions page appears, as shown in Figure 12-7.

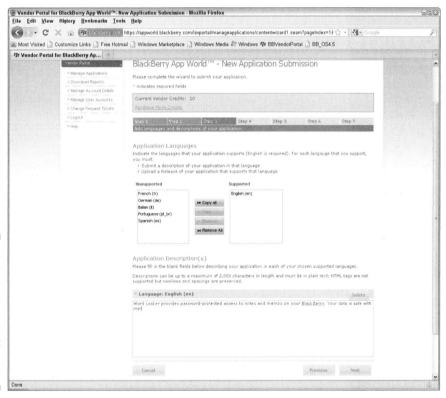

Figure 12-6: Add your application description and the languages you support in your app here.

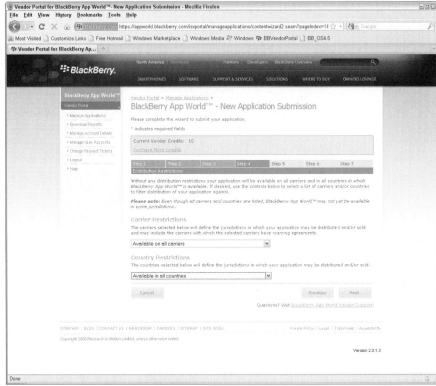

Figure 12-7:
Select the
carriers and
countries
your app
will be
running on
(or not).

10. **Select which carrier(s) your app was designed for and which country(ies) you want to sell your app to from the Carrier Restrictions and Country Restrictions drop-down lists, respectively; then click Next.**

    This stage allows you to set the restrictions on which wireless service providers' users might or might not be permitted to download your app — and, similarly, which countries' users may be permitted to download your app.

    The ScreenShots page appears, as shown in Figure 12-8.

11. **Click the Add Screenshot button and browse to the screen shot(s) you want to upload; then click Next.**

    You can add up to 50 screen shots on this page.

    When you click Next, the Releases page appears, as shown in upcoming Figures 12-9 and 12-10.

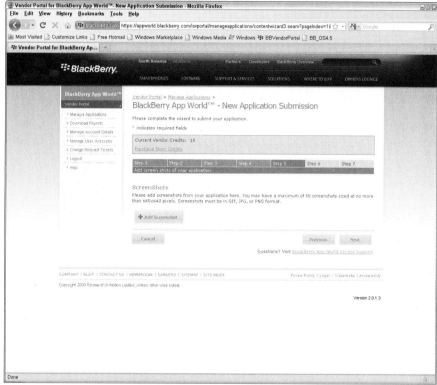

Figure 12-8:
Upload
screen
shots of
your app
for users to
view before
they buy.

12. **Click the Add Release button to expand the Web page. Provide the following information, and then click Next:**

- *Selected Release, Release Version, and Release Notes:* Select the release number and enter the version number. In the Release Notes text field, add any comments about the current release.

- *View Bundle, Bundle Name, and Minimum OS:* If you have different COD files for different devices or OS versions, create a separate File Bundle for each by clicking the Add New Bundle button. Enter the name in the Bundle Name text box, and then select the OS version number from the Minimum OS drop-down list.

- *Supports All Devices:* Select this check box if your app will run on all devices; deselect if you are targeting a specific device.

- *Filebundle Language:* Select the language from this drop-down list.

- *COD Files:* Click the Add button and then navigate on your machine to the COD file for each File Bundle for your app.

Figures 12-9 and 12-10 show a completed Releases and File Bundle page for my sample app The Word Locker. You can see in Figure 12-10 that all devices running OS 4.5.0 should be able to download and run my app.

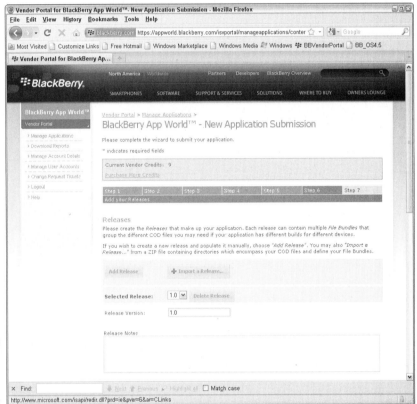

Figure 12-9:
The Release
page.

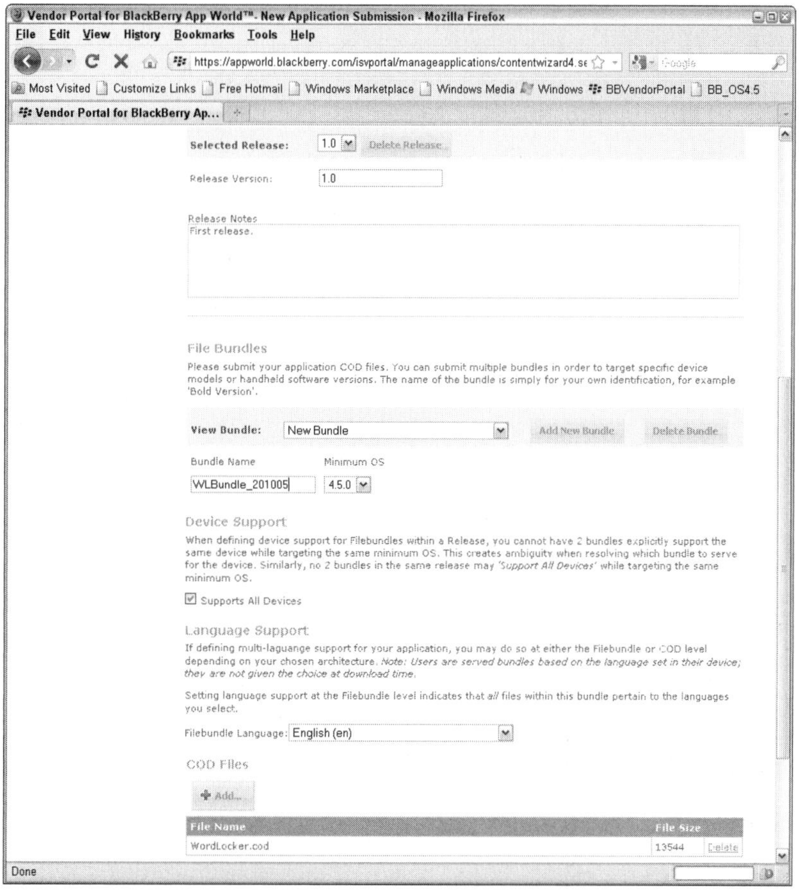

Figure 12-10:
A completed
File Bundle
page.

After you click Next, the Application Summary page appears, as shown in Figure 12-11.

Figure 12-11:
The
submission
summary
page.

13. **Review the settings you selected in the previous screens, and then select either the Leave Application and Releases(s) in Draft and Submit for Review Later radio button or the Submit Application and Release(s) for Review Immediately radio button.**

    Leaving your app as a draft does not cost you any submission points. As illustrated in Figure 12-12, I left my Word Locker app as a draft while I tracked down some bugs. When I returned to complete the submission process, the Manage Application page (reached in Step 5) showed The Word Locker status as Draft, and clicking the link of its name brought me to the Edit Application Submission page, as shown in Figures 12-13 and 12-14.

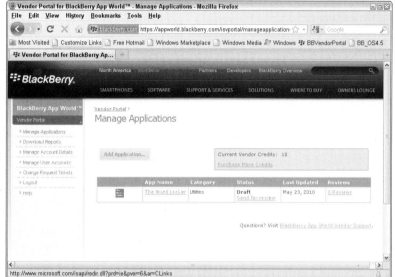

Figure 12-12:
Word
Locker sits
in limbo
while its
author goes
bug hunting.

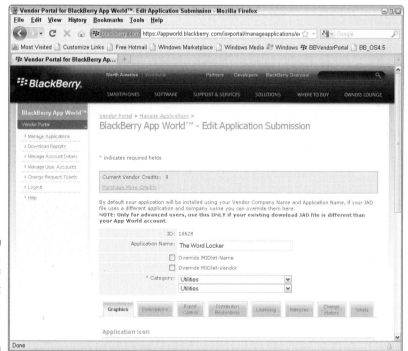

Figure 12-13:
The top half
of the Edit
Application
Submission
page.

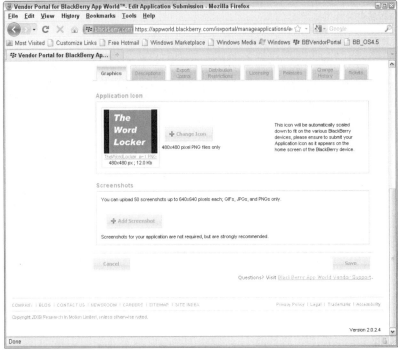

Figure 12-14:
The
bottom half
of the Edit
Application
Submission
page.

14. **Click Finish.**

    When you complete your submission, RIM has your app and will review it over the next week or so.

And that's it. Your application is ready for review by RIM. If you were careful about your application development, there should be no difficulty in your app being selected to appear in the BlackBerry App World.

After I submitted my Word Locker app for review, I got an e-mail from RIM indicating that the app was in queue for review.

If RIM approves your app, you will receive an e-mail indicating that your app has been approved and that you will need to login to the App World Vendor portal to finalize the process. Follow these steps:

1. **Log in to the App World Vendor Portal.**

2. **Click the Manage Applications link.**

    You will be shown the applications that you've uploaded for review.

3. For the application that has been approved, click the Post for Sale link in the Status column.

Figure 12-15 shows the applications page at the Vendor portal after RIM approved the app (top) and after I instructed RIM to post it for sale at the App World (bottom).

If RIM rejects your app, you have to review the reasons provided for rejection and address those reasons.

For example, The Word Locker was held up on its first submission because of export control restrictions. I received an e-mail from RIM exactly two weeks after I submitted the app, asking me to fill out a PDF form indicating the encryption that my app performed and to send the form back to RIM. I did so, but I didn't include enough information about the export classification. I did include in the e-mail body a textual description of what my application used from the cryptographic library, and RIM's response was to provide me a different Export Classification form to precisely define which export classification my app fell into. After that, RIM accepted The Word Locker, and I was able to post it for sale in the App World.

Part V
Securing and Supporting Your App

The 5th Wave   By Rich Tennant

"Other than this little glitch with the landscape view, my app works great on the Storm."

In this part . . .

*I*f you were going to write just one app, you could probably ignore this part — but just like eating those famed potato chips, you can't stop at just one! Each app you write will itself generate ideas for new apps, or at least new ideas for a future version. So this part assists your understanding of what you can do to support not only your first app but also every other app you write or dream of writing.

You also discover the basics of source code control and why it's a good idea to track your bugs in an organized manner. (As you can read here, the best thing you can do when you find a problem is to record it, if only for posterity.) You also find out about the joy of creating your own wiki, where you can give your ideas a place to rest so you can find them again at will, and unload them from your head so that you have more space for more ideas.

Chapter 13

Best Practices for Application Development

In This Chapter

▶ Introducing coding styles

▶ Architecting maintainable code

▶ Finding and fixing memory leaks

▶ Making your app lean and mean

▶ Keeping your code safe and organized

Writing applications for BlackBerry can bring you satisfaction, frustration, joy, and sorrow — just like writing for every platform and operating system you can think of. A `Hello, World!` application is easy to write and take care of; anything more complicated is, well, more complicated both to implement and also to maintain. After you release your application to the App World, you will experience the "pleasure" of many users finding every nook and cranny of your app and all the different problems that result. Some of these problems will be user error, some will be the fault of the device or even the operating system. Still, most problems will be the result of something you neglected to prevent. And don't discount feedback: Your users will sometimes comment on things that a future version of your app might do.

Strive to write your application while keeping an eye toward the future. After all, at some point, you're going to have to modify, augment, or rewrite your code. And although actually making changes is something most of us don't want to think about, if you take the time to plan ahead and write your code *today* knowing that something *tomorrow* will require you to improve what you write now, you and your code will both be in a good position for whatever the future brings. This mindset does take discipline as well as a little more work, but the benefits of keeping your code maintainable from the beginning definitely outweigh the cost of making it maintainable.

You will also find that making your code readable is another worthwhile goal. When you go back to update your app, you have to get back into "rhythm" with your code: That is, you'll need to understand precisely what's going on. If your code isn't readable or if you find yourself taking a long time to remember why you implemented a specific approach to solving a problem, you could end up breaking the code you're trying to improve. If your code is easy to comprehend from the first moment you look at it, though, you can make changes faster and more effectively, with little risk of introducing more problems.

In this chapter, I introduce you to some of the elements of the coding style that I prefer (some of which you might have noticed from the code samples elsewhere in this book). I also go over some architectural concepts, ways to structure your code, and some design patterns that I use fairly frequently. Then, I talk a bit about memory leaks and how to avoid them, as well as how to streamline your app. And finally, I talk about backing up your data and using a source code control system to keep your code safe and organized.

Coding with Style

If you've been programming for awhile, you already have a coding style that you're comfortable with. If you're like me, your coding style has evolved, especially if you work with other software developers or if you've read many code samples in books. You might have gotten used to one particular style simply because of the amount of programming you've done for a particular platform using a specific tool. Maybe you just accept the default initial coding that a tool provides and adjust your coding accordingly to match the tool's style of coding. Sun Microsystems, the creator of Java, has its own coding style guidelines — not hard-and-fast rules, per se, but suggestions put together as the Java programming language evolved.

The following sections describe some of the coding style standards I've amassed over my software development career. Adhering to them helps me to come up to speed fairly quickly whenever I have to start working on my code again. That's what code styles is all about: Putting your code into a state where you can easily slide back into developing and improving it.

Naming classes and variables

The following sections describe the naming conventions I follow when creating classes and different types of variables.

Naming classes

I follow the Sun recommendation for naming classes. The names of classes in my applications are all in *camel case,* wherein the first letter of each word of the class name is capitalized and all the rest are lowercase, such as `NewPasswordScreen`. This is one of the places where Sun violates its own suggestion: For example, the Java URL class (`java.net.URL`) is clearly not in camel case, nor are several other URL-related classes. RIM occasionally violates this suggestion as well. However, my code always follows this style so it's easy to tell what is and is not a class name.

Naming member variables

Almost every class you write will have member variables; you'll store data for each object of your class for later reference. If your entire class fits on one screen, you can see which variables are member variables and which ones are not. Chances are, though, that you're adding a decent amount of code — more than one screen's worth — which means that you'll eventually be staring at a block of code far away from where the member variables are declared. And you'll want to have an easy way to determine which variable is which. Listing 13-1 shows an example of two classes demonstrating good and bad member variable naming.

Listing 13-1: The Good and the Bad of Naming Member Variables

```
public class GoodMemberVariable
{
  private int m_time;

  public void setTime( int time )
  {
    m_time = time;
  }

  public GoodMemberVariable()
  {
  }
}

public class BadMemberVariable
{
  private int time;

  public void setTime( int time )
  {
    // this will compile, but what value will be
    // assigned to which variable?
    time = time;
  }

  pubic BadMemberVariable()
  {
  }
}
```

I put m_ in front of all my member variables to distinguish them from any other member variable. In addition, I make sure that my member variable names are noticeably different from the names of any other variables used in the class's methods.

Naming parameter variables

Back in the days of C programming, I adopted a coding style for naming the parameters passed into a function, prefixing them with in, out, or io depending on whether the parameters were to be used (respectively) as data coming into the function, data the function would create and return, or data that acted as both. I still follow this approach in my Java coding because I find it very important to make obvious which variables were passed into a method, and which ones are local or member variables. Almost all the methods I write use in parameters; typically, my methods return new objects as opposed to setting data in an object that is passed in as a parameter. Simple data types such as int will only ever be input parameters because their values are copied into the method when the method is called, and are unchanged when the method returns to the code that called it.

Naming local variables

I find it useful to provide local variables with names longer than one character, and almost always much longer than that. The names will necessarily avoid the patterns I use for parameter variables and member variables, and generally these names will be very indicative of what the variables are used to accomplish. For instance, the loop variable in my for loops is always something like index (because I'm usually using it as an index into a set of items). Another example: If I write code to calculate the X and Y coordinates of items my application displays on a screen, I use xPos and yPos for the calculated values. This reduces the likelihood of my misunderstanding the use of x or y as it provides information specific to the position my code is calculating.

Keeping method and class sizes small

My rule for writing class methods is no longer than one screen — and preferably much shorter. The more code you stuff into a method — that is, the more you want the method to do — the greater the chance you will introduce an error, and the more difficult it will be for you to find the error when you discover the problems it causes. Short methods are easy to debug, and you can build up lots of simple, short methods into large conglomerations that do just about anything.

Now, this doesn't mean that my methods are always small every moment that I work on them. I might violate this rule on a daily basis while creating and improving my code, and then later go back over what I produced to reduce it to a smaller size. My approach to coding is to write first, and re-factor second. But I do make sure the re-factoring gets done, which helps keep my methods readable and easy to understand when I come back to improve them.

In line with making methods as small as can be, you should try to keep your classes small as well. At the very least, you will find it easier to scroll through a few hundred lines of a class than you will to scroll through a few thousand lines of a class. (And yes, I've worked on classes that were more than a thousand lines long.)

Part of accomplishing this goal means that you will need to limit the capabilities of each of your classes. Putting too much functionality or too many features into a class will increase the size of the class. This leads to more methods, leading to greater likelihood of errors, and thereby more debugging. If you find your classes getting fatter and fatter, review each of the largest ones. Very likely, you can find a way to carve off some functionality to place in a separate, smaller class. In Listing 13-2, you see an example of a class that contains several pieces of data to support its usage as a text-editing screen. The text being edited, the time of the edit, and whether the edit has occurred are contained in the `TextEditScreenBig` object as separate member variables.

Listing 13-2: The TextEditScreenBig Class Contains Several Member Variables to Do Its Job

```
// all-in-one Big class
public class TextEditScreenBig extends MainScreen
{
  private String m_text;
  private long m_editTime;
  private boolean m_modified;
  public TextEditScreenBig( String inText )
  {
    super();
    m_text = inText;
    m_modified = false;
    m_editTime = Calendar.getInstance().getTime().getTime();
  }

  public String getText()
  {
    return (m_text);
  }

  public boolean isModified()
  {
    return (m_modified);
  }

  public long getEditTime()
  {
    return (m_editTime);
  }
}
```

In Listing 13-3, you see that `TextEditScreenSmall` contains only one member variable of the class `TextClass`. `TextClass` contains as its member variables the same members that `TextEditScreenBig` carried. The `TextClass` object is easier to work with because it keeps all the related pieces of information together — the text, when it was modified, and whether it was modified.

Listing 13-3:   TextEditScreenBig Broken Up into Two Classes

```
public class TextClass
{
  private String m_text;
  private long m_editTime;
  private boolean m_modified;
  public TextClass( String inText )
  {
    m_text = inText;
    m_editTime = 0L;
    m_modified = false;
  }

  public void setText( String inText )
  {
    if (false == inText.equals( m_text ))
    {
      m_text = inText;
      m_editTime = Calendar.getInstance().getTime().getTime();
      m_modified = true;
    }
  }

  public String getText()
  {
    return (m_text);
  }

  public long getEditTime()
  {
    return (m_editTime);
  }

  public boolean isModified()
  {
    return (m_modified);
  }
}

public class TextEditScreenSmall extends MainScreen
{
  private TextClass m_textObj;
```

```
public TextDisplayScreenSmall( TextClass inTextObj )
{
  m_textObj = inTextObj;
}

public TextClass getTextObj()
{
  return (m_textObj);
}
}
```

Assigning protection

If you're familiar with Java, you've seen the three protection classifications: public, protected, and private. You can use them on the following items in your code:

- ✔ Classes
- ✔ Methods
- ✔ Member variables

Class protection

Most of the time you want your classes to be public. This is true for classes in one part of your package hierarchy that make use of classes in another part of the hierarchy: Only classes declared to be public can be used in other parts of the hierarchy. You can provide a minimal kind of security by creating classes in a package with no protection declared: This creates *"package private" classes,* which are classes that can only be accessed from classes within that particular piece of the hierarchy.

In Listing 13-4, you see three classes that are in two different places in the package hierarchy:

- ✔ com.karlgkowalski.wordlocker.util.FirstUtility: Declared as a public class, your code in another part of the package hierarchy can create and use this class of object.

- ✔ com.karlgkowalski.wordlocker.util.SecondUtility: This class is not declared public, so only classes within the com.karlgkow alski.wordlocker.util package can create and use these objects.

- ✔ com.karlgkowalski.wordlocker.storage.WordLockerStorage: WordLockerStorage: A class defined in a separate part of the package hierarchy. A WordLockerStorage object can create FirstUtility objects, but not SecondUtility objects.

Note that the three classes shown in Listing 13-4 would be implemented in three separate files.

Listing 13-4:   The WordLockerStorage Class Can Create and Use FirstUtility Objects, But Not SecondUtility Objects

```
// FirstUtility.java
package com.karlgkowalski.wordlocker.util;

public class FirstUtility
{
  // class implementation
}

// SecondUtility.java
package com.karlgkowalski.wordlocker.util;

class SecondUtility
{
  // class implementation
}

// following code in different package
// WordLockerStorage.java
package com.karlgkowalski.wordlocker.storage;

import com.karlgkowalski.wordlocker.util;

public class WordLockerStorage
{
  public WordLockerStorage()
  {
    FirstUtility u1 = new FirstUtility();
    // the Java compiler will refuse to compile
    // this next line and display an error
    SecondUtility u2 = new SecondUtility();
  }
}
```

Method protection

You can control access to the methods in your application by setting protection levels for each. The important points to remember about method access control are that

- ✔ A public method is usable by any code that creates an instance of your class.

- ✔ A protected method is usable by any code within the class, as well as any code within any subclass of it.

- ✔ A private method is usable only by your class.

I generally use protected and public protections on methods. There's usually a reason to subclass one of my classes in the future, and using private methods makes that a little difficult. Use your own judgment to determine which methods to make public and which should have greater protection.

Member variable protection

Member variables follow the same rules of behavior as methods:

✔ A public member variable is usable by any code that creates an instance of your class.

✔ A protected member variable is usable by any code within the class, as well as any code within any subclass of it.

✔ A private member variable is usable only by your class.

My own approach to using member variable protection is that member variables should almost always be private, rarely protected, and never public.

Your code can only directly modify private member variables from within the class where they are defined. Not even subclasses can modify them directly. Sometimes you might want a subclass to be able to access a member variable in a parent class; the best way to do that is to provide public or protected methods in the parent class to get and set the data of the member variable. In Listing 13-5, you find two classes that demonstrate the use of private member variables within a parent class and its child.

Listing 13-5: A Parent Class with a Private Member Variable That Its Child Class Can't Access

```
// parent class
public class ParentClass
{
  private int m_parentInt;
  public ParentClass()
  {
    m_parentInt = 5;
  }

  public int getParentInt()
  {
    return (m_parentInt);
  }
}

// child class
public class ChildClass extends ParentClass
{
  private int m_childInt;
```

(continued)

Listing 13-5 *(continued)*

```
public ChildClass()
{
  // compiler will accept this
  // next line
  m_childInt = 2*this.getParentInt();
}

public int getSum()
{
  // compiler will display an error and
  // refuse to compile this next line because
  // the ChildClass is not permitted to access
  // the private member variable of the parent
  return (m_childInt+m_parentInt);
}
}
```

This channels all the efforts to modify data within an object through specific gateways. You can control and monitor all such modifications, thereby reducing the possibility that the data your object uses to get its job done is not what you expect it to be.

Avoid using magic numbers

A *magic number* is a number entered into the code without any explanation of its origin or its use. I confess that I still sometimes put magic numbers into my code because it's easy and quick just to type it while I'm typing code. But when shipping code — namely, code that will reach the App World — I replace them with constant variables that have meaningful names. I do this because I will forget why I picked a particular value, and if it's sitting there with no explanation of what it is or why it was typed in that particular line of code, I will have to spend more time to research why the value is as I left it.

Listing 13-6 demonstrates a code snippet indicating how to properly create magic numbers and incorporate them and other constant data in your app.

Listing 13-6: Adding a Magic Number

```
public class MagicNumberClass
{
    public static final int MAGIC_INTEGER  =  173;
    public static final String MAGIC_TEXT  =  "Waterfall";
    // the remainder of the class code
}
```

You can modify the protection level, currently set to `public`, to suit your app's needs for using the data outside of this class.

The `static` keyword tells the compiler that there will only ever be one of these values for all the instances of this class that your code creates. The `final` keyword tells the compiler that no code is permitted to modify what this item (I won't call it a "variable" because it doesn't *vary*) is initialized to be. As a result, your app can depend on the value of this item being constant while your application is running.

Using Singleton patterns

One of my favorite design patterns is the Singleton. A *Singleton* ensures that one and only one instance of the class exists, and provides a global point of access to it.

In my application, I use a Singleton to restrict access to the stored data. By using a Singleton class for this task, I rely on only the code developed in the Singleton class to deposit and retrieve information from the BlackBerry persistent storage mechanism. This gives me one-stop shopping for stored data, and I am only ever creating one object and one set of code to perform the operations necessary for interacting with the data in the storage. You will no doubt find uses for Singleton patterns in your code as well, beyond providing access to data storage. Listing 13-7 demonstrates the simplicity of setting up a Singleton class.

Listing 13-7: Defining and Implementing a Singleton Class

```
public class StorageAccess
{
   private static StorageAccess m_instance;

   public static StorageAccess getInstance()
   {
      if (null == m_instance)
      {
         m_instance = new StorageAccess();
      }
      return (m_instance);
   }

   private StorageAccess()
   {
      // do your initialization here
   }

   // other methods for the StorageAccess object to perform
}
```

The constructor of a Singleton must not be made public because a public constructor allows any code to create and make use of an instance of the class, and you don't want to allow any code that kind of access to your Singleton classes. You should make the constructor private.

Commenting code

Small applications that do simple things generally don't need comments. However, as you develop larger and more complicated apps, you will discover that your memory of why you did something a specific way fades over time. No one I've worked for demanded that I provide comments in my code, but I use comments because some issue inevitably comes up later on in the development that requires me to question why I did something that particular way. Without a solid explanation to justify what I did, I have to waste time figuring it out all over again.

You'll get a feel for how and where to comment as you gain experience developing applications. Here are a few cases where commenting your code is beneficial:

- ✔ **Positive justification:** Your approach to solving a particular problem is based on experience you had in similar situations. You found a solution that you can use again, so marking the code with a comment to that effect is helpful.

- ✔ **Negative justification:** In this case, although you don't have evidence that your approach is the best way to solve a problem, you know of several other ways that *don't* work. So, you put a comment in your code to note a workaround for something you can't get to work any other way.

Plugging the Leaks

One of the most challenging problems in software development came about when programming languages such as C allowed developers to request chunks of memory from the operating system. This was a truly wonderful thing: Instead of having to calculate precisely how much memory your app was going to use in its operations and implement your app to use only that much, your app could now just ask for whatever memory space was required, at the moment it needed it. This was truly freedom: I remember developing applications using programming languages where I had to guess what the utmost maximum amount of data I was going to need to run my application. In addition, the size of the application grew: The memory was allocated as part of the entire application. With the advent of C, though, the application was as large as it needed to be, and would grow when and if it needed to do so.

However, there was a disadvantage to on-demand memory. The price for the benefit of your app being allowed to request memory from the OS whenever your app needed it was that your app also had to return that memory to the OS — for use by a future request — when the memory was no longer needed. Your app now lived a very dynamic existence. It could grab memory while running, but it also would be required to free up that memory as well.

Your app could hold onto all the memory it requests from the OS, but that would only eventually bring the amount of unused memory lower and lower, and most applications use some amount of temporary memory to execute. This means that as your app requests and retains all the memory it wants, the execution of the application can eventually cause the OS to halt your app because it has run out of memory in which to operate. So developers of C programs had to discipline themselves to balance the moments where their apps requested memory from the OS with moments when their apps freed that same memory. And sometimes something bad happened: a *memory leak*.

Then Java came along. The developers of Java knew that memory leaks were a real problem for pre-Java applications. So Java was developed to address this problem, and its solution was *garbage collection*. Every Java application — including BlackBerry apps — runs as a process within a Java Virtual Machine (JVM). Part of the JVM is a *garbage collector,* a process that coexists with every other Java application and pays attention to blocks of memory requested by each application. The garbage collector is especially interested in blocks of memory no longer able to be referenced by applications as a result of resetting the value stored in the container of the reference to the memory block to something other than what was allocated. The code snippet in Listing 13-8 demonstrates this.

Listing 13-8: Intentionally Losing a Reference to a Block of Memory

```
public void memoryLost()
{
   // requesting memory for a ClassA instance
   ClassA a = new ClassA();
   a = new ClassA();
   // the original request has now gone missing
}
```

In the second line of the method, the variable a has had its original contents — a reference to a ClassA object — replaced by a new reference to a new ClassA object. When this happens, the first object is no longer referenced by the application; its memory block is just sitting, unused. The garbage collector *eventually* picks up on this fact and releases the memory automatically, returning it to the pool of available memory. Because your app has lost its reference to the object, it's obvious that your app no longer wants access to the contents of this object, and so losing it isn't a horrible thing.

Don't depend on the garbage collector to take care of leaks

The garbage collector is supposed to free up blocks of memory that were requested by your app but which your app retains no reference it can use to access the data. However, the BlackBerry garbage collector doesn't run all the time. Instead, it appears to execute to resolve all the leaked memory only when the OS runs out of unused memory and can't oblige a request for more. And this might not happen for quite some time.

As I mention previously, you can get rid of leaked memory simply by terminating your app. In other words, when the user shuts down your application, the OS frees all the memory that was requested by your app. However, here are two situations in which your app can cause memory leaks to happen while your app is running:

- ✔ **When users use the Switch Application feature to keep your app running while they do something else**

- ✔ **When your app chooses to go into the background, even if the user has selected the Close menu option**

  Ordinarily, your application should terminate when the user selects Close. However, if the user has set your app to perform some background processing, closing the app would terminate this feature, so your app will continue to run in the background instead of actually closing.

Operating in the background

One of the great features of the BlackBerry is that users can run multiple applications, much like they can on desktop PCs. A user may run the Browser to grab the latest stock quotes while writing a response to a corporate e-mail. Users access the range of running applications by selecting the Switch Application menu item, as shown in Figure 13-1.

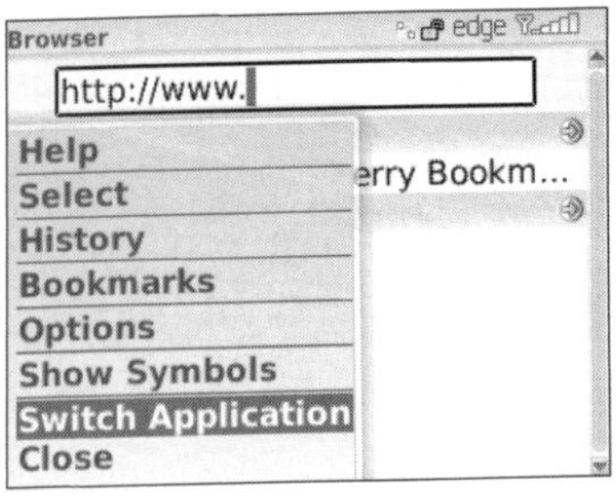

Figure 13-1: Jump from one application to the next.

When a user selects Switch Application, the applications that are running on the BlackBerry are displayed in a window, and the user can select one to use in place of the current application. This window is shown in Figure 13-2.

Figure 13-2:
Select
the app to
switch to.

The Call Log application is highlighted in Figure 13-2. This is the app that will be brought into the foreground for the user to interact with (while the Browser is sent to the background).

This means that your users expect your app to provide this capability as well. Your application must support being placed into the background when a user wants to check e-mail, and being brought back into the foreground later. Apps support moving between the background and foreground through two methods that override in the subclass of UiApplication:

- ✔ void UiApplication.activate(): This method is called by the BlackBerry OS when your application is moved from the background into the foreground. This is the primary location for memory leaks to arise.

- ✔ void UiApplication.deactivate(): This method is called by the BlackBerry OS when your application is moved from the foreground into the background. Here, you will make sure that your application performs any tasks needed before it gets suspended.

The good news is that the activate() method is really the only place where you have to worry about memory leaks creeping in as a result of a user switching your application into the background.

Your application can create a memory leak as a result of creating new objects when activate() is executed. One of the easy ways to do this is to push a screen onto the screen stack within the activate() method. If you look closely at the code in Listing 13-9, this pushes a new screen onto the screen stack whenever the user switches out of the application and returns to it.

Listing 13-9:   The activate() Method from Chapter 3

```
public void activate()
{
   this.pushScreen( new FirstBlackBerryScreen() );
}
```

Why? Because the app is simply pushing a new screen, created as a parameter into the `pushScreen()` method when it gets called. And the previous screen pushed the last time the app was launched has now been leaked. You can use the `UiApplication.getScreenCount()` method to find out how many screens are already on the stack, and handle the situation accordingly when your application again runs through the `activate()` method. Listing 13-10 (an implementation of `activate()` that checks whether the app already has a screen displayed) shows a better way to implement the `activate()` method found in Listing 13-9.

Listing 13-10:   Check for the Presence of a Screen to Avoid Memory Leak

```
public void activate()
{
   if (this.getScreenCount() > 0)
   {
      this.updateDisplay();
   }
   else
   {
      this.pushScreen(new FirstBlackBerryScreen() );
   }
}
```

This `activate()` method checks for any screens already on the stack, and just tells them all to update themselves if there are any. If no screens are on the stack, the code creates one. This ensures that only one screen will end up being placed on the stack as a result of switching out of and back into the application. Your code also has to provide for this possibility as well because a user who moves from one application to another fairly frequently might cause `activate()` to be executed numerous times in your application. And if your app is creating and pushing screens onto the stack using `activate()`,the amount of available memory will decrease, and your app's performance will suffer.

Memory leaks are your responsibility. The garbage collector present in the BlackBerry JVM doesn't run frequently enough to recover memory blocks, such as objects your app creates when your app no longer maintains a reference to them. Just a glance through the first few results of an online search engine looking for "blackberry memory leak" demonstrates that more than a few applications aren't keeping a close eye on their use of memory.

The official RIM statement regarding review of your application as part of the process for submitting your app to the App World does not specifically mention memory leakage as a reason for disqualification. A memory leak is not an error that will destroy data or cause harm to the device or user, and a leak is easily removed simply by terminating the offending application (or rebooting the smartphone). However, because checking for memory leaks while executing applications is a simple process, you're better off locking down every piece of your code that could lead to one. The description in this section should help you hunt down memory leaks in your BlackBerry app.

Streamlining Your App

Your application development will undoubtedly cover many paths as you prototype and experiment with different ideas. You'll also find some things that work according to plan, and others that just plain don't. I have developed enough applications, BlackBerry and others, to know that the code I end up with doesn't always look as pretty as it should. I enjoy experimenting with different ways of getting problems solved, and this leads to leftovers and no-longer-used code modules that clutter up the entire application. You will likely discover that when you come back to a previously published application after some time, you'll find a lot of stuff that you meant to get to later now has to be reevaluated or removed.

The following sections provide simple tips to keep your application manageable.

Don't reinvent the wheel

The BlackBerry class framework has hundreds of classes, and chances are that one of them already has the features or functions you're looking for. Your app can use one of these directly, or else subclass it and extend its capabilities. If you create your own class, you add to the size of your application, which will affect your users in the following ways:

- **Longer start times:** The more code the OS has to pull in, the longer your app will appear to take to start up.

- **Longer download times:** Each byte of your application gets downloaded from the App World; the more there are, the more time it takes.

- **Greater storage space requirements:** BlackBerry devices have a limited amount of space to store applications into. You want your app to be as small as possible.

Group source files using the package hierarchy

The desktop version of Java — Java Standard Edition — requires that Java source code modules must reside in a file-system hierarchy of folders that matches the "package" locations of the class. This means that a Java class that has the following line representing its location in the package hierarchy

```
package com.karlgkowalski.myblackberryapp.util;
```

must reside in a folder path that looks like this (following the Windows file system):

```
{current directory}\com\karlgkowalski\myblackberryapp\util
```

Discipline yourself to place appropriate types of source modules into the appropriate spots in the file system hierarchy. This makes it easier to find things in the future as well as keep track of things while you're working on them. I usually use the following in all my application projects (all packages start with `com.karlgkowalski.{application_name}`):

- ✔ `ui`: This folder consists of all the user interface classes I implement for the application. I may create subfolders for more specific UI classes.

- ✔ `util`: This folder contains utility classes; usually, it's a catch-all folder for everything that doesn't quite fit anywhere else.

- ✔ `network`: I put network-related classes into this folder; usually, I will implement a class that encapsulates the network functionality, and place it within this folder so that I know the kind of work it's doing.

- ✔ `data`: In applications where I'm storing data, especially if the data requires a particular grouping of different types of information, I create classes inside this folder.

Keep method sizes small

One of the principles of object-oriented programming is that smaller pieces of code are much easier to debug. My experience has been that if a method takes more than one screen's worth of vertical space to implement, it's time to break up that method. Granted, it's easy to add just ten more lines of code to a method to fix something now. So again, you will need to discipline yourself to avoid the easy path. However, taking the simpler way first sometimes is beneficial — that is, as long as you schedule yourself to review and re-factor the eventually bloated method (all 17 pages of it) to something easier to figure out.

Each class should accomplish just one purpose

Similar to the warning about keeping your methods small, you should extend that idea and keep your classes to a small size in terms of functionality. That's part of what's required when you use the *MVC* (Model-View-Controller) approach: keeping the classes that make up each component of MVC limited to doing one thing each, and doing it well. (See Chapter 4 for more about the MVC approach.)

Reduce the public methods in your classes to the bare minimum

Each method in a class that you declare public is, effectively, a method that can be executed by any other class in your application. This creates a great many paths for a particular class's methods to be executed. And that will make tracking down problems more of a challenge. Limiting access to a class's methods for manipulating data reduces the footprint of the class and thereby restricts the options for other classes to interact with the class's internal data.

Backing Up and Organizing Your Code

The more software you write, the more stuff you have to manage. Every software project requires a multitude of different pieces that all have to work together. After a few projects, you might need a bigger hard drive! If something in your development machine fails, all your efforts are at risk. "Save early, save often" may not be enough to recover your code if your entire machine collapses into a pile of virtual dust.

The following sections introduce you to some basic concepts regarding the care and maintenance of your application code *outside* the immediate tasks of getting the app uploaded to the App World. I might sound like a parent in the following sections. However, the practices outlined here can potentially save you an enormous amount of headache and heartache should the worst-case scenario occur.

Backing up your precious data

I admit it: For the longest time, I refused to do backups. I justified this childish refusal with the belief that even if the worst thing possible happened, I could always recover the data on my computer even if it meant writing it all over again.

And nothing bad ever happened (nope, no story of how failing to back up data cost me time, money, or something else very important). What did happen was I realized that I didn't want to spend days or weeks re-creating my work, especially when I undertook a contract job where I wrote all my code on my machine. Losing all the work I had done was not something worth taking a chance on.

So, I now back up all my crucial files and projects, complete with source code and other files from the development environment — everything I can't easily re-create myself — on both CD-Rs and an external drive. My startup company does complete backups on a daily basis, and monthly backups to more permanent storage.

Make sure you back up all the important components of your BlackBerry application development projects. The most critical components are your source modules — these are the containers of your Java code — and your image files, which are the crown jewels of your application. You don't want to have to start from scratch should your hard disk fail. The other components include the project and workspace files used by the JDE, and the files containing the data you use to sign your application. Anything the JDE creates for you — such as the COD, ALX, or JAD files — you don't need to back up.

The preceding set of components should all be backed up onto a reliable storage system. My recommendations are to do

- ✔ **A daily backup onto an external hard drive:** I don't recommend using memory sticks (USB flash drives) because they are small and easily misplaced. I recommend using an external hard drive, preferably connected to your local area network. This is the simplest and easiest way to back up your crucial files. It's less guaranteed than recordable media, but it's faster so you can do it every day.

- ✔ **Less-frequent backups onto recordable media:** CD and DVD burners are cheap, as are blank CDs and DVDs. There's no reason to avoid doing this kind of backup. If saving your development efforts to a disk saves you a few hours' worth of rewriting, the backup system is worth its cost.

  This kind of backup is more permanent and therefore more secure than backing up to a hard drive. You don't need to do this every day, but once weekly or perhaps even monthly will suffice. The best thing about recordable media is you don't have to worry about a failure after the data is verified on the disk; the usable lifetime of the disk is generally longer than the time period over which the data is useful.

Discipline yourself to get the backups done regularly. Fortunately, most operating systems can support scripts to back up parts or even all of your desktop PC hard drives. And a number of third-party solutions are dedicated to this as well. In addition, several third-party solutions allow you to back up your data to a network server on the Internet, which will relieve you of any worry about data recovery because these services, in turn, back up their own data regularly.

Keeping your code organized with a source code control system

You will find it difficult to work anywhere in the software industry today without coming into contact with a source code control system (SCCS). You use an SCCS to organize and manage the files you use in your application's development. These files include but are not limited to the following (identical to the list for backups):

✔ Source code

✔ Images

✔ JDE files

✔ Other files

What makes this different from doing a backup? An SCCS performs some management functions beyond those of a simple backup. These functions include

✔ **Diff-ing:** You can see the differences between the current version of a file and every version that came before it. This feature can be extremely helpful when you want to find out precisely where things went wrong. And it's even more useful if you're working on a team, where everyone can modify any file, at any moment.

✔ **History:** Each time you add, update, or delete a file from the source code repository, you add a note to the action. With a minimal amount of discipline, you can keep these notes simple and informative. The SCCS can provide a list of the changes that were made over time as a summary of the life of your application's pieces.

✔ **Snapshot:** At some point, you will decide that your app is as done as it's going to be. All your app's modules and components are ready to be put together for delivery to the App World, so you tell the SCCS to mark all the components for your app. You use this as a *snapshot* — a moment in time where you know everything is ready to ship. In the future, no matter what changes you make to the components, this snapshot is always available from the SCCS to bring you back to a known good point.

✔ **Branching:** Most SCCSes support *branching:* making a complete copy of your app's components to enable you to try something new. A new branch of the application is a completely separate app, as far as the SCCS knows. You would use branching to build a specialized version of your app for a particular customer: for example, you create a version of your app that's modified for a customer's specific business. Using a different branch of the source code and other components to build a specialized version of your app allows you to keep the two versions separate. Later, you can merge the two branches so that new features in the specialized version can be made available to a new set of customers.

I find SCCSes to be an annoying and generally unpleasant necessity. However, as projects get larger, a good SCCS becomes even more necessary. The same is true when you start working on many different projects. If you're planning to do more than one BlackBerry application, you should invest in an SCCS that you are comfortable with and that suits your needs and abilities. The following list provides several free source code control systems:

- **Perforce:** A free, two-user version of Perforce is available at www.perforce.com. Perforce comes with a Windows GUI client that makes using it pretty easy. There's also a command line interface. Perforce provides you with the basic features of an SCCS, plus a lot more. Perforce is the easiest SCCS to set up and get working with.

- **Subversion (SVN):** SVN is a Web-based SCCS, from the open source Apache project, available at http://subversion.apache.org. One important challenge with this SCCS is that it requires a Web server to operate. Apache (www.apache.org) provides a Web server you can install yourself, also for free, but this choice does make for more work at your end.

- **Concurrent Versioning System (CVS):** CVS (available at www.nongnu.org/cvs) is the oldest SCCS and perhaps has the steepest learning curve to set up and use. After you get used to its syntax, though, you'll find it actually pretty easy to use. For my startup company, we settled on CVS because we needed more than a two-user capability (which ruled out the free version of Perforce). CVS is also open source. CVS was originally a command line tool, but you can download several free Windows-based client applications.

Do you really need source code control?

Is an SCCS absolutely necessary? No. But you will find it very useful as you develop more and more applications for the BlackBerry App World, as well as for any other mobile device development you may choose to do in the future. And you should always be thinking beyond your current development work.

One of the best features of a source code control system is that you can do backups very easily because all the files you need to back up are conveniently located in the source code control system area. That makes it easier for you to get into the habit of doing backups regularly. An SCCS requires more input from you to perform its tasks and do them well, but you will find that using an SCCS is less of a headache than trying to remember to do its tasks yourself.

Chapter 14

Application Deployment and Upgrades

*A*lthough this book is mostly about BlackBerry application delivery through the BlackBerry App World, a couple of other deployment options for BlackBerry applications are available. The advantage of using BlackBerry App World is that it provides a simplified approach to making your application available to the millions of BlackBerry users:

✔ **One-stop shopping experience:** Every user knows to go to the App World to search for more apps.

✔ **Centralized payment mechanism:** You don't need the extras of handling checks, processing credit card payments, and so on.

The App World certainly makes it easier for you to offer your app, and easier for users to purchase it. However, other options are available:

✔ **Desktop download:** Just like you deployed your app to your own BlackBerry to really test its features as users would experience them, you can also deliver your app to your users and let them deploy your app via the BlackBerry Desktop Manager application.

✔ **BlackBerry Enterprise Server (BES) download:** For corporate enterprise BlackBerry users governed by a BES, your app can be delivered wirelessly to some or all BES-activated users from the BES itself.

✔ **Web download:** Your BlackBerry application can be placed on a Web server with the appropriate settings to allow users to download your app through the BlackBerry Browser.

In this chapter, I go over these different deployment options and show you what you need to know about each one, to give you the greatest range of opportunities for delivering your application to anyone who wants it. I also cover upgrading your app, and how to make upgrading your app seamless for users so they don't lose any data they created with the previous version of your app.

Delivery from a Desktop PC

For a user to deploy your application from their desktop PC to their BlackBerry, you need to deliver two files to the user (see Figure 14-1):

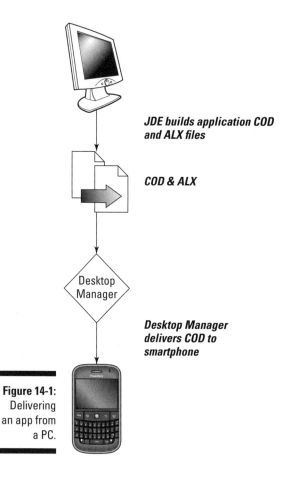

JDE builds application COD and ALX files

COD & ALX

Desktop Manager

Desktop Manager delivers COD to smartphone

Figure 14-1: Delivering an app from a PC.

✔ **Your application's signed COD file:** This is your application's executable, so it's necessary no matter what delivery mechanism you choose.

✔ **Your application's ALX file:** This is the file that you create apart from your application (and I still wonder why RIM hasn't made this something the build process does by default), which provides information to Desktop Manager.

I discuss the creation of the COD file in Chapter 3, and the ALX file in Chapter 10.

The Desktop Manager application (provided with every BlackBerry) provides users the ability to add and remove applications to their BlackBerry smartphones across a USB cable (also provided with every BlackBerry). The steps to deploying your application using Desktop Manager are the same as those described in Chapter 10. In Figure 14-2, you can see that The Word Locker application is highlighted and the check box has been checked so that Desktop Manager will install the application onto my BlackBerry Curve 8900.

Figure 14-2: Desktop Manager shows that The Word Locker will be installed.

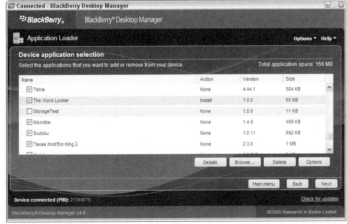

 When a corporate BES controls a user's BlackBerry smartphone, the restrictions placed on the BlackBerry will still apply when the user attempts to use Desktop Manager to deliver applications to the smartphone. If the BES administrator prevents users from installing applications onto their smartphones, the Desktop Manager can't install your app onto the BlackBerry. I went through this exact problem with the BlackBerry smartphone I bought through eBay.

To use this approach, you will have to find a way to deliver these two files to your end users. This can be achieved by e-mailing a ZIP file containing the two files to each user who has requested and paid for your app. You can also automate the process through the use of a Web site to collect payment information and upon successful authorization allow the user to download the two files.

Delivery through a BES

Most BlackBerry users use their BlackBerry smartphones to gain access to their corporate network. This is achieved when users activate their smartphones to the corporate BES, which establishes a secure connection from the BlackBerry smartphone to the internal corporate network. However, this means that the user gives up some control over the operation of their smartphone because the BES administrator can dictate certain rules of behavior over the device, as I detail in Chapter 8.

In certain cases, the BES administrator may restrict the users' ability to download applications from BlackBerry App World, and it is possible that third-party applications can be deployed only through the BES. To that end, your application will have to be delivered to the BES administrator, who will then schedule the deployment of your app through the BES.

This approach to application delivery is not as glamorous as using the BlackBerry App World. If your application has a strong appeal to corporate enterprise BlackBerry users, though, you will want to be prepared for delivery in this fashion.

When delivering your app for distribution to the App World, you need a lot of different pieces of information, but there's really only one important file: your application's COD file. (True, there's an image file used by App World for visual display, but it's not really very important.)

Comparatively, just like Desktop Manager delivery, BES delivery requires two files (see Figure 14-3):

- ✔ The signed COD file
- ✔ The ALX file

However, the BES uses a tool that takes these two files and creates a package that it can deploy to users' BlackBerry smartphones. You can use the same approaches described in the previous section to deliver the ALX and COD files to any company that wants to purchase your app for its users: Package the two files into a ZIP file and e-mail them, or deliver them via a Web site. (You can find more information about setting up a Web site for selling your app in *Starting an Online Business For Dummies,* 6th Edition, by Greg Holden [Wiley].)

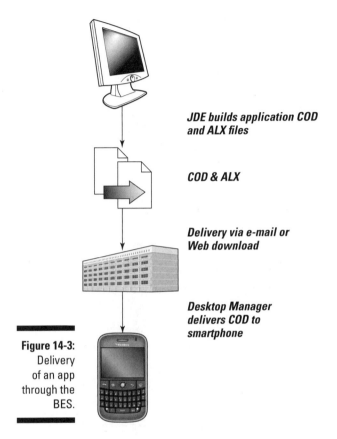

JDE builds application COD
and ALX files

COD & ALX

Delivery via e-mail or
Web download

Desktop Manager
delivers COD to
smartphone

Figure 14-3:
Delivery
of an app
through the
BES.

Delivery via the Web

BlackBerry users also download applications onto their smartphones by
using the BlackBerry Browser on their phone. Given a URL for a particular file
sitting on a Web site, the BlackBerry Browser will prompt users who want to
download your application with a dialog box, as shown in Figure 14-4.

You need two files to allow users to download your app from your Web site
(you do not need the ALX file):

✓ Your application COD file (of course!).

✓ Your application Java Application Descriptor (JAD) file. You can find
more information about the JAD file in Chapter 3.

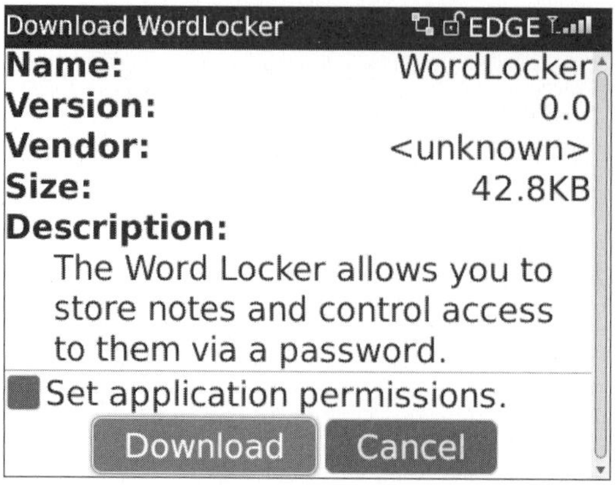

Download WordLocker	EDGE
Name:	WordLocker
Version:	0.0
Vendor:	<unknown>
Size:	42.8KB

Description:

The Word Locker allows you to store notes and control access to them via a password.

■ Set application permissions.

[Download] [Cancel]

Figure 14-4: Users can download your app by navigating their browser to your app.

Both files must be available at the same place on the Web server. Users navigate their browser to the JAD file. BlackBerry Browser is smart enough to determine that the user is trying to download a COD file application, and displays the dialog box shown in Figure 14-4 as a result. The user is presented with a choice of downloading the application or canceling the download.

Using a Web server to deliver your application allows you to control access to your app: No one who hasn't gone through your process to allow users to download your app will be able to install it onto their device. This means that you have the ability to charge users for downloading your application in a way that can prevent other users from making copies of your app and distributing it without your permission or compensation. Of course, you will have to set up the Web site and the payment process yourself, but there are a variety of tools for that task. Some of the available options for online sales processing include the following:

✔ PayPal

✔ Yahoo! Merchant Solutions

✔ Google Checkout for Merchants

✔ ProStores

✔ 1&1 Internet

✔ PayLoads

You will have to configure your Web server to permit users to download your app COD files as a result of the user navigating their BlackBerry Browser to the location of your app's JAD file. Your Web server comes with a default configuration that permits users to access the HTML and HTM file types. Because your server doesn't know anything about COD or JAD files, you must configure the server to allow users to access those types of files. You will have to add MIME (Multipurpose Internet Mail Extension) types to your Web server's configuration. There are two you need to add:

✔ **For JAD files:** `text/vnd.sun.j2me.app-descriptor`

✔ **For COD files:** `application/vnd.rim.cod`

Consult your Web server's guide to modify its permitted MIME types.

Upgrading Your App

Upgrading your app is the best way to get new features and functionality into the hands of your users. Through the App World, users can review and comment on your application, providing you with feedback on what they like and dislike about the different features of your application. You can use this information to develop improvements and provide an updated version when you've implemented the right amount of new and improved functionality. And when your upgraded application has survived the rounds of review performed by RIM, the BlackBerry App World notifies owners of your app about the update, prompting them to download the latest and greatest version of your application.

Progress marches on

The world of software development is constantly changing. New hardware, new equipment, new smartphones — and new software to run on them. Your application can sit still: That is, you can develop it once and never touch it again. Or, hmm, your application can grow with the BlackBerry platform as it evolves into a better, stronger, more powerful future.

To illustrate, consider that the BlackBerry smartphones of 2010 are much more powerful and capable than the original BlackBerry smartphones of 2002. Today's users expect that next-generation BlackBerry smartphones will offer them more features and functionality than their current-generation devices. And you will have to keep your app up to date with respect to newer BlackBerry smartphones — after all, your competitors surely will.

For instance, a BlackBerry application built in 2007 to run on the top of the line devices at that time would be unable to take advantage of the touchscreen- and accelerometer-enabled BlackBerry Storm, which came out the following year. RIM introduces approximately four new models every year. In addition to introducing new models, RIM also updates its operating systems for its prior models. Although this is usually a beneficial change, there is a chance that your app might break as a result of changes under the hood. To keep your app from falling behind others, and maintain your users' appreciation of your app as a valuable tool in their BlackBerry toolkit, you will have to keep your application updated on a regular basis.

You must consider several points when creating an upgrade of your application. These items are easily overlooked, and if you do, you can make the path from "I'd really like to have this feature" to "Version 2 now available at the App World, New and Improved!" much longer than expected. You need to be careful about the following points:

- ✔ **A new version of your application delivered to the BlackBerry App World requires you to use up another submission credit.** RIM doesn't care whether your issue is a bug fix or a completely revamped edition. Another submission credit will be subtracted for a new application version delivered for RIM to review and submit for App World distribution. You must decide exactly what qualifies as enough of a modification to be worthy of the effort and the expenditure of another submission. You can find out more about the submission process and your submission credits in Chapter 12.

- ✔ **The new version of your app must have the same name as the old version of your app.**

- ✔ **The version number of your application must change to a greater value.** This sounds obvious, but it's easy to overlook: You must modify the project Properties to set the version number of your application. See Figure 14-5. Of course, you also want to change it everywhere you use the version number within your application to keep everything aligned. For example, you must change the version number in the project Properties screen. Figure 14-5 shows you the version number field highlighted in the project Properties screen. If you've included an About box within your app, you need to change it there as well. For the alternate delivery options mentioned in this chapter, you have to regenerate the ALX file as well, because it includes the version number.

- ✔ **Any object within your application that you have implemented as `Persistable` must also exist in the new version of your application,** with *precisely* the same fully qualified class name and also must have *precisely* the same member variables. Chapter 6 covers the details of using the `Persistable` interface in your apps.

If your older application is storing its own objects in the persistent storage system of a user's BlackBerry, the upgraded version of your application must be able to retrieve those exact same objects. In the next section, I go over a means by which you can handle this in your application, which reduces the restrictions of maintaining classes in an unchanging state.

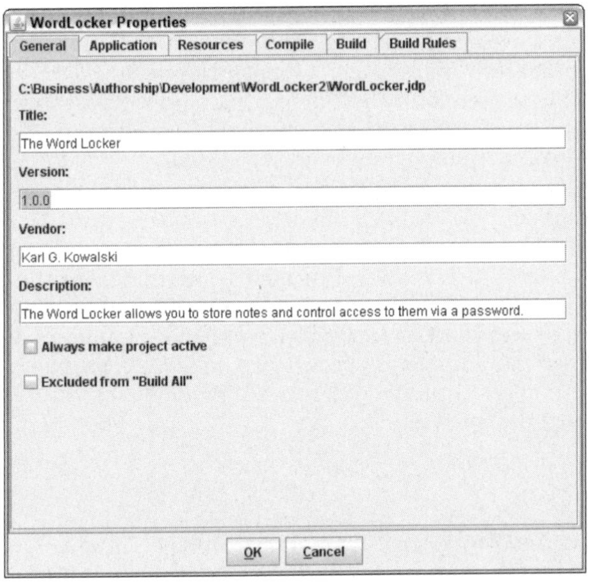

Figure 14-5:
The
Properties
screen.

Insistent persistence

As I mention in Chapter 6, your app can take advantage of storing its own information by using the persistent storage mechanism available in the BlackBerry OS. Your app's data can be stored as a set of objects specific to your application if the classes that define those objects implement the RIM interface Persistable. You can also store basic Java class objects, which means that your application will have to create a basic Java object for each piece of information that your app needs to store. In Chapter 6, I mention the following issues:

- ✔ If your app stores Persistable objects, those objects will be removed after your application is deleted.

- ✔ If your app stores basic Java objects, those objects will still be maintained in the persistent store even after your app is deleted.

When a user upgrades your application, the Persistable objects that your app stores must be present in the upgraded application. Otherwise, the upgrade will fail. The failure will happen because the upgrade process checks that the classes that are marked Persistable in the installed version of the app are not available in the upgrade version of the app.

I have not yet created an update to The Word Locker at the App World, but my experience with upgrading applications via Desktop Manager has convinced me that RIM will investigate this as part of the App World submission review of your application upgrade, and I expect the upgrade will fail (through the App World) the same way it will via Desktop Manager. The Persistable objects must match both in their fully qualified class names and in their set of member variables. Otherwise, well, I'm sure you get the picture.

My application, The Word Locker, stores user-entered text in the persistent storage area of the BlackBerry smartphone. The objects stored in the persistent storage area contain basic Java elements as member variables such as int, long, and String types. My app also defines as Persistable the classes that contain the stored data, and so my app can store these objects directly in the persistent storage. Any upgrade version of The Word Locker must contain the same classes that were stored by the previous version of The Word Locker.

The following list provides solutions to this problem:

- ✔ **Maintain the legacy persistent data classes and migrate to newer persistent data classes as part of the upgrade.** Your upgraded application reads through the old persistent storage and retrieves the legacy data, converting the old objects into objects of the new data classes. Then your new app creates a new persistent store with the new objects. Lastly, the old persistent store is deleted. As a result, the new application will maintain copies of the older code simply for migration purposes. The older code can be dropped in a future upgrade because no objects of the older classes exist. Listing 14-1 shows you a snippet of code that demonstrates how an object from a previous version stored in persistent storage can be used to generate a replacement object in a new version of your application. You would have to implement UpgradeObject to know what elements of OldObject to extract and make use of.

- ✔ **Serialize the data stored in the persistent store.** Your application should store data as String objects, created by the class objects that your app uses to maintain the data. During the upgrade, the new application reads the old data String objects from the persistent store and converts them into the new classes. In this manner, your app doesn't have any classes that are Persistable, so there's no issue with changing the class names or their member variables. The only issue in this approach is that your app's data is maintained even if the application is deleted from the device. This approach might not be appropriate for your application, especially if you're storing sensitive data.

Listing 14-1:   Old Version of an Object Initializes a New Version

```
public void upgradeToNewData()
{
  PersistentObject storage = PersistentStore.getPersistentObject( STORAGE_KEY );
  OldObject oldObj = (OldObject)storage.getContents();
  // use prior version object to initialize the new version object
  UpgradeObject upgradeObj = new UpgradeObject( oldObj );
}
```

Serializing your data

You need to implement code that serializes your data. *Serialization* is the act of turning the data contained within your objects into a neutral form, such as a string. You can structure your internal data by using XML, and turn each basic type of data within your objects into name-value pairs within the XML. The BlackBerry OS provides standard XML classes to assist in this process. Listing 14-2 demonstrates the serialization of the `WordLocker Category` class.

Listing 14-2:   Turning WordLockerCategoryRecord into a Block of XML for Serialization

```
String m_name; // name of the category
long m_creationTimestamp; // creation date

public  String  serialize()
{
   StringBuffer   buffer   =   new StringBuffer();
   buffer.append( "<? xml version=\"1.0\" ?>\n" );
   buffer.append( "<WordLocker version=\"1.0\">\n" );
   buffer.append( "<Category name=\"" );
   buffer.append( m_name );
   buffer.append( "\">\n" );
   buffer.append( "<CreationDate timestamp=\"" );
   buffer.append( m_creationTimestamp );
   buffer.append( "\"/>\n" );
   buffer.append( "</Category>\n" );
   buffer.append( "</WordLocker>\n" );
   return (buffer.toString());
}
```

The output of the `serialize()` method is a `String` object that contains the XML representation of both the category name and the category's creation date:

✔ `<Category name=""/>`: This block contains the name of the category as an attribute called `name`.

✔ `<CreationDate timestamp=""/>`: This block contains the long data value representing the creation date of the category as an attribute called `timestamp`.

Deserializing data

When you store serialized data like this, you can easily retrieve it in a future version of your application by providing an implementation that will *deserialize* the string data and initialize the member variables of a new object. Listing 14-3 demonstrates the reverse operation:

Listing 14-3: Deserializing the String Version of a Category and Creating a New WordLockerCategoryRecord Object

```
private void deserialize( String inSerial )
{
    if (null != inSerial && inSerial.length() > 0)
    {
        ByteArrayInputStream bais = new ByteArrayInputStream( inSerial.getBytes()
            );
        try
        {
            DocumentBuilderFactory dbf = DocumentBuilderFactory.newInstance();
            DocumentBuilder db = dbf.newDocumentBuilder();
            Document doc = db.parse( bais );
            NodeList categoryNodes = doc.getElementsByTagName( "<Category>" );
            if (null != categoryNodes && categoryNodes.getLength() > 0)
            {
                // only want the first
                Node categoryNode = categoryNodes.item( 0 );
                m_name = this.getAttributeValue( categoryNode, "name" );
            }
            NodeList creationDateNodes = doc.getElementsByTagName( "<CreationDate>"
                );
            if (null != creationDateNodes && creationDateNodes.getLength() > 0)
            {
                Node creationDateNode = creationDateNodes.item( 0 );
                String creationDateString = this.getAttributeValue( creationDateNode,
                    "timestamp" );
                if (null != creationDateString)
                {
                    m_creationTimestamp = Long.parseLong( creationDateString );
                }
                else
                {
                    m_creationTimestamp = new Date().getTime();
```

```
                }
            }
        }
        catch (Exception except)
        {
            // handle anything that goes wrong here
        }
    }
}

private String getAttributeValue( Node inNode, String inAttributeName )
{
    String attrValue = null;
    if (null != inNode && null != inAttributeName && inAttributeName.length() >
            0)
    {
        NamedNodeMap attrs = inNode.getAttributes();
        if (null != attrs && attrs.getLength() > 0)
        {
            Node attrNode = attrs.getNamedItem( inAttributeName );
            if (null != attrNode)
            {
                attrValue = attrNode.getNodeValue();
            }
        }
    }
    return (attrValue);
}

public WordLockerCategoryRecord( String inSerial )
{
    this.deserialize( inSerial );
}
```

The work of deserializing the incoming String data is handled within the
deserialize() method by using the XML parser found in the BlackBerry
OS: net.rim.device.api.parsers.DocumentBuilder. This class does
all the work to split up the standard XML data that comes in. Here's the basic
process:

✔ The incoming String data is converted to a ByteArrayInputStream
  because that's what the DocumentBuilder object requires for
  performing its parsing operation.

✔ A new instance of DocumentBuilderFactory is created.

✔ The DocumentBuilderFactory is used to create the
  DocumentBuilder object.

✔ The DocumentBuilder object parses the ByteArrayInputStream to
  produce a Document object.

- ✔ The Document object is used to extract a `NodeList` of the set of all XML tags that match `<Category>`.

- ✔ Because I know I care only about the first `Node` in the `NodeList`, the code only retrieves that one item.

- ✔ That first `Node` is passed to the `getAttributeValue()` method to retrieve the named attribute, which is used to initialize the `m_name` member variable. Because `m_name` is a `String`, no further processing is required.

- ✔ The process is repeated for the `m_creationTimestamp` member variable. In this case, because the `m_creationTimestamp` is a long value, the `String` returned from `getAttributeValue()` is converted to the original type.

Figure 14-6 shows you the deserialization process.

You can use the BlackBerry OS XML objects to serialize the data as well. I chose not to do so in this instance because the XML structure needed to represent a `WordLockerCategoryRecord` is relatively small and easily put together by using a `StringBuffer`. For more complex XML, you might find it useful to implement serialization while you do deserialization. If your data objects contain other complex objects as member variables, your XML structure may include hierarchies of XML tag data, in which case using the XML objects to perform the serialization would be your best choice.

By serializing your data, you provide a standard format for future versions of your application to retrieve the data. When users upgrade from an older to a newer version of your application, they want to be assured that all their work done in the prior version smoothly migrates to the new version. They don't want to lose any of their information, and they don't want to be required to put it all back in again, even assuming they can remember it all. And that's why users use smartphones: to keep track of the wide variety of information that enters their lives. Your users will appreciate the effort you put into your application to make your app easy to use, and maintaining the information that they contribute.

Handling multiple versions of your app

Because you're thinking about the future of your app, you will want to consider the possibility that the next version of your app that a user installs might be several versions newer than the one they originally installed. Version 3 of your application has to be able to handle data being migrated from version 1, and not just data from version 2. As a result, you will likely want to serialize a version number of the objects storing the data in serialized form so that some future version of the same object can deserialize appropriately.

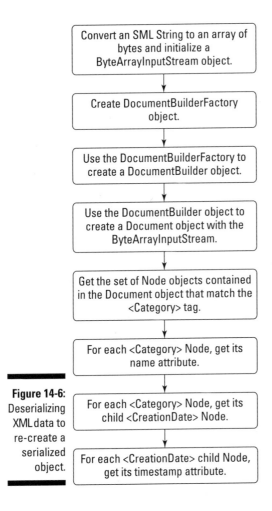

Figure 14-6:
Deserializing
XML data to
re-create a
serialized
object.

Flowchart boxes:

- Convert an SML String to an array of bytes and initialize a ByteArrayInputStream object.
- Create DocumentBuilderFactory object.
- Use the DocumentBuilderFactory to create a DocumentBuilder object.
- Use the DocumentBuilder object to create a Document object with the ByteArrayInputStream.
- Get the set of Node objects contained in the Document object that match the <Category> tag.
- For each <Category> Node, get its name attribute.
- For each <Category> Node, get its child <CreationDate> Node.
- For each <CreationDate> child Node, get its timestamp attribute.

The best way to do that is to add a data-version component into your serialized output, and react to it when the data is read back in. In your implementation of the specific class that's being serialized, you implement a `deserialize()` method that pays attention to the version attribute of the data `String`. In Listing 14-4, you can see the XML that the code in Listing 14-3 would create, with random values inserted for the name and creation timestamp.

Listing 14-4:   The XML Created for the Serialized Category "On The Road"

```
<?xml version="1.0" ?>
<WordLocker version="1.0">
   <Category name="On The Road">
      <CreationDate timestamp="12791109568"/>
   </Category>
</WordLocker>
```

The version attribute for the WordLocker tag is set to 1.0. You can use this as the indicator for which data elements were present when the data was written into the serialized form. Although a newer version of WordLocker might add more member variables to a Category object — in fact, could even completely replace the WordLockerCategoryRecord class used to represent different categories — the data contained in an older record can still be imported and interpreted in the new application. You could similarly add a version attribute to the Category tag itself, although that is probably more than is required. Any changes to the structure or contents of a Category record would very likely result from an update (and thus a new version number) for the entire application.

Part VI
The Part of Tens

In this part . . .

With every new BlackBerry come new features as well as new ways for you to take charge of the smartphone and deliver its power to your users. And with every version of the Java Development Environment (JDE), RIM provides a new set of sample code, increasing the library of applications that show off what your coding skills can accomplish.

This part delivers my ten favorite sample applications, where you can find examples of the interesting features that a BlackBerry will let you play with. But don't let those hold you back — check out the remainder of the samples. And you should look forward to each new version of the JDE for the examples that arrive with it.

Finally, in this part, I also give you tips for keeping your development efforts focused on the things that matter while you work on your app.

Chapter 15

Ten Most Useful Sample BlackBerry Apps

· ·

*L*onger ago than I prefer to recall, I was handed a book on programming in BASIC that contained the source code for more than 100 games. The book did not cover theory, data structures, or anything deeply philosophical. Most games worked as written, some required a work-around, and one horse-racing game never did work. (Perhaps I should rewrite it as a BlackBerry app?) The end result was that I learned to program by taking those examples and making them work. Today, I still look for example code when I need to solve problems.

You can find the RIM sample applications in the following default location. If you have a different version of the JDE, use its version number instead of 4.5.0:

```
C:\Program Files\Research In Motion\BlackBerry JDE 4.5.0\samples\samples.jdw
```

This workspace contains all the separate sample projects, each a separate application designed to show you the specific — and most importantly, *correct* — way of doing something. You can run them all from the BlackBerry simulator, or sign them to run on a real BlackBerry device. In this chapter, I describe the ten sample apps that I find to be the most interesting and useful.

contactsdemo

Most likely, your application will be storing data, one way or another. It's pretty difficult to avoid, and at the very least, your users will want to go right back to the place they were the last time they ran your app. The `contacts demo` application uses the persistent storage mechanism to store its data, and it also supports reacting to changes in the device's settings for content protection or compression. A second project, called `ContactsDemo_auto startup`, is included with this application. This project is known as an *Alternate Entry Point* (AEP), which provides your app a way to perform some initialization behind the scenes without displaying a screen. (I describe this in more detail in Chapter 3.)

custombuttonsdemo

The `custombuttonsdemo` is a small app that shows you how you can create just about any shape of button you like. In a broader sense, you see how you can extend a `Field` object to represent any UI element you can envision. The sample app contains a class that demonstrates the different aspects you must implement for a `Field` subclass when you want to use your own unique interface elements rather than standard ones.

httpdemo

The `httpdemo` sample app contains useful code samples for performing network operations. The app waits for you to input a URL, and then will fetch the HTML text from the Web server and display it all as text in the scrolling field below the URL. Don't forget to launch the MDS simulator if you run this app on a BlackBerry simulator. Read more about the MDS simulator in Appendix A.

gpsdemo

The Global Positioning System (GPS) is one of the most useful programs ever developed by the U.S. military, and now 21st century cell phones can use this 1960s-era technology to determine a location. Certain BlackBerry models come with GPS hardware and support the Java Micro Edition (JME) Location framework (`javax.microedition.location`), which provides classes that you can use to determine the latitude, longitude, and altitude of the user's BlackBerry device. Your application can then use this data to provide sight-seeing or public transit information for visitors to foreign cities. Imagine flying to a faraway city and using your BlackBerry to help you go to the cultural sites you want to visit.

localizationdemo

If you're looking to sell your application to people who don't speak English, look to the `localizationdemo` sample app for code examples to ensure that all your pieces of text are correctly *localized,* meaning your app shows its menus in French when running on a BlackBerry whose language is set to French. The demo provides English text also translated to four other languages (German, Spanish, French, and Italian); you'll need to use a simulator that comes with multiple languages already installed, or deploy a signed version of the application onto a device that is multilingual. You'll find that making your application speak different languages is actually pretty easy, but the first step is to separate the text your app will display to the user from the code that creates the display.

memorydemo

As painful as it is to admit, your application will consume memory. And the more you use, the greater the chance that the OS will run out of memory for you to use because other apps need it, too. If your app makes use of large data files (such as movies or music), a low-memory condition is likely to occur. The memorydemo sample app demonstrates how to set up your application to provide a means by which your app can free up *stale* memory blocks — data that isn't used frequently enough to keep in memory.

notificationsdemo

The BlackBerry OS allows your application to transmit and respond to notifications generated either by the OS or by your own application. A *notification* is essentially a message that your application can sign up to receive. In addition, your application can alert the BlackBerry user that it has something new for the user to know. An application that makes use of social networking to keep users informed of the status of others in the network could use this feature, and the techniques in the notificationsdemo sample app are worth reviewing.

phoneapidemo

Your application can reach into the phone records of a user's BlackBerry if the user gives the app permission to do so. The phoneapidemo is an application that can list the phone calls made and received by the BlackBerry. The source code for this sample shows the use of various UI components such as display lists, and how to integrate your app with the BlackBerry OS phone APIs. If you look at the phone APIs (net.rim.black berry.api.phone), you will find that your app can pay attention to all the different phone operations. Note, however, that if the user does *not* grant your application permission to access this information, any attempt to use a phone API will cause a ControlledAccessException to interrupt the execution of your app and prevent the use of that code.

smsdemo

A quarter of a century ago, SMS (Short Message Service) was defined for use with mobile handsets. With the exception of my parents, pretty much everyone in the world has used text messaging to communicate with, well, pretty much everyone else in the world. Your application can take advantage of the BlackBerry's ability to transmit and receive SMS messages. The sms demo application gives you sample code to do just that, showing you how to create a message connection object and use it to broadcast messages from and intercept messages received on a BlackBerry device.

tictactoedemo

Tic-tac-toe is a very simple game, and the tictactoedemo provides the basic game, you versus the BlackBerry, to demonstrate various UI elements. As a bonus, you can play a game against someone on another BlackBerry, using the BlackBerry Messenger service. This application demonstrates two-way communication using the APIs of the BlackBerry Messenger to transmit the game-move information from one player to the other. The demo sets up the communications service and coordinates transmission and reception of each player's move to the other.

xmldemo

Much of the information transmitted across the Internet is in the form of XML data. The BlackBerry contains a full XML DOM parser, which is a set of APIs that will load and interpret XML text, as well as create properly formatted XML text. The xmldemo project demonstrates how you can use the DOM parser to read and write XML data. The xmldemo application loads an XML file into the DOM parser and then proceeds to display the information in a hierarchy on the BlackBerry display.

Chapter 16

Ten BlackBerry Development Tips

I've been working with the BlackBerry platform for more than four years now, and while RIM keeps me hopping with new features and functionality to play with, a few things I do remain the same from one app to the next. When writing code, I have a closetful of reminders for standard tricks I've learned to keep the application in an easy-to-maintain, easy-to-improve state. I discovered almost all these tips as a result of doing something the wrong way first, and then rewriting the code to do it the right way. Here are ten tips that help you get your code right the first time.

Keep Your Constant Strings in One Place

RIM sells BlackBerry devices all around the world, in more than 100 countries. This means that your application has a market that includes people who don't speak English and don't want to use an application that only speaks English. To reach them — and their wallets — your application needs to display text in all the languages you want to sell to. The BlackBerry development environment comes with tools to enable your app to automatically deliver text strings in the language the user has set the device to use. To do this, you have to make an effort to pull out any hard-coded text strings from your classes, and replace them with code to retrieve the text from a `ResourceBundle` object. And remember that *concatenation* (creating a text string by combining two or more different strings) works differently in different languages, so you'll need to take note of where your app is doing something like this.

Manage All Screens

The primary object your application uses to communicate with your users is its screens. You have to master the knowledge of screen management; see Chapter 5 for basics of screens and their requirements. You also need to experience the actual screens running in the simulator and on a device. Keep the following rules in your mind when your app is dealing with screens:

✔ Push new screens on the top the screen stack before you *pop* (remove) old ones.

✔ Always use `Application.getEventLock()` or `Application.invokeLater()` to make changes on a screen from a process in the background.

✔ Except for transitions, keep only one screen on the screen stack at a time. With a little discipline, you should be able to achieve this goal. This assists you greatly throughout your app's existence because you always know what screen is the active one.

Don't Lose Your Memory

Unlike other programming languages, Java reduces the need for developers to keep track of all the memory their objects allocate. Your app doesn't have to match a `delete` or `free` operation with every `new` you use to create a new object. However, that doesn't mean you should leave unused objects just lying around, waiting for the Java garbage collector to pick up after you. BlackBerry devices have a limited amount of memory that can be used to hold data while your application is running, and Java starts the garbage collection process only when that memory is almost all gone.

Your app should be very strict in its use of memory, especially when it comes to creating new screen objects because these objects use up a significant amount of memory, and they're also the easiest objects to leave lying around. Ideally, your app will have as few screens as possible and create a new one only when absolutely necessary. One way to accomplish this is to only ever create one instance of a screen, and then recycle that instance (reinitialize it) when you need it again.

Keep Your Constants All Together

One of the biggest problems in development using older programming languages was the overuse of *magic numbers* — some unexplained and arbitrary number in the middle of the source code. The originator of the code might have an instinctive awareness of what the number meant and why it was that value, but future generations usually had a difficult time figuring out why that number couldn't be something different — or worse, where else that particular value came into play.

Java coding guidelines (and you've read them all, right? Check out `http://java.sun.com/docs/codeconv/CodeConventions.pdf`) dictate how you should set up your constants within the classes you create. I won't tell you to use all the coding conventions in the Sun Java guidelines, but the one on constants is both easy to implement and extremely helpful for handling problems that arise in the future.

Keep the Order Straight

Every application, whether written for a desktop PC or a BlackBerry or something else, has a predefined order of operation. From the moment the user tells the OS to launch the app until the moment the first screen is displayed for the user to see, your app follows a prescribed sequence of events. If you keep this order close at hand when you're programming your app, you're much more likely to know what stage your app is in at a given moment while it's running. Table 16-1 is a list of the major events, in order, that your application will move through.

Table 16-1	The Natural Order of Things	
Event	*Object*	*Method*
User launches app	UiApplication	main(String[] args)
OS tells app to begin	UiApplication	activate()
Screen is pushed onto stack	MainScreen	onDisplay()
Screen about to be drawn	MainScreen	onUiEngine Attached()
Menu or dialog is removed	MainScreen	onExposed()
Screen is closed	MainScreen	close()
OS puts app in background	UiApplication	deactivate()

This list of method calls — which are executed by the OS — gives you a sequence you will refer to again and again while you're developing your app and learning how it behaves.

Harmonize with RIM

RIM is constantly introducing new devices and new versions of its device OS. The good news is this means new features and functionality head your way several times a year. The bad news is that sometimes code that worked in a previous version of the OS no longer works in the new version. The real bad news is that when something breaks, you have to deal with it, one way or another.

You should periodically check the BlackBerry developer Web site (`http://na.blackberry.com/eng/developers`) and keep up with the latest and greatest of what's going on with RIM. For instance, as of this writing, the newest released device OS is 5.0, and the upcoming 6.0 device OS has been demonstrated at the 2010 Wireless Enterprise Symposium (WES). In addition, JDE 5.0 is now available.

Initialize at the Right Moment

Every object you create, every member variable of even the simple Java types, requires initialization. Many difficulties in your development result from variables being uninitialized when you expected them to be valid data. Sometimes this can be difficult to track, especially if your app does any background processing that hasn't finished when the mainline of your app tries to use the data delivered by the background process. The Java compiler initializes all member variables to one of several innocuous values:

- `Zero`
- `null`
- `false`

However, local variables must be initialized before being used, or else the compiler refuses to compile the code.

For certain objects, such as the `Application` object or any `Screen` object, you might have to wait for the right time to perform initialization. After the constructor has been executed, the OS goes through its own initialization phase. For `Application` objects, this is the time between the call to `enterEventDispatcher` and the execution of `activate`. For `Screen` objects, this is the time between pushing the screen onto the screen stack and the execution of its `onUiEngineAttached` method. So you want to make certain you override these two methods to finish your initialization just before you present the user with something on the screen.

Catch Those Exceptional Moments

Java provides you with a mechanism for handling unexpected behavior on the part of the device or the operating system by throwing exceptions. This allows you to write code that can react to unpredictable events through something called the try-catch mechanism. The BlackBerry APIs contain uncountable numbers of methods that can throw exceptions, and you want to make sure that your app can handle at least all of the most likely ones. Otherwise, your users will see something like the screen shown in Figure 16-1.

Figure 16-1: An app throws an exception that bubbles up outside the app.

One thing to keep in mind: Your app can't catch *all* exceptions. Some of them come from out of nowhere, and there's just nothing you can do about those. The BlackBerry API documentation provides you with the obvious ones, but I have come across some very subtle programming issues — usually involving at least another thread of execution — that throw not-so-obvious exceptions.

Remember the User

Your application is going to be downloaded and used by hundreds, thousands, millions (I hope!) of users. Users bring their own expectations and hopes when it comes to using your app, so you need to craft your app in a way that keeps their basic needs in mind. A BlackBerry user is almost always a high-energy, on-the-go, no-time-to-waste person, and your app needs to be built with this in mind. It's easy to scroll through several thousand vertical pixels' worth of information in a Web page on your desktop PC; a user trying to scroll through that much on a BlackBerry screen is going to go somewhere else. The same is true for non-Web applications: Your users depend on you to provide them with the information they want quickly and easily. Try to keep the pertinent information in one screen, with supporting screens just one click away.

RIM provides a User Interface Guide that you definitely should take a look at (http://docs.blackberry.com/en/developers/deliverables/6625). The guide contains information about all the different models and their characteristics, as well as design principles to help you develop your application to be useful across all the BlackBerry devices. Learning these principles will help you keep your app living up to its users' expectations.

Don't Take It All Too Seriously

I enjoy programming and have developed applications for many different platforms. The BlackBerry makes some things easy, and also provides challenges requiring me to be persistent and sometimes even creative. I still scream at the computer, the simulator, the JDE, and the application whenever they do something I didn't count on. At that point, it's easy to see I'm taking things too seriously, and I need to take a break. Hopefully you will learn this as well to reduce the stress that arises when your app just simply won't do what you tell it to do.

Programming is fun, which is what it should be. The fact that you've purchased this book suggests that you think so, too. When the code you're working on is frustrating and stymieing you, it's no longer much fun. That's when it's time to step away, for just a little bit, and escape from the problem at hand. You can come back to it in an hour, or a day, when emotions have died down and the problem is no longer a wall slammed down on the path you chose, but is instead a challenge to learn about and overcome. Programming is all about solving problems.

Part VII
Appendixes

The 5th Wave   By Rich Tennant

"The developers lived on Jolt and cheese sticks putting this product together, but if you wanted to just use 'cola and cheese sticks' in the Users Documentation, that's okay too. We're pretty loose around here."

In this part . . .

Sometimes chunks of valuable information are just better encapsulated as references in a "room of their own," which is why books have appendixes — and that's what this part is.

Here, you find a virtual debate between simulation and reality: the benefits and challenges of BlackBerry simulators versus the positives and negatives of using the real things. You discover why BlackBerry simulators can give you the next best thing to the real thing, and also why a real device will expose your app to the real world that real users experience.

Appendix A

Device and Service Simulators

*Y*ou can download and install all the tools you need to develop, build, and run your BlackBerry app for free. RIM provides the JDE complete with BlackBerry smartphone simulators in one package. These simulated smartphones operate exactly as the real smartphones using the same version of the BlackBerry OS, so you can be sure that if your app runs perfectly on the simulator, your app will run perfectly on the real thing. Okay, that's not always true — real smartphones can and do misbehave — but you'll find that your app does behave on a real smartphone pretty much as it does on a simulator. And you can be sure that if your app *fails* on a simulator, it will *definitely fail* on a real smartphone.

RIM also provides BlackBerry smartphone simulators apart from the JDE. See, RIM is developing new versions of its smartphone OS and new BlackBerry smartphones all the time, but you'll find that RIM doesn't update the JDE packages quite as quickly as it puts new smartphones on the market. You want to test your app on the new smartphones without waiting for RIM to release the next generation of the JDE.

In this appendix, you discover how to use the simulators that come with the JDE to test and stress-test your app before you bring it to the BlackBerry App World, without having to buy all the different smartphone models to test it on. I also show you where to find and how to install the latest BlackBerry smartphone simulators available at RIM so you can keep up to date and be sure that your app is good to run on the new hardware as well as the old.

Smartphone simulators won't be enough to fully capture the complete BlackBerry smartphone experience — real users holding real BlackBerry smartphones can get real e-mail and connect to real Web services. So in addition to device simulators, RIM provides a pair of *service* simulators that you use to provide network and e-mail capability to BlackBerry smartphone simulators. I show you where you can find these simulators at RIM so you can download, install, and set up so your BlackBerry smartphone simulators are connected just like their real physical cousins are.

Using BlackBerry JDE Device Simulators

All BlackBerry device simulators execute the exact same code as an actual BlackBerry device using the same operating system version number. That is, your application, running on a simulator, will execute its code just as if it were running on an actual device. This means you can be pretty certain how your application will behave on your users' BlackBerry devices just by running it on the BlackBerry simulators.

Each version of the JDE comes with its own set of simulated BlackBerry devices. The JDE version 4.5 comes with the following device simulators:

- ✔ 81xx Pearl series (8100, 8110, 8120, 8130)
- ✔ 83xx series Curve (8300, 8310, 8320, 8330)
- ✔ 8700 and 8703e
- ✔ 88xx series (8800, 8820, 8830)

The JDE version 4.7 comes with the following simulators:

- ✔ 8830
- ✔ 95xx series Storm (9500, 9530)

As you can see, the JDE v. 4.7 doesn't provide as many different device simulators as the JDE v. 4.5; however, the JDE v. 4.5 does not come with the BlackBerry Storm, which is one of the most popular BlackBerry models. That's because the Storm itself uses BlackBerry device OS 4.7 or later, and so the 4.7 JDE is required to create applications that can take advantage of the Storm's touchscreen.

You can launch your application using the simulators that come with the JDE in two ways:

✔ **From within the JDE itself, by pressing the F5 key:** This is the quickest way to get your app up and running, and the JDE will also build your application if needed.

✔ **From the command line by performing the steps in the following list.** The JDE simulators are found in the following directory, assuming that you installed the JDE at the default location:

```
C:\Program Files\Research In Motion\BlackBerry JDE x.y.z\simulator
```

Each separate simulator has a BAT file in this directory, and that file contains the `fledge.exe` command line command to launch an application. This application is the engine for all the simulated BlackBerry devices.

To launch your application in a simulator from the command line, follow this procedure:

1. **Open a command window.**

2. **Navigate to**

```
C:\Program Files\Research In Motion\BlackBerry JDE 4.5.0\simulator
```

For this example, I'm using the 4.5.0 JDE.

3. **In this directory is a collection of .BAT files, one for each simulator; pick your favorite simulator from the list.**

Figure A-1 shows a directory listing of the set of .BAT files that come with the 4.5.0 JDE.

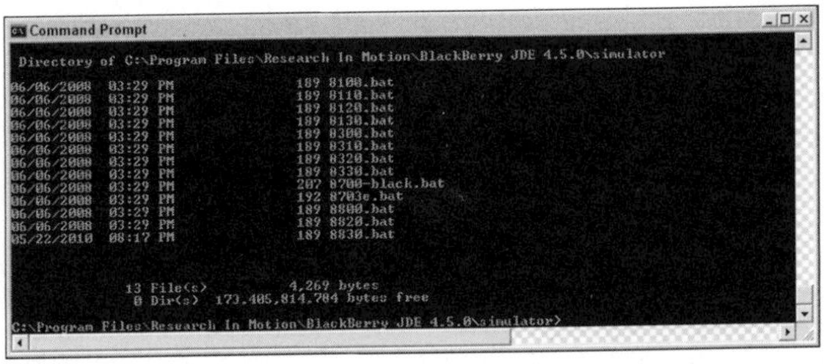

Figure A-1:
The default simulator BAT files installed with the BlackBerry 4.5.0 JDE.

Of all the smartphone simulators installed with the 4.5.0 JDE, my preferred is the BlackBerry 8310 Curve, so I use the BAT file `8310.bat` to launch it.

4. Execute the BAT file of your simulator.

When I type the following command — `8310.bat` — into the command window, the BlackBerry 8310 simulator launches. The BAT file is a script file that contains the commands needed to launch the simulator executable with the settings needed to simulate the BlackBerry 8310 Curve.

5. Choose File⇨Load Java Program.

The Windows Open File dialog box appears.

6. Navigate to the location of your app's COD file, select it, and click the Open button.

The COD file contains all the code in your application, and this is all you need the simulator to open. In Figure A-2, you can see the 8310 simulator's Open File dialog box ready to open `WordLocker.cod`.

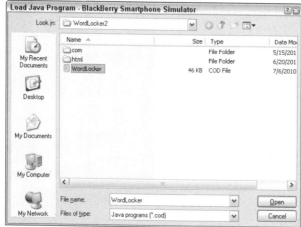

Figure A-2: WordLocker. cod is selected to be added to the simulator's set of apps.

The simulator installs your app, and your app's icon is displayed on the BlackBerry simulator screen.

7. Move the simulator's selection cursor to your app and click the app to launch it.

You operate the BlackBerry smartphone simulator just like you would a real BlackBerry. All the keys — as well as the operations of the trackball, trackwheel, trackpad, and touchscreen — are mapped to keys on your PC's keyboard. If you hold your mouse over the simulator's keys, you see in the bottom-left corner of the window the PC key that maps to the simulator key. In Figure A-3, you can see that the BlackBerry menu key (the button to the left of the trackball) maps to `Keyboard:Insert` (the mouse hovering over the menu button didn't get captured in the screen capture). You move the selection cursor (the yellow highlight at the topmost icon in Figure A-3) using the PC's arrow keys.

Keeping things tidy

Every time you build an application using the JDE and then execute that application with the JDE's simulator, a copy of your application's code files (COD files) is placed in the simulator directory, deleting any older version of your app. This copy will stay there until you delete it, which means that every other application you build and run will stay there as well. Fortunately, you can execute the BAT file in the simulator directory — `clean.bat` — to clean the simulator directory of all the COD files that shouldn't be there.

Selection cursor

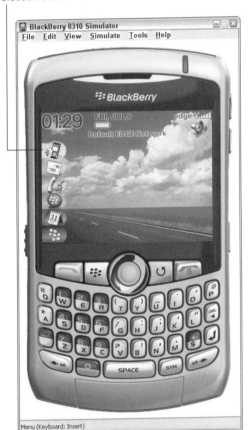

Figure A-3:
Mapping the
menu button
to the PC's
Insert key.

When you launch the simulator from a command line window, the JDE is not informed. This means that the JDE can't be used to debug or monitor the simulator or your app running on it. This sequence of steps prepares you for launching simulators you download directly from RIM, so you can test your app on the latest simulated smartphones. You can connect the JDE to the simulator as it is running so that you can monitor and debug your app just as if you had launched it from within the JDE. Here's how you do that:

1. **Launch your app using a simulator from the command line, as detailed earlier.**

2. **Launch the JDE.**

3. **Load your application workspace into the JDE if it's not already there.**

4. **Choose Debug⇨Attach To⇨Simulator.**

   Alternatively, you can also press Ctrl+Shift+O.

   The JDE connects to the simulator. You're now ready to test your app, and catch any piece of code that misbehaves.

Using the MDS Simulator

BlackBerry users are *networked* users. Their devices talk to the Internet through a wireless service provider or through a Wi-Fi connection; they receive e-mail, go to Web sites, push and pull data — everything you can do with an Internet connection. If your app is going to enhance the user's Internet experience, you definitely need to test that functionality before your app goes public. And seeing as how this is the appendix on simulators, this section is all about how a BlackBerry device simulator accesses the Internet.

The JDE you installed comes with an MDS simulator. MDS — Mobile Data Service — is a service of the BlackBerry Enterprise Server (BES) system. The MDS simulator is designed to provide access for device simulators to the Internet through the Windows operating system.

To launch the MDS simulator, choose Start⇨All Programs⇨Research In Motion⇨BlackBerry JDE 4.5.0⇨MDS-CS. The MDS simulator opens a command line window, like that shown in Figure A-4, which displays lines of text output, telling you what the MDS is doing. The last line

```
Admin. Task- pending push messages
```

indicates that the MDS has completed its initialization and is waiting for activity.

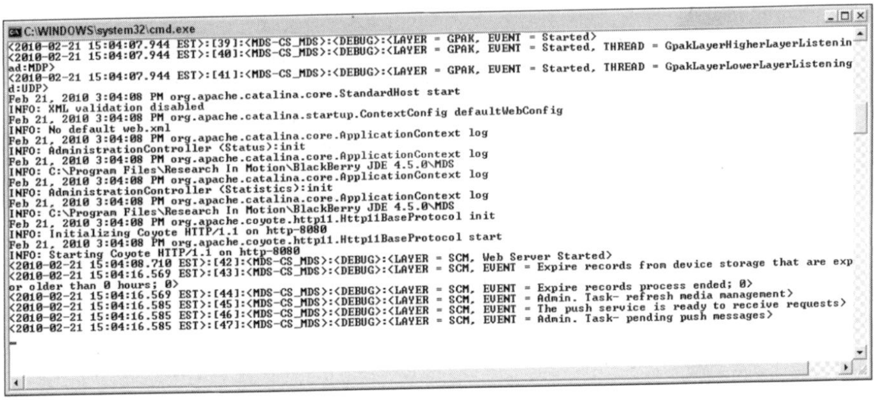

Figure A-4:
BlackBerry
MDS
simulator
after
initialization
and ready to
network.

With the MDS simulator launched, a BlackBerry device simulator can access the Internet, just as if it were a BlackBerry (even though it uses your PC's Internet connection). You can see this by following these steps:

1. **Launch a BlackBerry simulator.**

   It doesn't matter whether you launch it from the JDE or from the command line. In this example, I'm launching the AT&T BlackBerry 9700 simulator.

2. **Launch the BlackBerry Browser application on the simulator just like you would on a BlackBerry.**

3. **Type** yahoo.com **(or your favorite Web site) into the URL entry text box.**

   You can enter this by using the keys on your PC's keyboard. You can also click the onscreen keys using your mouse, but I find using the keyboard to be much faster.

4. **Press Enter.**

   You see the text in the MDS command window scrolling by as the MDS performs various operations. This confirms that the BlackBerry simulator is communicating with the MDS simulator and from there to the Internet. You can see some of this text in Figure A-5.

   After the MDS simulator retrieves all the information that the URL provided, the BlackBerry simulator will display the Web page you surfed to.

The MDS simulator can provide more functionality than simple outward-bound network access, but at the moment, this is all you need to know. I cover network communications from within a BlackBerry app in Chapter 9.

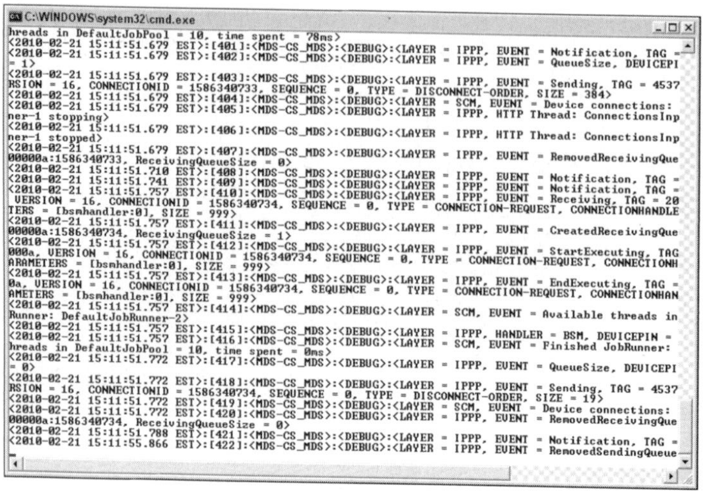

Figure A-5:
BlackBerry
MDS
simulator in
communica-
tion with a
BlackBerry
device
simulator.

Using the Email Service Simulator (ESS)

If your application will make use of e-mail messages or their attachments, you need to test this functionality. You can do this pretty easily by using a real device with a real wireless connection. However, when you're running on a simulator, you also need to simulate the e-mail service so that the simulated device can send and receive e-mail messages just like a real device would.

As of this writing, only the 4.1.4 ESS application seems to work as described. If your application requires testing e-mail interaction on a simulator, this version is the one you need. You don't require the 4.1.4 version of the JDE, however; the 4.1.4 ESS will work with current device simulators.

If your application is going to access e-mail, either to send or receive, your best bet is to buy a real device complete with a service plan that allows you to do this. The ESS isn't complicated or difficult to set up, but the hairs on the back of my neck stand on end whenever I think of using it because I've managed to successfully get only the 4.1.4 version to work correctly.

Downloading the latest ESS

To download the 4.1.4 ESS, perform the following steps:

1. Point your browser to

   `http://na.blackberry.com/eng/developers/resources`

   You see a screen that looks similar to that shown in Figure A-6.

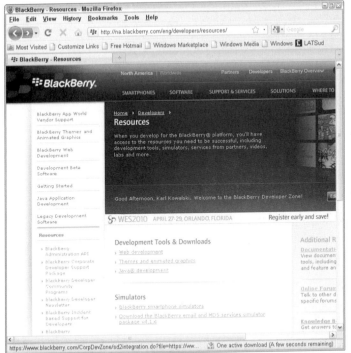

Figure A-6:
RIM
BlackBerry
resource
page.

2. **Click the Download the BlackBerry Email and MDS Services Simulator Package v4.1.4 link.**

   You are taken to a familiar "please enter your registration information" screen, hopefully with all the required text boxes filled out.

3. **Check all the required text boxes and fill in those that are missing.**

   Sometimes one or two don't get filled in. I think RIM just wants to make sure that a human being is at the controls.

4. **Click the Next button.**

   You are taken to the Eligibility screen.

5. **Check Agree (because I'm pretty sure you do!) and then click Next.**

   You'll be presented with the Software Download for Developers screen, showing you that you're about to download a file called `BlackBerry_Email_MDS_4.1.4.exe`.

6. **Click the Download button.**

   The usual download process will run.

7. **Navigate via Windows Explorer to the file you just downloaded and double-click the file to start the installation process.**

8. Accept all the defaults and let the installation run.

The ESS application and the MDS application can't be executed together. I haven't determined why this is, but when both are running, the ESS application doesn't receive any communication from either the smartphone simulator or Outlook if MDS is running, too. If you want to test your application's e-mail capabilities, you have to close MDS if it's already running. (It won't hurt your app or your PC if both are running at the same time; it's just that ESS won't work correctly.)

Running the ESS

To run ESS version 4.1.4, choose Start➪All Programs➪Research In Motion➪ BlackBerry Email and MDS Services Simulators 4.1.4➪ESS. You see the Email Server Simulator window (shown in upcoming Figure A-4) when the ESS is launched.

You can also run the ESS from a command line window. This has the added advantage of providing more information about what the ESS is doing, just in case you run into problems with its operation. I prefer launching ESS from the command line window because

- ✔ I enjoy the hum of debug messages scrolling across the window.
- ✔ When something goes wrong, it's obvious.
- ✔ When something should be going right, but doesn't, it's obvious. (This is how I discovered that the ESS wasn't getting any e-mail attempts from the smartphone simulator while MDS was also running.)

The ESS will operate in one of two modes:

- ✔ **Connected mode:** In this mode of operation, the ESS will communicate with a real e-mail server, one which you will need to provide enough information for ESS to act as a middleman between the device simulator and the e-mail service. Outgoing messages created on the BlackBerry device simulator will be delivered using the e-mail service you configure ESS to communicate with. Connected mode works well with corporate e-mail services, but does not work easily with services such as Gmail, Yahoo!, or Hotmail — I haven't yet gotten my BlackBerry simulator to work with my Gmail account.

- ✔ **Standalone mode:** Using this mode of operation turns the ESS into an e-mail server running on your PC. This is the best approach to using ESS because you can set up Outlook or Outlook Express to communicate with your BlackBerry simulator through ESS.

Configuring the ESS

I recommend running the ESS in Standalone mode when you want to test using e-mail with your application. Figure A-7 shows the ESS setup on my PC, before executing Standalone mode.

Email Server Simulator

- ● Standalone mode
  - Pop3 port 110
  - Smtp port 25
  - Clean FS
- ○ Connected mode
  - Outgoing: .... smtp.server
  - Incoming: pop3.server
  - User name:
  - Password:
  - Poll inbox every 2 seconds

- Name: .... Karl G. Kowalski
- Email: .... kgk@mymachine.com
- PIN: 2100000A

  Launch | Help | Load Test

To start the ESS, all you need to do is the following. This sequence of steps sets the ESS to act as a mail server running on your PC, but only for the BlackBerry simulator. In this example, I'm using Standalone mode; see the preceding section.

1. **Select the Standalone Mode radio button.**

   The POP3 port and SMTP port values are prefilled for you, and you don't want to change them. Your local e-mail client (such as Outlook) will by default expect the ESS to use those values.

   The ESS uses your PC to store the e-mail messages that the BlackBerry simulator sends out, and the e-mail messages your e-mail client sends to the BlackBerry simulator. The ESS is acting as a post office, except it keeps copies of the e-mail messages sent in either direction, just like a real e-mail service does. The Clean FS button removes all those copies, so you should click it every time you launch the ESS, before you click its Launch button.

2. **Enter a name into the Name text box.**

This name can be anything you choose, so I usually put my own name, in all lowercase. This helps me pick out these messages in my Outlook inbox more easily — you might consider setting it to something like *BlackBerry Simulator* to make it stand out even more.

3. Enter the e-mail address that will be used in the Email text box.

I chose kgk@mymachine.com. The choice of e-mail address is completely up to you because you set up your favorite e-mail application, such as Outlook, to use that account. This isn't a real e-mail account — this is only for the ESS to manage. You create a new account in your e-mail client to use this e-mail address and tell it that this address is controlled by the ESS. Note that Web-based e-mail services can't be used with the ESS. After this step, you don't need to change any other information on the screen.

The PIN text box is the BlackBerry 8-hexadecimal digit Personal Identification Number. There's a different one for every real BlackBerry smartphone. For the simulator, the PIN is assigned and can be set to any 8-hexadecimal digit value you'd like. The default is 2100000A. If you take a peek inside the BAT file for the BlackBerry simulator you launch, you see that one of the pieces of information used to launch the simulator is this PIN value. You can change it, but I've found it better to stick with the default because then I don't have to remember what I've changed it to.

4. Click the Launch button.

That's all you need to do to run ESS and have it act as a mail server specifically for BlackBerry device simulators. If you launch a BlackBerry device simulator (such as the 9700 AT&T Bold 2), it will connect by default to the ESS for messages. You can create e-mail messages, using the device simulator, and send them to the ESS.

If you want to access the messages sent by the BlackBerry device simulator to the ESS, you need to set up a Windows mail application (such as Outlook Express) to connect to the ESS.

To configure Outlook 2007 to communicate with the BlackBerry simulators, follow these steps:

1. Launch Outlook 2007.

2. Select Tools⇨Account Settings.

Outlook 2007 shows you the list of e-mail accounts it's aware of. Figure A-8 demonstrates my Outlook BlackBerry simulator e-mail account. The account kgk@mymachine.com is set to talk to the ESS and the BlackBerry simulator.

3. Click New.

This starts the process of creating a new e-mail account.

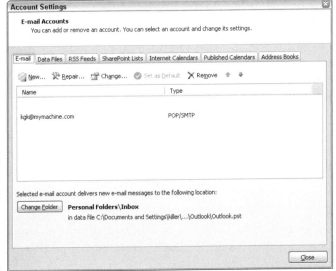

Figure A-8:
The list
of e-mail
accounts in
my Outlook
2007.

4. **Select Microsoft Exchange, POP3, IMAP, or HTTP, and click Next.**

5. **Select the Manually Configure Server Settings or Additional Server Types check box, and then click Next.**

   This disables all the other entry fields.

6. **Select Internet E-mail and click Next.**

   Apparently, the only reason you need to do this is so Outlook knows you're not trying to connect to Microsoft Exchange.

7. **Fill in the page as follows:**

   - In the Your Name text box, enter any name you wish.

   - In the E-mail Address text box, enter the same e-mail address you entered for the ESS.

   - From the Account Type drop-down list, select POP3 (it should be that already).

   - In both the Incoming Mail Server and the Outgoing Mail Server (SMTP) text boxes, enter **localhost.**

   - In the User Name text box, enter the username of the e-mail address you entered in the E-mail Address text box.

   - Leave the Password text box blank.

   - Make sure the Remember Password and Require Logon Using Secure Password Authentication (SPA) check boxes are unchecked.

   Figure A-9 shows the settings for my `kgk@mymachine.com` account in Outlook 2007.

Figure A-9:
The e-mail
account
allows
Outlook to
send e-mail
messages
to the
BlackBerry
simulator
through
the ESS
simulator.

Change E-mail Account

Internet E-mail Settings
Each of these settings are required to get your e-mail account working.

User Information

Your Name: Karl G. Kowalski

E-mail Address: kgk@mymachine.com

Server Information

Account Type: POP3

Incoming mail server: localhost

Outgoing mail server (SMTP): localhost

Logon Information

User Name: kgk

Password:

☐ Remember password

☐ Require logon using Secure Password Authentication (SPA)

Test Account Settings

After filling out the information on this screen, we recommend you test your account by clicking the button below. (Requires network connection)

[Test Account Settings ...]

[More Settings ...]

[< Back] [Next >] [Cancel]

8. **Click Next and then click Finish on the last screen to finish the account creation.**

If you use another e-mail client, check the user documentation for your e-mail application to determine how to connect it to the ESS as if it were the mail server.

After you have your ESS running and your mail client communicating to it, a BlackBerry device simulator can send e-mail messages to ESS for your mail client to receive, and your mail client can send e-mail messages to ESS for the BlackBerry device simulator to receive.

In my experiments setting up the ESS and Outlook 2007 to work together to send and receive e-mail messages between Outlook and the BlackBerry simulator, I got frustrated when the BlackBerry simulator was sending e-mail to the ESS, but nothing was showing up in my Outlook Inbox. The ESS messages flashing by in the command-line window looked good, no errors were reported, but nothing was showing up in Outlook no matter how many times I clicked the Send/Receive button. Worse, Outlook's little window displaying the steps it was taking was showing no errors or failures either. Then I noticed my Junk E-mail folder was getting more messages. Apparently, Outlook didn't trust the BlackBerry simulator or the ESS. After I told Outlook to stop treating those messages as junk, it all worked fine. Lesson learned: Always check your Junk E-mail folder!

Appendix B

Real Devices and Services

In This Appendix

▶ Using a BlackBerry device for development

▶ Getting familiar with BlackBerry Internet Service (BIS)

▶ Getting familiar with BlackBerry Enterprise Server (BES)

*Y*our development efforts in creating The Greatest BlackBerry App can be performed almost completely using the device simulators and the service simulators downloaded from RIM. Before you send your app to the BlackBerry App World, though, you must run it on a real device at least once to properly test it. If you've ever developed an application for a mobile platform, you already know this. If creating an app for a BlackBerry is your first mobile device experience, just take my word for it. An app only works as well as it's tested, and because the final destination for your BlackBerry app is a real device, you have to test it on a real BlackBerry. And if your BlackBerry app wants to access the Internet, you'll need to test that as well.

In this appendix, I give you a solid background of BlackBerry devices and cover basic details about the BIS and the BES so you'll have a good understanding of what you need to do to ensure your application runs on real hardware.

Picking Out a BlackBerry Device

You can acquire a BlackBerry in two ways:

✔ **Buy a new or refurbished device from a wireless service provider.** This requires a service contract with the wireless service provider, which might not fit into your budget.

✔ **Buy a used device.** This way is usually less expensive than buying from a wireless service provider but comes with its own set of advantages and disadvantages.

Chapter 1 provides a list of the BlackBerry models available as of this writing.

Keep in mind that if you want to write an app for a particular BlackBerry model, you may have to purchase it from a particular carrier — for example, you can only purchase a Storm from Verizon.

Buying new or refurbished

Purchasing a new BlackBerry from one of the wireless service providers is the most expensive way to go. You can, of course, find refurbished devices from the providers for significantly reduced cost. In both cases, though, you have to purchase at least a data plan. Wireless service providers are always looking to increase the number of subscribers, so they usually have some rebate or discount available (although it usually requires signing a one-year or two-year contract). Be sure to read the fine print. For example, the BlackBerry I bought (keep reading) wasn't eligible for a rebate because I didn't purchase a voice plan for it.

I chose a new BlackBerry Curve 8900 from AT&T. I also own another touch-screen smartphone from AT&T, which got me a little discount in the service contract. Because I already have a voice plan for that *other* phone, I selected only a data plan for my BlackBerry to keep my costs down. The 8900 comes with Wi-Fi, so I can connect via either 3G speeds when I'm out and about or faster Wi-Fi when I'm near a network I trust. AT&T and T-Mobile offer BlackBerry models that come with Wi-Fi; Verizon and Sprint are starting to do the same. I recommend buying a BlackBerry smartphone that will support the app you want to create. My Word Locker app doesn't depend on the smartphone having a touchscreen, so the BlackBerry Curve I bought works perfectly fine for testing the app on a real device. If you choose the 4.5.0 version of the JDE, your app will execute the same on all BlackBerry smartphones running OS 4.5.0 or later, with the exceptions as noted in Chapter 2.

So should you go with a refurbished model? My experience with refurbished equipment in other areas of electronics such as computers has led me to believe that refurbished hardware is just as good as new — that is, as long as the manufacturer is trustworthy and the hardware comes with a warranty that is equivalent to that of new hardware. And a refurbished model is certainly more trustworthy overall than buying a used device. I have seen cost savings of 25 to 30 percent, depending on the model. One disadvantage is that you may not find the particular BlackBerry model that you're looking for, and the carrier may only have limited numbers available. My recommendation is to investigate what refurbished models are available at each carrier, and then determine whether a new model is within your budget.

The carrier assumes responsibility for making sure that the refurbished BlackBerry you purchase works just as if it had come fresh from the factory. As you see later in this chapter, used BlackBerry smartphones don't come with this guarantee, and this can cause problems. I recommend talking with a representative of the carrier, either by phone or through e-mail, to make sure of the carrier's responsibility and the warranty status when you buy a refurbished BlackBerry smartphone.

Buying used

BlackBerry devices, like other smartphones and cellphones in general, are now coming to be seen as *consumables*. RIM is developing new BlackBerry smartphones every three to six months, and wireless service providers attract their customers with discounted prices on top phone models that come with two-year contracts. Many BlackBerry users replace their 2-year-old devices with new ones when they renew their wireless service contracts. And that means that all the old devices replaced by new devices have to go somewhere.

As the largest marketplace for used equipment, eBay (www.ebay.com) is probably the first place you should look for used BlackBerry devices. Craig's List (www.craigslist.org) is another great place to search, especially for sellers who are close by. My experience has been with eBay, and I purchased a used AT&T BlackBerry 8820 from an online auction. This device had been used by the seller in a corporate environment, and the seller got a new phone with a new contract, prompting him to sell his old device.

The 8820 comes with Wi-Fi, so a service contract wasn't necessary to access the Internet through a WiFi connection. I offered the high bid, and the seller shipped me the device along with a USB cable and the password.

There was just one problem: The device had previously been Enterprise Activated. *Enterprise Activation* means the BlackBerry device is connected to your corporate e-mail account and can access corporate network services such as intranets. This process is known as *BES-ing* (*bezz*-ing) a device because the device is being associated with a BlackBerry Enterprise Server (BES). The benefits of Enterprise Activation are discussed in the later section "BlackBerry Enterprise Server (BES)"; my focus here is on what can happen when you purchase a used BlackBerry that was originally associated with a BES.

When I charged up the used 8820 and turned it on, I discovered two anomalies: There was no Browser application installed, and the device refused to let me install applications I created and signed myself. This state seemed rather strange. I knew from some development experience, though, that there were a great many rules that could be enforced on a BlackBerry that were associated with a BES, and which would continue to be enforced even after that BlackBerry was no longer connected to that BES. When my development team and I first discovered this lingering rules enforcement, we were very surprised. And that is what had happened to my used BlackBerry: The original owner had used it under the authority of his corporate BES environment, and that environment included rules that dictated the following:

- The user would not be allowed to access the Web via a browser.
- The user would not be allowed to install applications.

That left me with one problem: how to get these rules reversed. My development team determined that even erasing and reinstalling the device OS (*wiping* the device) didn't remove these rules.

The only way to undo the rules assigned to the device by the BES was to Enterprise Activate the device to a BES under my control, and then set the rules to be more flexible. The company I work for grants me access to a BES, and so that was the solution to my 8820's problems.

The lessons for you to take away from my experience are

- ✔ Buying a used BlackBerry is cheaper than buying a new or refurbished BlackBerry.
- ✔ *But* a used BlackBerry might have restrictions placed on it that limit its usefulness and that might be difficult or even impossible to remove.

So, before purchasing or even bidding on a used BlackBerry, ask the seller these questions:

- ✔ Was the device originally purchased for personal use?
- ✔ Was the device ever Enterprise Activated for access to a corporate network? This question might be difficult for the seller to answer if the device was bought and sold more than once.
- ✔ If the device was Enterprise Activated for the seller's use, can the administrator remove any restrictions before you purchase the device?

Some online tools claim to remove rules that have been placed on a device associated with a BES, but be careful using them. It turns out that rules can't actually be removed: They can only be replaced by less-restrictive rules.

BlackBerry Internet Service (BIS)

The reason why most people choose BlackBerry smartphones is simple: BlackBerry smartphones do e-mail well. The first BlackBerry devices worked with a BES, something that only medium to large businesses could afford. Then RIM introduced BlackBerry Internet Service (BIS). Using BIS, a BlackBerry user can create an e-mail account managed by RIM and connected to the user's wireless service provider. After purchasing my BlackBerry 8900, I set up an account through the AT&T portion of BIS, and now have an e-mail account specifically for my BlackBerry device in the `att.blackberry.net` domain.

BIS provides BlackBerry users with an e-mail account hosted by RIM, and it also allows access to other e-mail providers, including

✔ Gmail

✔ Yahoo!

✔ Hotmail

✔ Any Web-based e-mail provider that supports POP3 or IMAP

BIS doesn't impose rules on BlackBerry devices, so if you bought a used BlackBerry that had BIS service, your app won't be affected by that service. However, BIS is a service that is owned, operated, managed, and maintained by RIM, and that can sometimes indirectly cause issues for your app, such as e-mail attachments not being delivered to the smartphone or even service interruptions. Because the BIS is primarily an e-mail service, the issues will show up around your app's interactions with e-mail.

The BlackBerry device OS allows applications to interact with all of a user's e-mail — if the user gives your app permission to do so. Because BIS acts as a mail service for a BlackBerry device, anything your app expects from the BlackBerry Email application programming interfaces (APIs) will be dependent upon BIS performing its e-mail duties correctly. Like every piece of software ever written, BIS can sometimes fail in achieving this goal. These issues can be difficult to diagnose seeing as how your app isn't the reason for the failure. This is one of the reasons I include a discussion about logging information on a running device in Chapter 11.

BlackBerry Enterprise Server (BES)

BlackBerry Enterprise Server is one of the most important components of the realm of BlackBerry. BES is deployed within a corporate environment, which provides employees in a corporation the ability to connect to and access resources within the internal corporate network from their BlackBerry devices.

Here are the main features that a BES provides to BlackBerry users in an enterprise:

✔ **E-mail:** BES synchronizes users' BlackBerry devices with their corporate e-mail server. This is accomplished using *push technology:* BES delivers new e-mail to a BlackBerry device when it arrives at the e-mail server, and the user never needs to request it.

✔ **Web access:** The BES acts as a gateway to the Internet for corporate BlackBerry users. This means that a corporate user might be prevented from accessing URLs that the IT department within the enterprise determined to be undesirable or not serving the needs of the business. Your app, if used on a BES-ed device, might need to handle a situation where it's prevented from making network connections.

✔ **Internal network access:** In addition to its duties protecting the corporate BlackBerry users from nasty Web sites, BES also provides access to the network resources behind the corporate firewall. Your app may be permitted to access these resources as well.

✔ **Push technology:** BES uses push technology to deliver e-mail messages to a user's device. The same push technology can also be used to deliver other data to your application running on a device. However, this also requires the administrator of a BES to execute an application behind the corporate firewall to deliver the data to the BES for forwarding on to your application that's running on a specific user's device.

A BES can establish rules — known to BES administrators as *IT Policy Settings* — for any and all devices that the BES manages. Administrators can impose a great many rules upon devices under management of the BES, and some of them can interfere with the operation of your app. Here are just a few of the rules that can change the behavior of your application:

✔ Disabling the camera (photo and video)

✔ Requiring the user to confirm sending messages via SMS (Multimedia Messaging Service), MMS (Multimedia Messaging Service), and e-mail

✔ Disabling SMS messaging

✔ Restricting outgoing calls

✔ Disallowing network connection

✔ Disallowing applications' use of the persistent storage on the smartphone. (I go over the storage capabilities of BlackBerry smartphones and how your app can use them in Chapter 6.)

✔ Disabling use of an external memory card

✔ Disabling Wi-Fi access

✔ Disabling Bluetooth access

If your app expects to make use of any of the preceding features, keep in mind that users whose devices are Enterprise Activated will potentially be subject to the security settings imposed by BES.

Some of the devices that your app ends up on will be monitored by and affected by a BES. You will want to keep your users informed about what your application does before they purchase it. Your application may access features and functionality that a BES administrator has determined are not allowed for the BlackBerry devices the BES manages — *and that will prevent your app from operating fully or possibly at all.*

Consider the following before releasing your app to the App World. This is by no means a complete list, but you'll get the basic ideas for handling situations regarding the use of your app in a BES environment where your app's functionality may be affected by something outside your control:

✔ **Give a warning before users download the app.** As part of the description of your app on display at BlackBerry App World, you should include information about what your app uses that might conflict with rules set on a BES, if the user's device is associated with one. Users can decide before downloading your app whether they can live with the consequences of your app's functionality being limited by the BES administrator's choice of restrictions. For instance, if your application uses persistent storage to remember recorded audio notes a user makes while using your app, you should point this out in your app's App World description and mention this as a requirement for anyone running your app. Most BES administrators don't prevent use of persistent storage, but you'll provide better customer service if your users are aware that this is a requirement.

✔ **Make sure your apps fail safely.** Your app will need to gracefully handle situations where a user's BlackBerry is prevented from operating as your app wishes. Your app should be able to operate even if all restrictions given in the preceding list are enforced. For instance, your game app may attempt to connect to a Web-based service to post and retrieve high scores, but a BES administrator could block your app's access to the external network. This should not prevent users from being able to play the game. When a BES administrator's policies prevent your app from operating normally, your app will receive an Exception when it tries to perform a forbidden operation. For instance, if a BES policy prevents network access by third-party applications (such as yours), your app's attempt to open a network connection using the `Connector` class will cause a `ControlledAccessException` to be thrown by the smartphone OS. Your app should catch the exception (your app will already be wrapping the use of `Connector` with a `try/catch` block) and should display an appropriate error message for this specific exception, such as "The policies assigned to your smartphone do not permit this application to communicate with the network." I discuss networking in detail in Chapter 9.

✔ **Allow users to try before buying.** BlackBerry App World provides a Try & Buy option: Users can download your app from the App World for free for a limited time period, after which they must pay for your app to continue using it. You are responsible for implementing any control features with respect to Try & Buy such as enforcing the time limit as well as activating the application when the user purchases the full version. The sidebar "Try & Buy applications" shows you a simple algorithm to keep track of how long your app has been in use.

You are responsible for your app's success or failure to operate correctly on the devices where it's installed. You might be unable to prevent your app's failure when faced with running on a device protected by strong BES restrictions. I prefer a combination of all three approaches.

Try & Buy applications

As a Try & Buy application, your app is downloaded by users for free from the App World for a trial period. Your app is responsible for enforcing this trial period. You can add code similar to the following to determine whether the user has been using your app longer than a week. If the app detects a Long object stored in persistent storage, it assumes that this object is the date stored (in a value of milliseconds since January 1, 1970, as returned by the OS) when the app was launched for the first time — if the user never launches your app, there's no reason to worry about how long it's been used. If the difference in milliseconds between the current time and the stored time is greater than the value of a week's worth of milliseconds, the application displays a screen that tells the user the trial period is over. If the current date is less than that of a week, the application displays its main screen. Your own version of the timer will have to include logic that determines whether the user has performed the Buy part of the Try & Buy approach in addition to simply determining whether a week has passed since the app's first use. I present more details about BlackBerry persistent storage in Chapter 6.

```java
// this method is implemented inside the
// UiApplication subclass you create for your app
    public static final long WEEK_DURATION_MILLISECONDS = 60L*60L*24L*7L*1000L;
    public void activate()
  {
    PersistentObject persistentStorage =  PersistentStore.getPersistentObject(
        TRYANDBUY_PERSISTENT_STORAGE_KEY );
    if (null != persistentStorage)
    {
      Long storedStartDate   =   (Long)persistentStorage.getContents();
      if (null != storedStartDate)
      {
        Calendar now = Calendar.getInstance();
        long nowMilliseconds =   now.getTime().getTime();
// get current date in milliseconds since epoch
        long deltaMilliseconds   =   nowMilliseconds - storedStartDate.longValue();
        // get time in milliseconds since the start date
        if (deltaMilliseconds > WEEK_DURATION_MILLISECONDS)
        {
          this.pushScreen( new TrialPeriodOverScreen() );
        }
        else
        {
          this.pushScreen( new MainApplicationScreen() );
        }
      }
      else
      {
        // this is the first time
        Long startDate = new Long( System.currentTimeMillis() );
        persistentStorage.setContents(startDate);
        persistentStorage.commit();
      }
    }
  }
```

So how do you get a BES?

A BlackBerry Enterprise Server is, to put it bluntly, a very expensive and complicated piece of software. If your employer has a BES setup for its employees, you will likely be able to develop your application without having to set one up. Your test BlackBerry smartphone will have to be Enterprise Activated to your employer's BES.

However, in early 2010, RIM released BlackBerry Enterprise Server Express as a fully functional BES for small businesses. BES Express comes free with service for 1 user; additional users may be added for $99 each, up to 30 users. For testing your app against a fully functional BES equivalent, this would be an appropriate selection. Watch out for a few things, however:

- **Hardware:** BES requires a powerful PC, with lots of speed and memory and storage space. Even for only one user, BES demands high performance.

- **Operating system:** BES and BES Express run only on Microsoft Windows Server 2003 or 2008.

- **E-mail server:** BES Express operates only in conjunction with Microsoft Exchange. The BES can use Microsoft Exchange, IBM Lotus Domino, and Novell GroupWise.

- **Database server:** BES and BES Express require Microsoft SQL Server to maintain its operational information.

- **Internet access:** BES requires access to the Internet: specifically, inward and outward access through a particular port (3101), which your firewall has to open. This is the port that BES uses to communicate with the RIM servers, and from there to the wireless service providers.

Table B-1 summarizes the requirements for BES and BES Express.

Table B-1		BES and BES Express Requirements			
Enterprise Server	Hardware	OS	E-mail Server	Database Server	Internet Access
BES	Pentium IV-class processor, 2+ GHz, 1.5GB RAM	Microsoft Windows Server 2003 or 2008	Microsoft Exchange, IBM Lotus Domino, Novell GroupWise	Microsoft SQL Server	Port 3101 open
BES Express	Same as BES	Same as BES	Microsoft Exchange	Same as BES	Same as BES

Installing, configuring, and operating a BES are beyond the scope of this book.

Exploiting BES push technology

As I mention earlier, BES uses push technology to deliver e-mail from the mail server to a user's BlackBerry. This approach is automated, and no action is required by the user to acquire new mail — the e-mail arrives on its own and is waiting in the user's Inbox.

Your application can make use of the same technology if your app is intended to run on enterprise BlackBerry devices. For instance, you could create an app to listen for proprietary sales terms, delivered only to BlackBerry smartphones used by the corporate enterprise's salespeople. This requires two pieces:

- Your app must be "listening" for incoming data deliveries coming from the BES. This is the client side of the push.

- You must provide a standalone PC application that will deliver data to the BES for transmission to a particular device. This is the server side of the push.

The server application must be running on a machine that's permitted to communicate directly with the BES. The server application must perform the following operations:

- Collect the data to be delivered to the device.

- Open an HTTP connection to the BES on a specific port. This port defaults to 8080, and is known as the HTTP-Push port. The parameters of the HTTP request are given in the following list.

- Deliver the data as the POST data in the HTTP connection.

- Retrieve the HTTP response from the BES.

The HTTP request delivers the identification parameters as well as authentication data (account and password, if the BES is secured) as part of the URL for the request. The URL will look something like this:

```
http://<host>:<port>/push?DESTINATION=<device_PIN>&PORT=<device_port>
&REQUESTURI=localhost
```

The parameters (items within the angle brackets < >) are

- <host>: This is the hostname or the IP address of the BES, which the server application attempts to connect to for delivery of the data.

- <port>: This is the port the BES used for HTTP-Push; the default is 8080.

✔ <device_PIN>: This is the 8-digit (hexadecimal) unique identifier for the BlackBerry device that will receive the data. This can also be the user's precise e-mail address that the BES maintains for that user, which enables the BES push technology to work correctly even if the user gets a new device.

Sometimes corporate e-mail servers use one e-mail address that looks good to humans and another that is stored internally — for instance, you might send e-mail to me as karlkowalski@blazingapps.com, but inside the e-mail server, that e-mail address is actually kkowalsk0@ ponyexpress.blazingapps.com. If you use the e-mail address instead of the device PIN, you *must* use the e-mail address that the BES uses for the user.

✔ <device_port>: This is the port that your client application, running on the BlackBerry device, has to open to receive incoming HTTP-Push attempts.

The code in Listing B-1 shows Java code opening a connection to a BES for delivering HTTP-Push data to an app running on a BlackBerry device:

Listing B-1:   Server "Push" Code in Java

```java
String data = "this is the pushed data";
// dummy data to be delivered
String devicePIN = "1234ABCD"; // dummy device PIN
String appPort = "7117"; // dummy application port
URL theURL = new URL( "http", "localhost", 8080,
"/push?DESTINATION="+devicePIN+"&PORT="
+appPort+"&REQUESTURI=localhost";
HttpURLConnection conn = (HttpURLConnection)
theURL.openConnection();
conn.setDoInput(true); // to receive the confirmation
conn.setDoOutput(true); // to send the data
conn.setRequestMethod("POST");
OutputStream outStream = conn.getOutputStream();
// to write the data
outStream.write( data.getBytes() );
// data written as byte array
outStream.close();
InputStream inStream = conn.getInputStream();
// contains the response
int contentLength = conn.getContentLength();
if (contentLength > 0)
{
   byte[] bArray = new byte[contentLength];
   DataInputStream dataInStream = new DataInputStream
( inStream );
   dataInStream.readFully( bArray );
   String responseString = new String( bArray ); //
}
```

Two possible responses are returned by a BES to an HTTP-Push connection request:

> ✔ **A response starting with 200:** This is the good response, and means that the BES accepted the data you handed to it to be delivered via HTTP-Push to the device-ID/user–e-mail specified.

> ✔ **Any other response:** These are the bad responses. Most times, you will see a bad response returned because of an incorrectly specified user e-mail or device ID.

The code snippet in Listing B-2 shows code your application must be executing on the BlackBerry device, in a thread separate from the main thread, to listen for and receive HTTP-Push data deliveries. This code is taken from one of the 4.5.0 JDE sample applications, HTTPPushDemo. You will see a lot of try/catch blocks, which leads to lots of indenting and sectioning of code. These blocks are placed around calls to OS functions that can throw Exceptions that must be caught. For instance, the call to Connector.open() can fail if the requested port (7117) is already in use. If the Connector.open() call succeeds, the code then executes the StreamConnectionNotifier.acceptAndOpen() call, operating on the notify variable. This is a blocking call, which is why this code must be placed within a Thread object (and I go over these details in Chapter 7). The remaining code creates and fills a buffer with the incoming data, and then calls a method — updateMessage() — to handle the data that came in. The end of the snippet is devoted to handling exceptions while trying to make sure all the appropriate objects get closed correctly.

Listing B-2:   BlackBerry Code Snippet to Listen for Push Connection

```
// flag so an outside process can signal to stop listening
private boolean _stop = false;
// size of data buffer, to read in data in small chunks
public static final int CHUNK_SIZE = 256;
// the URL to open for listening to incoming Pushes
// the port number matches that in Listing B-2
private static final String URL = "http://:7117";

public void run()
{
    StreamConnection stream = null;
    InputStream input = null;
    MDSPushInputStream pushInputStream=null;

    while (!_stop)
    {
        try
        {
// Synchronize here so that we don't end up creating a connection
// that is never closed.
```

```
        synchronized(this)
        {
// Open the connection once (or re-open after an IOException), so we don't
// end up in a race condition, where a push is lost if it comes in before
// the connection is open again. We open the url with a parameter that indicates
// that we should always use MDS when attempting to connect.
            _notify = (StreamConnectionNotifier)Connector.open(URL +
                ";deviceside=false");
        }
        while (!_stop)
        {
// NOTE: the following will block until data is received.
// so this snippet needs to be within a Thread
            stream = _notify.acceptAndOpen();
            try
            {
                input = stream.openInputStream();
                pushInputStream= new MDSPushInputStream((HttpServerConnection)
                stream, input);
// Extract the data from the input stream.
                DataBuffer db = new DataBuffer();
                byte[] data = new byte[CHUNK_SIZE];
                int chunk = 0;
                while (-1!= (chunk=input.read(data)))
                {
                    db.write(data, 0, chunk);
                }
// the following call makes use of the data
                updateMessage(data);

// This method is called to accept the push.
                pushInputStream.accept();
                input.close();
                stream.close();
            }
            catch (IOException e1)
            {
// A problem occurred with the input stream, however, the
// original StreamConnectionNotifier is still valid.
                if ( input != null )
                {
                    try
                    {
                        input.close();
                    }
                    catch (IOException e2)
                    {
                    }
```

(continued)

Listing B-2 *(continued)*

```
                }
                if ( stream != null )
                {
                    try
                    {
                        stream.close();
                    }
                    catch (IOException e2)
                    {
                    }
                }
            }
        }
        _notify.close();
        _notify = null;
    }
    catch (IOException ioe)
    {
// Likely the stream was closed. Catches the exception thrown by
// notify.acceptAndOpen() when this program exits.
        if ( _notify != null )
        {
            try
            {
                notify.close();
                notify = null;
            }
            catch ( IOException e )
            {
            }
        }
    }
}
```

Keep in mind that the HTTP-Push technology works only with BES-ed BlackBerry devices, and using the technique for delivering data to BlackBerry devices works only in conjunction with a server-side application that a BES administrator will execute. This feature is possible only for corporate, enterprise-class BlackBerry applications.

Index